Heart Healthy cookbook

Delicious and Easy Low Sodium, Low Fat Recipes. Smoothie For Eating Well Every Day. 28-day meal plan. Includes Bonuses:Shopping List and 100 Tips for Heart Health.

Introduction

In the beautiful mosaic of life, the heart stands as both sentinel and maestro, orchestrating the rhythm of our existence. It is a silent hero, pumping vitality into every fiber of our being, quietly working to sustain our journey through time. Yet, in the whirlwind of our modern lives, we often overlook the heart's whispered plea for nourishment, for care, and for a harmonious partnership.

But here , within the pages of "Heart Health Cookbook," you'll discover the key to unlocking the extraordinary synergy between your heart and your culinary choices. This is not just another cookbook; it is a heartfelt invitation to embrace a lifestyle that nourishes not only your palate but the very core of your well-being.

As a seasoned author with a track record of Amazon bestsellers, I've embarked on a journey of discovery, one that has led me to the crossroads of health and taste. Through this book, I share with you the culmination of years of research, passion, and a profound belief that your heart's health should be a celebration, not a sacrifice.

"Heart Health cookbook" is a testament to the idea that you can indulge your love for food while nurturing your heart's well-being. Within these pages, you will encounter a symphony of flavors, a palette of colors, and a collection of recipes meticulously curated to harmonize your senses and invigorate your heart.

From crisp, refreshing salads that awaken your taste buds to hearty, comforting dishes that warm your soul, each recipe has been crafted to embrace the principles of hearthealthy living without compromising on taste. In these dishes, we celebrate the abundant palette of nature's bounty, where nourishment and pleasure unite.

But "Heart Health cookbook" is more than a cookbook; it's your trusted companion on a journey towards lifelong wellness. Alongside delectable recipes, you'll find insights into the science of heart health, practical tips for making informed dietary choices, and guidance for creating a sustainable, heart-loving lifestyle.

Together, we'll explore the profound connection between the food we eat and the heart that beats within us. We'll embark on a journey that celebrates your heart's wisdom, your body's vitality, and the culinary artistry that binds them together.

So, whether you're taking your first steps towards a heart-healthy life or seeking fresh inspiration in the kitchen, "Heart Health cookbook" is your passport to a world where health and taste merge seamlessly. Prepare to embark on a culinary adventure that nourishes not only your heart but your soul, and savor the symphony of flavors that will echo in your life for years to come.

Font design by Vernon Adams, photo by Victoria Shes, The Fry Family Food Co. Layout design by Yuliia Diiuk.

Contents

Introduction 2

Chapter 1: Understanding Heart Health:
General Disease of the Heart and their Consequences.................5

Chapter 2: The Heart of Heart-Healthy Eating:
Understanding the Heart-Healthy Diet 7

Chapter 3: Breakfast 8

Chapter 4: Salad 18

Chapter 5: Snack & Appetizers...24

Chapter 6: Soups & Stews 38

Chapter 7: Lean Meats & Poultry...49

Chapter 8: Seafood...60

Chapter 9: Smoothie recipes (fruits, vegetables) 69

Chapter 10: Vegetable 77

Chapter 11: Diabetic Mains 87

Chapter 12: Dessert..99

Chapter 13: Measurement conversion...................................... 106

Chapter14: 28-Day Meal plan 107

TWO BONUSES: 100 Tips for Heart Health 109

Shopping list... 110

Chapter 15: Conclusion... 111

Chapter 1: Understanding Heart Health: General Disease of the Heart and their Consequences

In the ever-changing world of health and wellness, few topics garner as much attention and importance as heart health. It is no secret that the heart is the epicenter of our life force, a symphonic conductor that orchestrates the rhythms of life itself. I am excited to share with you the essential aspects of heart health on this journey to a healthier and happier you.

The heart: a miracle of nature. Our hearts, those tirelessly beating powerhouses that sit within our chests, are nothing short of amazing. They pump life-giving blood, oxygen, and nutrients to every corner of our body. This continuous circulation is the life force that sustains us. Understanding the intricacies of our heart's functions is the first step to appreciating the critical role it plays in our overall well-being.

Common heart diseases and their consequences: In heart health, knowledge isn't just power; it's a lifeline. We'll cover some of the most common heart conditions that affect millions of people around the world, including:

Coronary heart disease (CHD): CHD, often called heart disease, occurs when the arteries that supply blood to the heart become narrowed or blocked. This can lead to chest pain (angina) or even heart attacks.

Hypertension (high blood pressure): High blood pressure is a silent threat that increases the risk of heart disease, stroke, and other complications.

Heart failure: Contrary to its name, heart failure does not mean that the heart has stopped working; rather, it struggles to pump blood efficiently, leading to fatigue and shortness of breath.

Arrhythmias: An irregular heart rhythm can impair the heart's ability to pump effectively and can cause palpitations, dizziness, or fainting.

Risk factors: known culprits. Understanding heart health also means recognizing the culprits that can lead to heart problems. While some risk factors, such as genetics, are beyond our control, others can be modified through lifestyle choices:

Diet: The food we eat has a big impact on our heart health. We'll delve into the role of diet in supporting a healthy heart, including the effects of saturated fat, trans fat, sodium, and sugar.

Lack of physical activity: A sedentary lifestyle can contribute to obesity and other risk factors. Discover the transformative power of regular physical activity.

Smoking: Smoking damages blood vessels and can lead to atherosclerosis, the leading cause of heart disease.

Alcohol consumption: While moderate alcohol consumption may have some heart benefits, excessive consumption can raise blood pressure and contribute to heart problems.

Stress and Mental Health: The mind-heart connection runs deep. Chronic stress, anxiety, and depression can affect heart health.

The link between weight and heart health: As we continue our exploration of heart health, we turn our attention to a critical factor that often stands at the crossroads of well-being: weight. I have witnessed the profound effects of weight control on heart health. That's why it's important to understand how the choices you make can tip the scales in favor of a healthier and happier life.

Weight is largely a reflection of our lifestyle. It's not just about aesthetics; it's a window into our overall health, where the heart takes center stage in this narrative.

In recent decades, obesity has reached epidemic proportions around the world. This is an alarming trend, and the profound impact it has on heart health. From inflammation and cholesterol levels to the stress on the heart from being overweight.

Vicious cycle: obesity and heart disease

Obesity is a known risk factor for heart disease, but the relationship is far from one-dimensional. It contributes to heart disease, including its role in:

Atherosclerosis: Excess fat in the body can cause fatty deposits to build up in the arteries, limiting blood flow to the heart.

High blood pressure: Obesity is a significant factor in hypertension, putting more strain on the heart and increasing the risk of heart disease.

Cholesterol Imbalance: Obesity often disrupts the balance of good (HDL) and bad (LDL) cholesterol, contributing to heart-damaging plaque.

Impact of weight loss: The good news is that even moderate weight loss can lead to significant improvements in heart health.

Remember, weight management isn't just about the numbers on the scale; it's about nurturing your heart and overall well-being. The food choices you make can either feed your heart or weigh it down. In the next section, we'll focus on a key aspect of maintaining a healthy heart: your diet.

Chapter 2: The Heart of Heart-Healthy Eating: Understanding the Heart-Healthy Diet

In the previous chapter, we embarked on our journey toward heart-healthy cooking, understanding the importance of nurturing our most vital organ, the heart. Now, it's time to delve deeper into the fundamentals of heart-healthy eating. To cook with love for our hearts, we must first comprehend the ingredients and principles that will guide us on this flavorful path to wellness.

Understanding the Heart-Healthy Diet

A heart-healthy diet is not a one-size-fits-all approach but rather a flexible set of guidelines that emphasize nutrient-rich foods while limiting those that can harm our cardiovascular system. Here are some key components:

Fruits and Vegetables: Nature's gift to heart health. These colorful gems are packed with vitamins, minerals, fiber, and antioxidants that promote a strong, healthy heart. Aim to fill half your plate with fruits and vegetables at every meal.

Whole Grains: Opt for whole grains like brown rice, quinoa, and whole wheat bread over refined grains. These grains provide essential nutrients and fiber, helping to maintain steady blood sugar levels.

Lean Proteins: Choose lean sources of protein, such as poultry, fish, beans, and legumes. These options are lower in saturated fat than red meats and provide essential amino acids for overall health.

Healthy Fats: Include sources of healthy fats like avocados, nuts, seeds, and olive oil. These fats can help reduce bad cholesterol levels and lower the risk of heart disease.

Portion Control: Be mindful of portion sizes. Even healthy foods can contribute to weight gain if consumed excessively.

Sodium Moderation: Limit sodium intake by minimizing processed and restaurant foods. Opt for herbs, spices, and other flavorful seasonings to enhance the taste of your dishes.

Sugar Awareness: Keep an eye on added sugars in foods and beverages. High sugar consumption can contribute to heart problems and weight gain.

Hydration: Stay hydrated with water, herbal teas, and other low-calorie beverages. Avoid excessive consumption of sugary drinks.

Cooking with Heart: Tips and Techniques

To master heart-healthy cooking, it's essential to adopt cooking techniques that preserve the nutritional value of your ingredients while enhancing flavor. Here are some tips to get you started:

Saute and Stir-Fry: Use non-stick pans and a small amount of heart-healthy oil when sautéing or stir-frying. This method allows you to use less fat while maintaining flavor.

Baking and Roasting: These techniques help lock in flavors without adding excessive fat. Season your ingredients with herbs and spices to enhance taste.

Grilling: Grilling is a heart-healthy way to prepare lean proteins like chicken and fish. Marinate your proteins to add flavor without excess calories.

Steaming: Steaming vegetables helps retain their nutrients and natural flavors. It's a quick and easy way to prepare a variety of heart-healthy side dishes.

Homemade Sauces: Make your own sauces and dressings using heart-healthy ingredients. This allows you to control sodium and sugar content.

Your Heart-Healthy Pantry.

A well-stocked pantry can make heart-healthy cooking more accessible and convenient. Ensure your kitchen is equipped with staples like whole grains, legumes, canned tomatoes, low-sodium broths, and a variety of herbs and spices. Having these ingredients on hand makes it easier to prepare nutritious and flavorful meals at a moment's notice.

As we continue our culinary journey together, remember that heart-healthy eating isn't about deprivation but rather a celebration of delicious, nourishing foods. In the chapters ahead, we'll put these principles into practice with an array of mouthwatering recipes designed to satisfy your palate while nurturing your heart.

So, are you ready to dive into the world of heart-healthy cuisine?

chapter3
Breakfast

Oatmeal with Berries and Nuts 9

Greek Yogurt Parfait 9

Avocado Toast.. 10

Whole Grain Pancakes.................................... 10

Egg White Omelet 11

Chia Seed Pudding... 11

Smoothie Bowl 12

Quinoa Breakfast Bowl 12

Muesli with Almonds and Dried Fruits 13

Veggie Breakfast Burrito 13

Baked Sweet Potato with Cottage Cheese 14

Berry and Banana Whole Wheat Muffins...... 14

Peanut Butter and Banana Sandwich 15

Homemade Granola Bars 15

Smoked Salmon and Whole Grain Bagel 16

Quinoa and Berry Breakfast Bowl 16

Avocado and Spinach Breakfast Wrap 16

Chia Seed and Green Tea Smoothie 17

Salmon and Dill Scrambled Eggs 17

Sweet Potato and Spinach Breakfast Hash ... 17

Oatmeal with Berries and Nuts

Prep Time: 5 minutes / Cook Time: 10 minutes
Yield: 1 serving

Ingredients

- 1/2 cup rolled oats
- 1 cup almond milk (unsweetened)
- 1/4 cup mixed berries
  (strawberries, blueberries, raspberries)
- 1 tablespoon chopped nuts (walnuts or almonds)
- 1 tablespoon honey or maple syrup (optional)
- 1/4 teaspoon ground cinnamon
- A pinch of salt

Directions

1. In a saucepan, combine the rolled oats, almond milk, and a pinch of salt. Bring to a simmer over medium heat.

2. Reduce the heat to low and stir the oats occasionally. Cook for about 5-7 minutes or until the oats are tender and the mixture has thickened to your desired consistency.

3. While the oats are cooking, wash and prepare the mixed berries.

4. Once the oats are cooked, remove the saucepan from heat and stir in the ground cinnamon.

5. Transfer the oatmeal to a serving bowl. Top with the mixed berries and chopped nuts.

6. If desired, drizzle honey or maple syrup over the oatmeal for added sweetness.

7. Serve hot and enjoy your heart-healthy oatmeal with berries and nuts!

Nutritional Information (Approximate)

Calories	300	Dietary Fiber	7g
Protein	8g	Sodium	150mg
Carbohydrates	49g	Cholesterol	0mg
Total Fat	9g	Potassium	310mg
Saturated Fat	1g		

This delicious oatmeal is not only satisfying but also packed with fiber, antioxidants from the berries, and healthy fats from the nuts, making it a perfect choice for a heart-healthy breakfast. Adjust the sweetness to your preference and enjoy a nutritious start to your day!

Greek Yogurt Parfait

Prep Time: 10 minutes / Cook Time: 0 minutes
Yield: 1 serving

Ingredients

- 1/2 cup non-fat Greek yogurt
- 1/4 cup fresh mixed berries
  (strawberries, blueberries, raspberries)
- 1 tablespoon honey or maple syrup (optional)
- 1 tablespoon chopped nuts (almonds or walnuts)
- 1 tablespoon granola (choose a low-sugar option)
- 1/4 teaspoon vanilla extract

Directions

1. In a mixing bowl, combine the Greek yogurt and vanilla extract. Mix well until the vanilla is evenly incorporated into the yogurt.

2. Wash and prepare the mixed berries. You can slice the strawberries if desired.

3. Start assembling your parfait in a glass or a bowl. Begin with a layer of Greek yogurt at the bottom.

4. Add a layer of mixed berries on top of the yogurt.

5. Drizzle honey or maple syrup over the berries for extra sweetness if desired.

6. Sprinkle chopped nuts on top of the berries for some healthy fats and crunch.

7. Finish by adding a layer of granola for additional texture and fiber.

8. Repeat the layering process if you have more ingredients or want a larger parfait.

9. Serve immediately and enjoy your heart-healthy Greek Yogurt Parfait!

Nutritional Information (Approximate)

Calories	250	Dietary Fiber	4g
Protein	14g	Sodium	60mg
Carbohydrates	40g	Cholesterol	0mg
Total Fat	4g	Potassium	280mg
Saturated Fat	0,5g		

This Greek Yogurt Parfait is a delightful and nutritious way to start your day. It's rich in protein, fiber, and antioxidants from the berries, while the nuts and granola provide healthy fats and crunch. Customize it to your taste and enjoy a delicious and heart-healthy breakfast or snack.

Avocado Toast

Prep Time: 5 minutes / Cook Time: 5 minutes
Yield: 1 serving

Ingredients

- 1 ripe avocado, 1/2 teaspoon lemon juice
- 1 slice of whole-grain bread (preferably low-sodium)
- 1/2 teaspoon olive oil (for toasting)
- A pinch of salt (optional)
- A pinch of black pepper (optional)
- A pinch of red pepper flakes (optional, for added flavor and heat)
- 1 small tomato, thinly sliced
- Fresh cilantro leaves or microgreens for garnish (optional)

Directions

1. Slice the ripe avocado in half, remove the pit, and scoop the flesh into a bowl. Mash it with a fork until you reach your desired level of creaminess.

2. Add lemon juice to the mashed avocado and mix well. This helps enhance the flavor and prevents browning.

3. Toast the whole-grain bread to your preferred level of crispiness. You can use a toaster or a pan with a light drizzle of olive oil for added flavor.

4. If desired, lightly brush the toasted bread with a small amount of olive oil for extra richness.

5. Spread the mashed avocado evenly onto the toasted bread.

6. Season with a pinch of salt, black pepper, and red pepper flakes for added flavor and spice.

7. Top your avocado toast with thinly sliced tomatoes. You can also add fresh cilantro leaves or microgreens for a burst of freshness and color.

8. Serve immediately and enjoy your heart-healthy Avocado Toast!

Nutritional Information (Approximate)

Calories	250	Dietary Fiber	20g
Protein	5g	Sodium	3mg
Carbohydrates	17g	Cholesterol	9mg
Total Fat	0g	Potassium	650mg
Saturated Fat	170g		

This Avocado Toast is a nutritious and satisfying option for breakfast or as a snack. Avocado provides healthy fats and fiber, while whole-grain bread adds complex carbohydrates. Customize your toppings to suit your taste, and enjoy a delicious and heart-healthy meal.

Whole Grain Pancakes

Prep Time: 10 minutes / Cook Time: 10 minutes
Yield: 2 servings

Ingredients

- 1 cup whole wheat flour, 1 cup low-fat or skim milk
- 2 tablespoons ground flaxseed, 1 tablespoon sugar (or a natural sweetener like honey or maple syrup)
- 2 teaspoons baking powder, 1/2 teaspoon baking soda
- 1/4 teaspoon salt (optional),
- 1 large egg, 1 tablespoon vegetable oil (preferably canola or olive oil)
- 1 teaspoon vanilla extract (optional)
- Cooking spray or a small amount of oil for the pan

Directions

1. In a large mixing bowl, whisk together the whole wheat flour, ground flaxseed, sugar (or sweetener), baking powder, baking soda, and salt (if using).

2. In a separate bowl, beat the egg and then add the milk, vegetable oil, and vanilla extract (if using). Mix well.

3. Pour the wet ingredients into the dry ingredients and stir until just combined. Be careful not to overmix; it's okay if there are a few lumps.

4. Heat a non-stick skillet or griddle over medium heat and lightly grease it with cooking spray or a small amount of oil.

5. Pour 1/4 cup portions of the pancake batter onto the hot skillet. Use the back of a spoon to spread the batter into a round shape.

6. Cook the pancakes for about 2-3 minutes on each side or until they are golden brown and have bubbles on the surface.

7. Transfer the cooked pancakes to a plate and keep them warm while you cook the remaining batter.

8. Serve your whole grain pancakes with your choice of heart-healthy toppings such as fresh berries, sliced bananas, a dollop of Greek yogurt, or a drizzle of pure maple syrup.

9. Enjoy your heart-healthy Whole Grain Pancakes!

Nutritional Information (Approximate)

Calories	250	Dietary Fiber	4g
Protein	14g	Sodium	60mg
Carbohydrates	40g	Cholesterol	0mg
Total Fat	4g	Potassium	280mg
Saturated Fat	0,5g		

These Whole Grain Pancakes are a nutritious and delicious breakfast option. The whole wheat flour and ground flaxseed add fiber and essential nutrients, while limiting added sugar keeps them heart-healthy. Top them with your favorite healthy toppings for a satisfying meal.

Egg White Omelet

Prep Time: 5 minutes / Cook Time: 5 minutes
Yield: 1 serving

Ingredients

- 4 large egg whites
- 1/4 cup diced bell peppers (any color)
- 1/4 cup diced onions, 1/4 cup diced tomatoes
- 1/4 cup chopped spinach or kale
- 1/4 cup diced mushrooms (optional)
- Cooking spray or a small amount of oil for the pan
- Salt and pepper to taste
- Fresh herbs (such as parsley or chives) for garnish (optional)

Directions

1. In a bowl, whisk the egg whites until they are slightly frothy. Season with a pinch of salt and pepper to taste.

2. Heat a non-stick skillet over medium heat and lightly grease it with cooking spray or a small amount of oil.

3. Add the diced bell peppers, onions, and tomatoes to the skillet. Sauté for about 2-3 minutes until they become slightly tender.

4. Add the chopped spinach (or kale) and mushrooms (if using) to the skillet. Continue to sauté for another 1-2 minutes until the greens are wilted and the mushrooms are cooked.

5. Pour the whisked egg whites over the sautéed vegetables in the skillet.

6. Cook the omelet for about 2-3 minutes, occasionally lifting the edges with a spatula and tilting the pan to allow uncooked egg to flow to the edges.

7. Once the egg whites are mostly set but still slightly runny on top, fold the omelet in half with a spatula.

8. Continue cooking for another 1-2 minutes until the omelet is fully set but not overcooked.

9. Slide the omelet onto a plate, garnish with fresh herbs if desired, and serve hot.

Nutritional Information (Approximate)

Calories	120	Dietary Fiber	0g
Protein	25g	Sodium	0mg
Carbohydrates	5g	Cholesterol	1mg
Total Fat	0g	Potassium	300mg
Saturated Fat	280g		

This Egg White Omelet is a low-calorie, high-protein breakfast option that's perfect for a heart-healthy diet. It's packed with colorful vegetables and free of saturated fat, making it a nutritious and delicious way to start your day. Customize the filling with your favorite vegetables and herbs.

Chia Seed Pudding

Prep Time: 5 minutes (plus overnight chilling)
Cook Time: 0 minutes / Yield: 1 serving

Ingredients

- 2 tablespoons chia seeds
- 1/2 cup unsweetened almond milk (or any milk of your choice)
- 1/4 teaspoon vanilla extract
- 1/2 tablespoon honey or maple syrup (optional, for sweetness)
- Fresh berries or sliced fruit for topping (e.g., strawberries, blueberries)
- Chopped nuts (e.g., almonds, walnuts) for garnish (optional)

Directions

1. In a bowl or jar, combine the chia seeds, unsweetened almond milk, vanilla extract, and honey or maple syrup if you want your pudding sweetened. Stir well to combine all ingredients.

2. Cover the bowl or jar with plastic wrap or a lid and refrigerate it for at least 2 hours, or preferably overnight. The chia seeds will absorb the liquid and thicken to create a pudding-like consistency.

3. Before serving, give the pudding a good stir to ensure it's evenly mixed and no clumps remain.

4. Transfer the chia seed pudding to a serving dish or bowl.

5. Top the pudding with fresh berries or your choice of sliced fruit. Berries like strawberries and blueberries work exceptionally well.

6. If desired, garnish your pudding with chopped nuts for added texture and healthy fats.

7. Serve your heart-healthy Chia Seed Pudding chilled and enjoy!

Nutritional Information (Approximate)

Calories	150	Dietary Fiber	7g
Protein	4g	Sodium	0,5mg
Carbohydrates	18g	Cholesterol	8mg
Total Fat	0g	Potassium	160mg
Saturated Fat	90g		

This Chia Seed Pudding is a nutritious and satisfying dessert or breakfast option. Chia seeds are rich in fiber, omega-3 fatty acids, and antioxidants, making them a heart-healthy choice. Customize your pudding with your favorite toppings and enjoy a delicious and guilt-free treat.

Smoothie Bowl

Prep Time: 10 minutes / Cook Time: 0 minutes
Yield: 1 serving

Ingredients

- 1/2 cup frozen mixed berries (strawberries, blueberries, raspberries)
- 1/2 banana, frozen or fresh
- 1/2 cup low-fat Greek yogurt (unsweetened)
- 1/4 cup unsweetened almond milk (or any milk of your choice)
- 1 tablespoon chia seeds
- 1 tablespoon honey or maple syrup (optional, for sweetness)
- 1/4 cup whole-grain granola (choose a low-sugar option)
- Fresh fruit slices (e.g., kiwi, berries) for topping
- Chopped nuts (e.g., almonds, walnuts) for garnish (optional)

Directions

1. In a blender, combine the frozen mixed berries, banana, low-fat Greek yogurt, unsweetened almond milk, chia seeds, and honey or maple syrup if you prefer a sweeter smoothie bowl.

2. Blend until the mixture is smooth and creamy. You may need to stop and scrape down the sides of the blender to ensure all ingredients are well incorporated.

3. Once the smoothie base is ready, pour it into a bowl.

4. Top your smoothie bowl with whole-grain granola for added crunch and fiber.

5. Add fresh fruit slices on top of the granola. Kiwi and additional berries work well for a burst of color and flavor.

6. If desired, garnish your smoothie bowl with chopped nuts for extra texture and healthy fats.

7. Serve your heart-healthy Smoothie Bowl immediately and enjoy!

Nutritional Information (Approximate)

Calories	350	Dietary Fiber	9g
Protein	14g	Sodium	150mg
Carbohydrates	55g	Cholesterol	0mg
Total Fat	8g	(if using yogurt with cholesterol)	
Saturated Fat	1g	Potassium	570mg

This Smoothie Bowl is a delicious and heart-healthy way to start your day. It's packed with fiber, antioxidants from the berries, and protein from Greek yogurt. Customize your toppings to your preference and enjoy a nutritious and satisfying breakfast or snack.

Quinoa Breakfast Bowl

Prep Time: 5 minutes / Cook Time: 15 minutes
Yield: 1 serving

Ingredients

- 1/2 cup quinoa, 1 cup water
- 1/2 cup low-fat Greek yogurt (unsweetened)
- 1/4 cup fresh berries (e.g., blueberries, strawberries)
- 1/4 cup chopped nuts (e.g., almonds, walnuts)
- 1 tablespoon honey or maple syrup (optional, for sweetness)
- 1/4 teaspoon ground cinnamon
- 1/4 teaspoon vanilla extract
- A pinch of salt (optional)
- Fresh fruit slices (e.g., banana, kiwi) for topping (optional)

Directions

1. Rinse the quinoa thoroughly under cold running water to remove any bitterness.

2. In a saucepan, combine the rinsed quinoa and water. Add a pinch of salt if desired. Bring to a boil over high heat.

3. Reduce the heat to low, cover, and simmer for about 15 minutes or until the quinoa is cooked and the liquid is absorbed. Fluff the quinoa with a fork and let it cool for a few minutes.

4. While the quinoa is cooling, prepare your toppings. Wash and slice fresh berries and chop the nuts.

5. In a small bowl, mix the low-fat Greek yogurt with honey or maple syrup (if using), ground cinnamon, and vanilla extract. Adjust sweetness to your preference.

6. In a serving bowl, place the cooked quinoa as the base.

7. Spoon the sweetened Greek yogurt over the quinoa.

8. Top the yogurt with fresh berries and chopped nuts for added flavor, texture, and heart-healthy fats.

9. If desired, garnish your Quinoa Breakfast Bowl with fresh fruit slices for an extra burst of freshness.

10. Serve your heart-healthy Quinoa Breakfast Bowl immediately and enjoy!

Nutritional Information (Approximate)

Calories	350	Dietary Fiber	7g
Protein	15g	Sodium	60mg
Carbohydrates	53g	Cholesterol	0mg
Total Fat	10g	(if using yogurt with cholesterol)	
Saturated Fat	1g	Potassium	350mg

This Quinoa Breakfast Bowl is a nutritious and satisfying way to start your day. Quinoa is rich in protein and fiber, while the Greek yogurt provides additional protein and probiotics. Customize your toppings to your taste, and enjoy a hearty and heart-healthy breakfast.

Muesli with Almonds and Dried Fruits

Prep Time: 5 minutes / Cook Time: 0 minutes
Yield: 1 serving

Ingredients

- 1/2 cup rolled oats (old-fashioned oats)
- 1/4 cup low-fat Greek yogurt (unsweetened)
- 1/4 cup unsweetened almond milk
  (or any milk of your choice)
- 1 tablespoon chopped almonds
- 1 tablespoon mixed dried fruits
  (e.g., raisins, apricots, cranberries)
- 1/2 tablespoon honey or maple syrup
  (optional, for sweetness)
- 1/4 teaspoon ground cinnamon
- Fresh fruit slices (e.g., banana, apple)
  for topping (optional)

Directions

1. In a bowl, combine the rolled oats, chopped almonds, and mixed dried fruits.

2. Add the ground cinnamon and mix well to distribute the spices evenly.

3. In a separate small bowl, mix the low-fat Greek yogurt with honey or maple syrup (if using) to sweeten it to your preference.

4. Pour the unsweetened almond milk over the oat mixture. Stir well to combine. Allow it to sit for a few minutes to let the oats absorb some of the liquid.

5. After a brief rest, spoon the sweetened Greek yogurt over the oat mixture.

6. If desired, top your Muesli with Almonds and Dried Fruits with fresh fruit slices for extra-natural sweetness and flavor.

7. Serve your heart-healthy Muesli immediately and enjoy!

Nutritional Information (Approximate)

Calories	320	Dietary Fiber	7g
Protein	12g	Sodium	90mg
Carbohydrates	45g	Cholesterol	5mg
Total Fat	9g	(if using yogurt with cholesterol)	
Saturated Fat	1g	Potassium	320mg

This Muesli with Almonds and Dried Fruits is a nutritious and quick breakfast option. The combination of oats, almonds, and dried fruits provides fiber and healthy fats, while Greek yogurt adds protein and probiotics. Customize your toppings and sweetness level to your liking and enjoy a heart-healthy meal.

Veggie Breakfast Burrito

Prep Time: 10 minutes / Cook Time: 10 minutes
Yield: 1 serving

Ingredients

- 1 whole-wheat tortilla (8-inch), 2 large egg whites
- 1/4 cup diced bell peppers (any color)
- 1/4 cup diced onions, 1/4 cup diced tomatoes
- 1/4 cup chopped spinach or kale
- 1/4 cup black beans (canned and rinsed)
- 1/4 cup salsa (low-sodium, if possible)
- 1/4 teaspoon ground cumin
- A pinch of salt and black pepper (optional)
- Cooking spray or a small amount of oil for cooking

Directions

1. In a non-stick skillet, heat a small amount of cooking spray or oil over medium heat.

2. Add the diced bell peppers and onions to the skillet. Sauté for about 2-3 minutes until they become slightly tender.

3. Add the diced tomatoes and chopped spinach or kale to the skillet. Continue to sauté for another 1-2 minutes until the greens are wilted.

4. In a bowl, whisk the egg whites and season with ground cumin, a pinch of salt, and black pepper if desired.

5. Push the sautéed vegetables to one side of the skillet and pour the whisked egg whites into the other side.

6. Scramble the egg whites until fully cooked and then mix them with the sautéed vegetables in the skillet.

7. Warm the black beans in the skillet for 1-2 minutes.

8. Heat the whole-wheat tortilla in the microwave or on a separate skillet for about 10-15 seconds to make it more pliable.

9. Lay the warmed tortilla flat on a plate and spoon the egg white and vegetable mixture onto the center of the tortilla.

10. Add salsa and black beans on top of the mixture.

11. Fold in the sides of the tortilla and then roll it up to form your Veggie Breakfast Burrito.

12. 1Serve your heart-healthy Veggie Breakfast Burrito immediately and enjoy!

Nutritional Information (Approximate)

Calories	300	Sodium	450mg
Protein	20g	(may vary based on salsa and	
Carbohydrates	45g	bean choices)	
Total Fat	5g	Cholesterol	0mg
Saturated Fat	1g	Potassium	600mg
Dietary Fiber	4g		

This Veggie Breakfast Burrito is a nutritious and satisfying breakfast option. It's packed with vegetables, egg whites for protein, and whole-wheat tortillas for fiber. Customize your burrito with your favorite heart-healthy toppings and enjoy a delicious meal to start your day.

Baked Sweet Potato with Cottage Cheese

Prep Time: 5 minutes / Cook Time: 45 minutes
Yield: 1 serving

Ingredients

- 1 medium-sized sweet potato
- 1/2 cup low-fat cottage cheese
- 1/4 teaspoon ground cinnamon
- 1/4 teaspoon honey (optional, for sweetness)
- Fresh parsley or chives for garnish (optional)

Directions

1. Preheat your oven to 375°F (190°C).

2. Wash and scrub the sweet potato thoroughly to remove any dirt.

3. Pierce the sweet potato several times with a fork to allow steam to escape during baking.

4. Place the sweet potato on a baking sheet and bake in the preheated oven for approximately 45 minutes or until it's tender and easily pierced with a fork.

5. While the sweet potato is baking, mix the low-fat cottage cheese with ground cinnamon and honey (if using) in a small bowl. Adjust the sweetness to your preference.

6. Once the sweet potato is fully baked, remove it from the oven and let it cool slightly for a few minutes.

7. Make a lengthwise slit in the center of the sweet potato, creating an opening.

8. Spoon the seasoned cottage cheese into the slit and on top of the sweet potato.

9. If desired, garnish with fresh parsley or chives for added flavor and presentation.

10. Serve your heart-healthy Baked Sweet Potato with Cottage Cheese immediately and enjoy!

Nutritional Information (Approximate)

Calories 250	Sodium (may vary based on cottage cheese) 350mg
Protein 15g	
Carbohydrates.............. 49g	Cholesterol (may vary based on cottage cheese) 10mg
Total Fat 2g	
Saturated Fat 1g	Potassium 800mg
Dietary Fiber 6g	

This Baked Sweet Potato with Cottage Cheese is a nutritious and filling meal. Sweet potatoes are rich in fiber and vitamins, while cottage cheese provides protein and calcium. Customize the seasoning and sweetness to your liking and enjoy a delicious and heart-healthy dish.

Berry and Banana Whole Wheat Muffins

Prep Time: 15 minutes / Cook Time: 20 minutes
Yield: 12 serving

Ingredients

- 1 1/2 cups whole wheat flour
- 1/2 cup rolled oats (old-fashioned oats)
- 1/2 cup unsweetened applesauce
- 1/2 cup honey or maple syrup (for sweetness, optional)
- 2 ripe bananas, mashed, 1/4 teaspoon salt (optional)
- 1/2 cup mixed berries (e.g., blueberries, raspberries)
- 2 large eggs, 1/4 cup low-fat yogurt (unsweetened)
- 1 teaspoon baking powder, 1/2 teaspoon baking soda
- 1/2 teaspoon ground cinnamon

Directions

1. Preheat your oven to 350°F (175°C). Line a muffin tin with paper liners or lightly grease it with cooking spray.

2. In a large mixing bowl, combine the whole wheat flour, rolled oats, baking powder, baking soda, ground cinnamon, and a pinch of salt (if using). Mix well.

3. In a separate bowl, whisk together the mashed bananas, unsweetened applesauce, honey or maple syrup (if using), low-fat yogurt, and eggs until well combined.

4. Pour the wet ingredients into the dry ingredients and stir until just combined. Be careful not to overmix; a few lumps are okay.

5. Gently fold in the mixed berries.

6. Spoon the muffin batter evenly into the prepared muffin tin, filling each cup about 2/3 full.

7. Bake in the preheated oven for approximately 18-20 minutes or until a toothpick inserted into the center of a muffin comes out clean.

8. Remove the muffins from the oven and let them cool in the tin for a few minutes before transferring them to a wire rack to cool completely.

Nutritional Information (Approximate)

Calories 140	Dietary Fiber 3g
Protein 3g	Sodium 120mg
Carbohydrates 32g	Cholesterol 25mg
Total Fat 1g	Potassium............... 170mg
Saturated Fat 0g	

These Berry and Banana Whole Wheat Muffins are a wholesome and delicious snack or breakfast option. They are made with whole wheat flour, oats, and natural sweetness from bananas and honey. Enjoy them as a heart-healthy treat anytime.

Peanut Butter and Banana Sandwich

Prep Time: 5 minutes / Cook Time: 0 minutes
Yield: 1 serving

Ingredients

- 2 slices of whole-grain bread
- 2 tablespoons natural peanut butter (unsweetened and unsalted)
- 1 small banana, sliced
- 1/2 teaspoon honey or maple syrup (optional, for sweetness)
- A pinch of ground cinnamon (optional)

Directions

1. Lay out the two slices of whole-grain bread on a clean surface.

2. Spread the natural peanut butter evenly onto one slice of bread.

3. Arrange the banana slices on top of the peanut butter.

4. Drizzle honey or maple syrup (if using) over the banana slices for added sweetness.

5. If desired, sprinkle a pinch of ground cinnamon on top of the banana slices for extra flavor.

6. Place the second slice of bread on top to create a sandwich.

7. Press the sandwich together gently to make it easier to eat.

8. You can enjoy the sandwich as is or cut it in half for easier handling.

9. Serve your heart-healthy Peanut Butter and Banana Sandwich immediately and enjoy!

Nutritional Information (Approximate)

Calories	350	Sodium	250mg
Protein	10g	(may vary based on bread
Carbohydrates	50g	and peanut butter choices)
Total Fat	14g	Cholesterol	0mg
Saturated Fat	2g	Potassium	310mg
Dietary Fiber	8g		

This Peanut Butter and Banana Sandwich is a nutritious and delicious option for a quick breakfast or snack. Whole-grain bread provides fiber, while natural peanut butter offers healthy fats and protein. Customize your sandwich with honey, cinnamon, or other toppings to suit your taste.

Homemade Granola Bars

Cook Time: 20 minutes (plus cooling time)
Prep Time: 15 minutes / Yield: 10 serving

Ingredients

- 1 1/2 cups rolled oats (old-fashioned oats)
- 1/2 cup unsweetened almond butter (or any nut or seed butter of your choice)
- 1/4 cup honey or maple syrup
- 1/4 cup chopped nuts (e.g., almonds, walnuts)
- 1/4 cup dried fruits (e.g., raisins, cranberries)
- 1/4 cup dark chocolate chips (optional)
- 1/2 teaspoon vanilla extract
- 1/4 teaspoon salt (optional)

Directions

1. . Preheat your oven to 350°F (175°C). Line an 8x8-inch (20x20 cm) baking pan with parchment paper, leaving some overhang on the sides for easy removal.

2. In a large mixing bowl, combine the rolled oats, chopped nuts, dried fruits, and dark chocolate chips (if using). Mix well.

3. In a microwave-safe bowl or a small saucepan, heat the almond butter and honey or maple syrup over low heat until they are easily stirrable. Stir in the vanilla extract and a pinch of salt (if using).

4. Pour the almond butter mixture over the dry ingredients in the mixing bowl.

5. Stir everything together until all the dry ingredients are well coated with the almond butter mixture. You may need to use your hands to press the mixture together.

6. Transfer the mixture to the prepared baking pan. Use a spatula or your hands to press it firmly into an even layer.

7. Bake in the preheated oven for approximately 18-20 minutes or until the edges are lightly golden.

8. Remove the pan from the oven and let it cool in the pan for about 10-15 minutes.

9. Use the parchment paper overhangs to lift the granola out of the pan. Place it on a cutting board and let it cool completely.

10. Once cooled, cut the granola slab into 10 bars.

11. Store your homemade granola bars in an airtight container at room temperature for up to a week or in the refrigerator for longer freshness.

Nutritional Information (Approximate)

Calories	200	Dietary Fiber	3g
Protein	5g	Sodium	50mg
Carbohydrates	22g	Cholesterol	0mg
Total Fat	11g	Potassium	180mg
Saturated Fat	1g		

Smoked Salmon and Whole Grain Bagel

Prep Time: 5 minutes / Cook Time: 0 minutes
Yield: 1 serving

Ingredients

- 1 whole-grain bagel (unsliced), 2 ounces smoked salmon
- 2 tablespoons low-fat cream cheese
- 1 tablespoon fresh dill, chopped, 1/4 red onion, thinly sliced
- 1/2 small cucumber, thinly sliced
- Fresh lemon wedges for garnish (optional)
- Fresh ground black pepper (optional)

Directions

1. Slice the whole-grain bagel in half horizontally.

2. Spread 1 tablespoon of low-fat cream cheese on each half of the bagel.

3. Lay the smoked salmon slices evenly over the cream cheese on both bagel halves.

4. Sprinkle chopped fresh dill on top of the smoked salmon.

5. Arrange the thinly sliced red onion and cucumber on top of the smoked salmon and dill.

6. If desired, squeeze fresh lemon juice over the toppings and add a pinch of fresh ground black pepper for extra flavor.

7. Place the bagel halves together to form a sandwich.

8. Serve your heart-healthy Smoked Salmon and Whole Grain Bagel immediately and enjoy!

Nutritional Information (Approximate)

Calories	350	Dietary Fiber	7g
Protein	20g	Sodium	600mg
Carbohydrates	40g	Cholesterol	25mg
Total Fat	12g	Potassium	310mg
Saturated Fat	3g		

Quinoa and Berry Breakfast Bowl

Prep Time: 10 minutes / Cook Time: 15 minutes
Yield: 1 serving

Ingredients

- 1/2 cup cooked quinoa, 1/4 teaspoon vanilla extract
- 1/2 cup fresh mixed berries (strawberries, blueberries, raspberries)
- 1/4 cup low-fat Greek yogurt
- 1 tablespoon honey or maple syrup (optional)
- 1 tablespoon chopped nuts (e.g., almonds, walnuts)
- 1 teaspoon chia seeds (optional)

Directions

1. Start by cooking the quinoa if it's not already cooked. Rinse 1/4 cup of quinoa in a fine-mesh strainer and then combine it with 1/2 cup of water in a saucepan. Bring to a boil, reduce heat to low, cover, and simmer for about 15 minutes or until the quinoa is tender and the liquid is absorbed. Fluff with a fork and let it cool.

2. In a bowl, mix the Greek yogurt with honey (or maple syrup) and vanilla extract. Stir until well combined.

3. In a serving bowl, place the cooked quinoa as the base. Top the quinoa with the fresh mixed berries. Drizzle the sweetened Greek yogurt mixture over the berries.

4. Sprinkle chopped nuts and chia seeds (if using) on top for added texture and nutrition.

5. Give it a gentle stir if desired and enjoy your heart-healthy Quinoa and Berry Breakfast Bowl!

Nutritional Information (Approximate)

Calories	320	Dietary Fiber	8g
Protein	11g	Sodium	35mg
Carbohydrates	58g	Cholesterol	2mg
Total Fat	6g	Potassium	380mg
Saturated Fat	1g		

Avocado and Spinach Breakfast Wrap

Prep Time: 10 minutes / Cook Time: 5 minutes / Yield: 1 serving

Ingredients

- 1 whole-wheat tortilla (8 inches in diameter)
- 1/2 ripe avocado, sliced
- 1/2 cup fresh spinach leaves
- 1 large egg
- 1/4 cup diced tomatoes
- 1 tablespoon diced red onion
- 1/4 teaspoon ground cumin
- Salt and pepper to taste
- Cooking spray or a small amount of olive oil for cooking

Nutritional Information (Approximate)

Calories	290	Dietary Fiber	9g
Protein	10g	Sodium	240mg
Carbohydrates	28g	Cholesterol	185mg
Total Fat	16g	Potassium	720mg
Saturated Fat	3g		

Directionsa

1. In a small bowl, whisk the egg and season it with ground cumin, salt, and pepper to taste. Heat a non-stick skillet over medium heat and lightly grease it with cooking spray or a small amount of olive oil.

2. Pour the whisked egg into the skillet and cook it, stirring occasionally, until it's fully scrambled, about 2-3 minutes. Remove from heat and set aside. Place the whole-wheat tortilla on a clean surface or a plate. Lay the fresh spinach leaves evenly on the tortilla.

3. Arrange the sliced avocado on top of the spinach. Spoon the scrambled egg onto the avocado and spinach.

4. Sprinkle diced tomatoes and diced red onion over the egg. Carefully fold in the sides of the tortilla and then roll it up from the bottom, creating a wrap.

5. Serve immediately, and enjoy your heart-healthy Avocado and Spinach Breakfast Wrap!

Chia Seed and Green Tea Smoothie

Prep Time: 5 minutes / Cook Time: 0 minutes
Yield: 1 serving

Ingredients

- 1 green tea bag, 1/2 cup hot water, 2 tablespoons chia seeds
- 1/2 cup unsweetened almond milk
- 1/2 cup fresh spinach leaves, 1/2 ripe banana
- 1/2 tablespoon honey (optional), ice cubes (optional)

Directions

1. Steep the green tea bag in 1/2 cup of hot water for about 3-5 minutes. Allow it to cool.

2. In a separate bowl, combine the chia seeds and almond milk. Stir well and let it sit for 10-15 minutes until it thickens into a gel-like consistency.

3. In a blender, add the cooled green tea, chia seed mixture, spinach, banana, and honey (if using). You can also add a few ice cubes for a colder and thicker smoothie.

4. Blend until all the ingredients are well combined and the smoothie is creamy.

5. Pour the smoothie into a glass and serve immediately.

Nutritional Information (Approximate)

Calories	180	Dietary Fiber	9g
Protein	3g	Sodium	85mg
Carbohydrates	32g	Cholesterol	0mg
Total Fat	6g	Potassium	300mg
Saturated Fat	0,5g		

Salmon and Dill Scrambled Eggs

Prep Time: 5 minutes / Cook Time: 5 minutes
Yield: 1 serving

Ingredients

- 2 eggs, 2 ounces smoked salmon, chopped
- 1 tablespoon chopped fresh dill, 1/4 cup diced red onion
- 1 teaspoon olive oil, salt and pepper to taste
- 1/4 cup diced red bell pepper

Directions

1. 1. In a bowl, beat the eggs until well mixed. Stir in the flaked salmon and chopped fresh dill. Season with salt and pepper to taste. Set aside.

2. Heat a non-stick skillet over medium heat and add the olive oil.

3. Once the oil is hot, add the diced red bell pepper and red onion. Sauté for about 2-3 minutes until they begin to soften. Pour the egg mixture into the skillet with the sautéed vegetables.

4. Cook the eggs, stirring gently and continuously, until they are fully scrambled and cooked to your desired level of doneness. This should take about 2-3 minutes.

5. Remove the skillet from heat and transfer the scrambled eggs to a plate.

6. Garnish with extra dill, if desired. Serve immediately, and enjoy your heart-healthy Salmon and Dill Scrambled Eggs!

Nutritional Information (Approximate)

Calories	260	Dietary Fiber	1g
Protein	23g	Sodium	360mg
Carbohydrates	5g	Cholesterol	385mg
Total Fat	16g	Potassium	400mg
Saturated Fat	3,5g		

Sweet Potato and Spinach Breakfast Hash

Prep Time: 10 minutes / Cook Time: 20 minutes / Yield: 1 serving

Ingredients

- 1 small sweet potato, peeled and diced, 1/4 cup diced red onion
- 1/2 cup fresh spinach leaves, chopped, 1 clove garlic, minced
- 1/4 cup diced red bell pepper, 1/2 teaspoon smoked paprika
- 1/4 teaspoon ground cumin, salt and pepper to taste
- 1 teaspoon olive oil, 1 large egg (optional)
- Fresh parsley or cilantro for garnish (optional)

Nutritional Information (Approximate)

Calories	220	Dietary Fiber	6g
Protein	4g	Sodium	90mg
Carbohydrates	36g	Cholesterol	0mg
Total Fat	7g	Potassium	660mg
Saturated Fat	1g		

Directions

1. Heat a non-stick skillet over medium heat and add the olive oil. Once the oil is hot, add the diced sweet potato. Cook for about 10-12 minutes, stirring occasionally, until the sweet potato is tender and lightly browned.

2. Add the diced red bell pepper, diced red onion, and minced garlic to the skillet. Sauté for an additional 2-3 minutes until the vegetables are softened. Season the mixture with smoked paprika, ground cumin, salt, and pepper. Stir well to coat the vegetables evenly with the spices.

3. Add the chopped spinach to the skillet and cook for an additional 2-3 minutes until the spinach wilts and is mixed in with the other vegetables.

4. If desired, create a well in the center of the hash and crack an egg into it. Cover the skillet and cook for about 5 minutes or until the egg white is set but the yolk is still runny (adjust cooking time to your egg preference).

5. Carefully transfer the Sweet Potato and Spinach Breakfast Hash to a plate.

6. Garnish with fresh parsley or cilantro, if desired. Serve immediately and enjoy your heart-healthy breakfast!

chapter4
SALAD

Caesar 19

Greek 19

Caprese 19

Cobb 20

Waldorf 20

Spinach and Strawberry 20

Thai Peanut 21

Quinoa 21

Mediterranean Chickpea 21

Taco 22

Chicken Caesar 22

Beet & Goat Cheese 23

Watermelon and Feta 23

Broccoli 23

Nicoise 24

Avocado and Black Bean 24

Kale Caesar 25

Tuna 25

Waldorf Chicken 25

Caesar Salad

Prep Time: 15 minutes / Cook Time: 0 minutes
Yield: 1 serving

Ingredients

- 2 cups fresh romaine lettuce, torn into bite-sized pieces
- 1/4 cup cherry tomatoes, halved
- 1/4 cup cucumber, sliced
- 2 tablespoons reduced-fat Caesar dressing
- 1 tablespoon grated Parmesan cheese (optional)
- 1/4 cup whole-grain croutons (optional)

Directions

1. Start by washing the romaine lettuce leaves thoroughly. Pat them dry with a paper towel or use a salad spinner to remove excess water.

2. Tear the lettuce into bite-sized pieces and place them in a salad bowl. Add the cherry tomatoes and cucumber slices to the bowl with the lettuce.

3. Drizzle the reduced-fat Caesar dressing over the salad ingredients. If you prefer, sprinkle grated Parmesan cheese on top for added flavor.

4. For some crunch, consider adding whole-grain croutons to the salad.

5. Gently toss all the ingredients together to evenly coat them with the dressing.

Nutritional Information (Approximate)

Calories	250	Dietary Fiber	4g
Protein	5g	Sodium	350mg
Carbohydrates	15g	Cholesterol	10mg
Total Fat	18g	Potassium	400mg
Saturated Fat	3g		

Greek Salad

Prep Time: 15 minutes / Cook Time: 0 minutes
Yield: 1 serving

Ingredients

- 2 cups fresh romaine lettuce, torn into bite-sized pieces
- 1/4 cup cucumber, diced, 1/4 cup cherry tomatoes, halved
- 1/4 cup red onion, thinly sliced
- 2 tablespoons reduced-fat feta cheese, crumbled
- 6-8 Kalamata olives, pitted and sliced
- 2 tablespoons extra-virgin olive oil
- 1 tablespoon red wine vinegar, 1/2 teaspoon dried oregano
- Freshly ground black pepper, to taste

Directions

1. Begin by preparing the vegetables. Wash and dry the romaine lettuce, then tear it into bite-sized pieces. Dice the cucumber, halve the cherry tomatoes, and thinly slice the red onion.

2. In a salad bowl, combine the romaine lettuce, cucumber, cherry tomatoes, and red onion.

3. Sprinkle the crumbled reduced-fat feta cheese over the salad. Add the Kalamata olives to the salad for a burst of flavor.

4. In a small bowl, whisk together the extra-virgin olive oil, red wine vinegar, dried oregano, and black pepper. This will be your dressing.

5. Drizzle the dressing over the salad ingredients.

6. Gently toss the salad to ensure all the ingredients are coated evenly with the dressing.

Nutritional Information (Approximate)

Calories	280	Dietary Fiber	4g
Protein	7g	Sodium	380mg
Carbohydrates	14g	Cholesterol	10mg
Total Fat	22g	Potassium	450mg
Saturated Fat	4g		

Caprese Salad

Prep Time: 10 minutes / Cook Time: 0 minutes / Yield: 1 serving

Ingredients

- 1 large ripe tomato, sliced, 1/4 cup fresh basil leaves
- 1/2 cup fresh mozzarella cheese, sliced or cubed
- 1 tablespoon extra-virgin olive oil
- 1 tablespoon balsamic vinegar (reduced sodium if available)
- Salt and freshly ground black pepper, to taste

Nutritional Information (Approximate)

Calories	300	Dietary Fiber	1g
Protein	12g	Sodium	350mg
Carbohydrates	6g	Cholesterol	25mg
Total Fat	25g	Potassium	400mg
Saturated Fat	10g		

Directions

1. Begin by slicing the ripe tomato into rounds, approximately 1/4-inch thick. Arrange the tomato slices on a serving plate.

2. Next, slice or cube the fresh mozzarella cheese and place it on top of the tomato slices.

3. Wash and dry the fresh basil leaves, then gently tear them or leave them whole for a rustic appearance. Scatter the basil leaves over the tomatoes and mozzarella.

4. In a small bowl, whisk together the extra-virgin olive oil and balsamic vinegar. Drizzle this dressing over the salad.

5. Season the salad with a pinch of salt and a grind of freshly ground black pepper to taste.

Cobb Salad

Prep Time: 15 minutes / Cook Time: 0 minutes
Yield: 1 serving

Ingredients

- 2 cups mixed salad greens (e.g., romaine and spinach)
- 3 ounces skinless, boneless grilled chicken breast, diced
- 1 hard-boiled egg, sliced 1/4 cup cherry tomatoes, halved
- 1/4 cup cucumber, diced, 1/4 avocado, diced
- 2 tablespoons crumbled reduced-fat feta cheese
- 1 slice turkey bacon, cooked and crumbled
- 2 tablespoons balsamic vinaigrette dressing (reduced sodium if available)

Directions

1. Start by washing and drying the mixed salad greens. Place them in a large salad bowl.

2. Dice the grilled chicken breast into bite-sized pieces and add it to the salad greens.

3. Slice the hard-boiled egg and place the slices on top of the salad.

4. Halve the cherry tomatoes and dice the cucumber. Scatter them over the salad.

5. Sprinkle the crumbled reduced-fat feta cheese and crumbled turkey bacon on top.

6. Dice the avocado and add it to the salad. Drizzle the balsamic vinaigrette dressing over the salad as your dressing.

Nutritional Information (Approximate)

Calories	380	Dietary Fiber	5g
Protein	30g	Sodium	600mg
Carbohydrates	15g	Cholesterol	185mg
Total Fat	20g	Potassium	600mg
Saturated Fat	4g		

Waldorf Salad

Prep Time: 15 minutes / Cook Time: 0 minutes
Yield: 1 serving

Ingredients

- 2 cups mixed salad greens (e.g., spinach and arugula)
- 1/2 medium apple, diced (with skin), 1/4 cup celery, thinly sliced
- 1/4 cup seedless grapes, halved
- 1/4 cup walnuts, chopped and toasted
- 2 tablespoons reduced-fat Greek yogurt
- 1 tablespoon honey, 1/2 tablespoon lemon juice
- 1/4 teaspoon ground cinnamon, a pinch of salt (optional)

Directions

1. Begin by washing and drying the mixed salad greens. Place them in a salad bowl.

2. Dice the apple (with the skin for added fiber and nutrients) and add it to the greens.

3. Thinly slice the celery and scatter it over the salad.

4. Halve the seedless grapes and add them to the salad.

5. Toast the chopped walnuts in a dry skillet over medium heat for a few minutes until they become fragrant. Be careful not to burn them. Once toasted, sprinkle them over the salad.

6. In a small bowl, whisk together the reduced-fat Greek yogurt, honey, lemon juice, ground cinnamon, and a pinch of salt if desired. This will be your creamy dressing.

7. Drizzle the creamy dressing over the salad ingredients.

Nutritional Information (Approximate)

Calories	350	Dietary Fiber	6g
Protein	5g	Sodium	40mg
Carbohydrates	45g	Cholesterol	0mg
Total Fat	18g	Potassium	400mg
Saturated Fat	2g		

Spinach and Strawberry Salad

Prep Time: 10 minutes / Cook Time: 0 minutes / Yield: 1 serving

Ingredients

- 2 cups fresh spinach leaves, washedand torn into bite-sized pieces
- 1/2 cup fresh strawberries, hulled and sliced
- 1/4 cup red onion, thinly sliced, 1/2 tablespoon honey (optional)
- 1 tablespoon slivered almonds, toasted
- 1 tablespoon balsamic vinaigrette dressing (reduced sodium if available)
- A pinch of black sesame seeds (optional)
- A pinch of salt and freshly ground black pepper (optional)

Nutritional Information

Calories	180	Dietary Fiber	4g
Protein	4g	Sodium	200mg
Carbohydrates	20g	Cholesterol	0mg
Total Fat	10g	Potassium	500mg
Saturated Fat	1g		

Directions

1. Start by washing and drying the fresh spinach leaves. Tear them into bite-sized pieces and place them in a salad bowl.Hull the fresh strawberries and slice them. Add the sliced strawberries to the spinach. Thinly slice the red onion and scatter it over the salad.

2. Toast the slivered almonds in a dry skillet over medium heat for a few minutes until they become golden and fragrant. Be careful not to burn them. Sprinkle the toasted almonds on top of the salad.

3. In a small bowl, whisk together the balsamic vinaigrette dressing and honey if you prefer a slightly sweeter taste. Drizzle this dressing over the salad.

4. For added texture and flavor, sprinkle a pinch of black sesame seeds over the salad. If desired, season the salad with a pinch of salt and freshly ground black pepper to taste.

Thai Peanut Salad

Prep Time: 15 minutes / Cook Time: 0 minutes
Yield: 1 serving

Ingredients

- 2 cups mixed salad greens (e.g., spinach, lettuce, and cabbage)
- 1/2 cup red bell pepper, thinly sliced
- 1/4 cup carrots, julienned or grated, 1/4 cup cucumber, thinly sliced
- 1/4 cup edamame beans (shelled), steamed and cooled
- 2 tablespoons unsalted peanuts, chopped
- 1 tablespoon fresh cilantro leaves, chopped
- 2 tablespoons Thai peanut dressing (reduced sodium if available)
- Lime wedges for garnish (optional)

Directions

1. Begin by washing and drying the mixed salad greens. Place them in a large salad bowl.

2. Thinly slice the red bell pepper and add it to the salad greens.

3. Julienne or grate the carrots and scatter them over the salad.

4. Slice the cucumber and add it to the salad.

5. Steam the edamame beans until tender, then let them cool before adding them to the salad.

6. Chop the unsalted peanuts and fresh cilantro leaves. Sprinkle them over the salad for added crunch and flavor.

7. Drizzle the Thai peanut dressing over the salad ingredients. Toss gently to coat everything evenly.

Nutritional Information (Approximate)

Calories	350	Dietary Fiber	7g
Protein	12g	Sodium	350mg
Carbohydrates	20g	Cholesterol	0mg
Total Fat	25g	Potassium	550mg
Saturated Fat	4g		

Quinoa Salad

Prep Time: 15 minutes / Cook Time: 15 minutes
Yield: 1 serving

Ingredients

- 1/2 cup quinoa, rinsed and drained, 1 cup water
- 1/4 cup cucumber, diced, 1/4 cup red bell pepper, diced
- 1/4 cup cherry tomatoes, halved
- 1/4 cup canned chickpeas, drained and rinsed
- 2 tablespoons fresh parsley, chopped
- 1 tablespoon extra-virgin olive oil, 1 tablespoon lemon juice
- 1/2 teaspoon ground cumin
- Salt and freshly ground black pepper, to taste

Directions

1. Start by rinsing the quinoa thoroughly in a fine-mesh sieve under cold running water.

2. In a saucepan, combine the rinsed quinoa and water. Bring it to a boil, then reduce the heat to low, cover, and simmer for about 15 minutes or until the quinoa is tender and the water is absorbed. Remove from heat and let it cool.

3. In a large salad bowl, combine the cooked and cooled quinoa, diced cucumber, diced red bell pepper, halved cherry tomatoes, chickpeas, and chopped fresh parsley.

4. In a small bowl, whisk together the extra-virgin olive oil, lemon juice, ground cumin, salt, and freshly ground black pepper to create the dressing.

5. Drizzle the dressing over the salad ingredients.

6. Gently toss everything together to ensure the dressing is evenly distributed.

Nutritional Information (Approximate)

Calories	400	Dietary Fiber	9g
Protein	12g	Sodium	250mg
Carbohydrates	62g	Cholesterol	0mg
Total Fat	12g	Potassium	500mg
Saturated Fat	2g		

Mediterranean Chickpea Salad

Prep Time: 15 minutes / Cook Time: 0 minutes / Yield: 1 serving

Ingredients

- 1 cup canned chickpeas, drained and rinsed
- 1/4 cup cucumber, diced, 1/4 cup cherry tomatoes, halved
- 1/4 cup red bell pepper, diced, 1/4 cup red onion, finely chopped
- 2 tablespoons Kalamata olives, pitted and sliced
- 2 tablespoons reduced-fat feta cheese, crumbled
- 1 tablespoon fresh parsley, chopped
- 1 tablespoon extra-virgin olive oil
- 1 tablespoon lemon juice, 1/2 teaspoon dried oregano
- Salt and freshly ground black pepper, to taste

Nutritional Information (Approximate)

Calories	350	Dietary Fiber	10g
Protein	15g	Sodium	400mg
Carbohydrates	40g	Cholesterol	5mg
Total Fat	16g	Potassium	500mg
Saturated Fat	3g		

Directions

1. Begin by draining and rinsing the canned chickpeas under cold running water.

2. In a salad bowl, combine the chickpeas, diced cucumber, halved cherry tomatoes, diced red bell pepper, finely chopped red onion, sliced Kalamata olives, crumbled reduced-fat feta cheese, and chopped fresh parsley.

3. In a small bowl, whisk together the extra-virgin olive oil, lemon juice, dried oregano, salt, and freshly ground black pepper to create the dressing.

4. Drizzle the dressing over the salad ingredients. Gently toss everything together to ensure the dressing is evenly distributed.

Taco Salad

Prep Time: 15 minutes / Cook Time: 10 minutes
Yield: 1 serving

Ingredients

- 1 cup mixed salad greens
  (e.g., romaine and iceberg lettuce)
- 1/2 cup lean ground turkey (or ground chicken),
  cooked and seasoned with taco seasoning
- 1/4 cup black beans, drained and rinsed
- 1/4 cup cherry tomatoes, halved, 1/4 avocado, sliced
- 1/4 cup red onion, finely chopped
- 1/4 cup bell pepper (any color), diced
- 2 tablespoons reduced-fat shredded cheddar cheese
- 2 tablespoons plain Greek yogurt
  (or low-fat sour cream)
- 1 tablespoon salsa (choose a lower-sodium option)
- 1/2 tablespoon fresh cilantro, chopped
- Baked whole-grain tortilla chips (optional, for crunch)

Directions

1. In a skillet, cook the lean ground turkey (or chicken) over medium heat until fully cooked, breaking it apart with a spatula as it cooks. Season it with taco seasoning according to package instructions. Set aside to cool slightly.

2. Wash and dry the mixed salad greens, then place them in a large salad bowl.

3. Drain and rinse the black beans, then add them to the salad greens.

4. Halve the cherry tomatoes, finely chop the red onion, and dice the bell pepper. Scatter them over the salad.

5. Sprinkle the reduced-fat shredded cheddar cheese over the salad for extra flavor.

6. In a small bowl, combine the plain Greek yogurt (or low-fat sour cream) and salsa to create a creamy taco dressing.

7. Top the salad with the cooked and seasoned ground turkey (or chicken), and drizzle the creamy taco dressing over it.

8. Garnish the salad with fresh cilantro and slices of avocado.

9. If desired, break whole-grain tortilla chips into smaller pieces and add them for added crunch.

Nutritional Information (Approximate)

Calories	400	Dietary Fiber	10g
Protein	25g	Sodium	550mg
Carbohydrates	35g	Cholesterol	50mg
Total Fat	18g	Potassium	650mg
Saturated Fat	4g		

Chicken Caesar Salad

Prep Time: 15 minutes / Cook Time: 15 minutes
Yield: 1 serving

Ingredients

- 2 cups fresh romaine lettuce, washed and torn into bite-sized pieces
- 4 ounces boneless, skinless chicken breast
- 1/4 cup cherry tomatoes, halved
- 1/4 cup cucumber, sliced
- 2 tablespoons reduced-fat Caesar dressing
- 1 tablespoon grated Parmesan cheese (optional)
- 1/4 cup whole-grain croutons (optional)

Directions

1. Start by washing the romaine lettuce leaves thoroughly. Pat them dry with a paper towel or use a salad spinner to remove excess water.

2. Tear the lettuce into bite-sized pieces and place them in a salad bowl.

3. Season the chicken breast with a pinch of salt and pepper. Heat a non-stick skillet over medium-high heat and cook the chicken breast for about 6-7 minutes per side or until fully cooked and no longer pink in the center. Remove from heat and let it rest for a few minutes before slicing it into thin strips.

4. Add the sliced chicken to the salad bowl with the romaine lettuce.

5. Add the cherry tomatoes and cucumber slices to the bowl.

6. Drizzle the reduced-fat Caesar dressing over the salad ingredients.

7. If you prefer, sprinkle grated Parmesan cheese on top for added flavor.

8. For some crunch, consider adding whole-grain croutons to the salad.

9. Gently toss all the ingredients together to evenly coat them with the dressing.

Nutritional Information

Calories	350	Dietary Fiber	4g
Protein	30g	Sodium	700mg
Carbohydrates	15g	Cholesterol	75mg
Total Fat	18g	Potassium	400mg
Saturated Fat	4g		

Enjoy your heart-healthy Chicken Caesar Salad! It's a delicious and satisfying option for a light meal or a flavorful side dish.

Beet and Goat Cheese Salad

Prep Time: 15 minutes / Cook Time: 0 minutes
Yield: 1 serving

Ingredients

- 2 cups mixed salad greens (e.g., arugula, spinach, and lettuce)
- 1 small beet, cooked, peeled, and sliced
- 1/4 cup crumbled goat cheese (reduced-fat if available)
- 1/4 cup walnuts, chopped and toasted
- 2 tablespoons balsamic vinaigrette dressing (reduced sodium if available)
- 1 tablespoon fresh basil leaves, torn (optional)
- Salt and freshly ground black pepper, to taste

Directions

1. Begin by washing and drying the mixed salad greens. Place them in a large salad bowl.

2. Cook the beet until tender, either by boiling, roasting, or microwaving it. Allow it to cool, then peel and slice it.

3. Scatter the sliced beet over the salad greens.

4. Sprinkle the crumbled goat cheese and chopped, toasted walnuts on top for a rich, creamy, and crunchy texture.

5. If desired, tear fresh basil leaves and add them to the salad for an extra layer of flavor.

6. In a small bowl, whisk together the balsamic vinaigrette dressing. Drizzle this dressing over the salad.

7. Season the salad with a pinch of salt and freshly ground black pepper to taste.

Nutritional Information

Calories	350	Dietary Fiber	5g
Protein	10g	Sodium	350mg
Carbohydrates	18g	Cholesterol	15mg
Total Fat	25g	Potassium	600mg
Saturated Fat	6g		

Watermelon and Feta Salad

Prep Time: 15 minutes / Cook Time: 0 minutes
Yield: 1 serving

Ingredients

- 2 cups fresh watermelon cubes, 1/4 cup cucumber, diced
- 1/4 cup crumbled feta cheese (reduced-fat if available)
- 1/4 cup red onion, thinly sliced
- 2 tablespoons fresh mint leaves, chopped
- 1 tablespoon extra-virgin olive oil
- 1 tablespoon balsamic vinegar, 1/2 tablespoon honey
- Salt and freshly ground black pepper, to taste

Directions

1. Begin by preparing the watermelon. Cut it into bite-sized cubes and place them in a salad bowl.

2. Crumble the feta cheese over the watermelon cubes for a salty and creamy contrast.

3. Dice the cucumber and add it to the salad.

4. Thinly slice the red onion and scatter it over the salad ingredients.

5. Chop fresh mint leaves and sprinkle them on top for a refreshing flavor.

6. In a small bowl, whisk together the extra-virgin olive oil, balsamic vinegar, honey, salt, and freshly ground black pepper to create the dressing.

7. Drizzle the dressing over the salad.

8. Gently toss all the ingredients together to ensure the dressing is evenly distributed.

Nutritional Information (Approximate)

Calories	250	Dietary Fiber	2g
Protein	6g	Sodium	280mg
Carbohydrates	30g	Cholesterol	10mg
Total Fat	13g	Potassium	450mg
Saturated Fat	4g		

Broccoli Salad

Prep Time: 15 minutes / Cook Time: 0 minutes / Yield: 1 serving

Ingredients

- 1 cup fresh broccoli florets, chopped into bite-sized pieces
- 1/4 cup red onion, finely chopped, 1/4 cup carrots, grated
- 1/4 cup raisins or dried cranberries
- 2 tablespoons plain Greek yogurt (reduced-fat if available)
- 1 tablespoon light mayonnaise, 1/2 tablespoon honey
- 1/2 tablespoon apple cider vinegar
- 1 tablespoon sunflower seeds (unsalted)
- Salt and freshly ground black pepper, to taste

Nutritional Information (Approximate)

Calories	250	Dietary Fiber	5g
Protein	7g	Sodium	200mg
Carbohydrates	40g	Cholesterol	5mg
Total Fat	8g	Potassium	450mg
Saturated Fat	1g		

Directions

1. Start by washing the fresh broccoli florets thoroughly. Drain them and chop them into bite-sized pieces. Finely chop the red onion and grate the carrots.

2. In a salad bowl, combine the chopped broccoli, chopped red onion, grated carrots, and raisins or dried cranberries.

3. In a small bowl, whisk together the plain Greek yogurt, light mayonnaise, honey, and apple cider vinegar to create a creamy dressing.

4. Drizzle the creamy dressing over the salad ingredients. Sprinkle sunflower seeds on top for added crunch and flavor.

5. Season the salad with a pinch of salt and freshly ground black pepper to taste. Toss everything together to ensure the dressing is evenly distributed.

Nicoise Salad

Prep Time: 15 minutes / Cook Time: 10 minutes
Yield: 1 serving

Ingredients

- 2 cups mixed salad greens
  (e.g., lettuce, arugula, and spinach)
- 1/2 cup canned tuna, drained (packed in water)
- 1/4 cup cherry tomatoes, halved
- 1/4 cup boiled baby potatoes, halved
- 1/4 cup blanched green beans,
  cut into bite-sized pieces
- 2 hard-boiled eggs, quartered
- 2 tablespoons Kalamata olives, pitted
- 2 tablespoons red onion, thinly sliced
- 1 tablespoon extra-virgin olive oil
- 1 tablespoon red wine vinegar
- 1 teaspoon Dijon mustard
- Salt and freshly ground black pepper, to taste

Directions

1. Begin by washing and drying the mixed salad greens. Place them in a large salad bowl.

2. Drain the canned tuna and add it to the salad greens.

3. Halve the cherry tomatoes and scatter them over the salad.

4. Halve the boiled baby potatoes and arrange them on the salad.

5. Cut the blanched green beans into bite-sized pieces and add them to the salad.

6. Quarter the hard-boiled eggs and place them on top of the salad.

7. Scatter pitted Kalamata olives and thinly sliced red onion over the salad.

8. In a small bowl, whisk together the extra-virgin olive oil, red wine vinegar, Dijon mustard, salt, and freshly ground black pepper to create the dressing.

9. Drizzle the dressing over the salad ingredients.

10. Gently toss all the ingredients together to ensure the dressing is evenly distributed.

Nutritional Information (Approximate)

Calories	450	Dietary Fiber	6g
Protein	35g	Sodium	680mg
Carbohydrates	30g	Cholesterol	370mg
Total Fat	20g	Potassium	750mg
Saturated Fat	4g		

Enjoy your hearty Nicoise Salad! It's a classic and satisfying dish with a balance of protein, vegetables, and flavor.

Avocado and Black Bean Salad

Prep Time: 15 minutes / Cook Time: 0 minutes
Yield: 1 serving

Ingredients

- 1 avocado, diced, 1/4 cup red bell pepper, diced
- 1/2 cup canned black beans, drained and rinsed
- 1/4 cup corn kernels (fresh, frozen, or canned)
- 1/4 cup red onion, finely chopped
- 1 tablespoon lime juice
- 2 tablespoons fresh cilantro, chopped
- 1 tablespoon extra-virgin olive oil
- 1/2 teaspoon ground cumin
- Salt and freshly ground black pepper, to taste

Directions

1. Begin by preparing the avocado. Cut it in half, remove the pit, and dice the flesh. Place it in a salad bowl.

2. Drain and rinse the canned black beans, then add them to the salad bowl with the diced avocado.

3. If using frozen corn, cook it according to the package instructions, then cool it before adding it to the salad. If using canned corn, drain it, and add it directly to the salad. Fresh corn can be used raw or lightly blanched, as desired.

4. Dice the red bell pepper and finely chop the red onion. Scatter them over the avocado and black beans.

5. Chop fresh cilantro leaves and sprinkle them on top.

6. In a small bowl, whisk together the lime juice, extra-virgin olive oil, ground cumin, salt, and freshly ground black pepper to create the dressing.

7. Drizzle the dressing over the salad ingredients.

8. Gently toss everything together to ensure the dressing is evenly distributed.

Nutritional Information (Approximate)

Calories	400	Dietary Fiber	13g
Protein	9g	Sodium	400mg
Carbohydrates	32g	Cholesterol	0mg
Total Fat	29g	Potassium	900mg
Saturated Fat	4g		

Enjoy your hearty Avocado and Black Bean Salad! It's a nutritious and satisfying dish with a burst of flavors and textures.

Kale Caesar Salad

Prep Time: 15 minutes / Cook Time: 0 minutes
Yield: 1 serving

Ingredients

- 2 cups fresh kale leaves, washed and chopped
- 1/4 cup cherry tomatoes, halved
- 2 tablespoons grated Parmesan cheese
- 2 tablespoons Caesar dressing (reduced-fat if available)
- 1/4 cup whole-grain croutons (optional)
- Freshly ground black pepper, to taste
- Lemon wedges, for garnish (optional)
- 1/4 cup cucumber, sliced

Directions

1. Start by washing the fresh kale leaves thoroughly. Remove the tough stems and chop the leaves into bite-sized pieces. Place them in a large salad bowl.
2. Halve the cherry tomatoes and scatter them over the kale. Slice the cucumber and add it to the salad.
3. Sprinkle the grated Parmesan cheese over the vegetables for added flavor.
4. Drizzle the Caesar dressing over the salad. If you prefer a lighter option, use reduced-fat dressing.
5. For some crunch, consider adding whole-grain croutons to the salad.
6. Season the salad with freshly ground black pepper to taste. Optionally, garnish with lemon wedges for a hint of citrus freshness.

Nutritional Information (Approximate)

Calories	300	Dietary Fiber	4g
Protein	8g	Sodium	480mg
Carbohydrates	20g	Cholesterol	10mg
Total Fat	22g	Potassium	600mg
Saturated Fat	4g		

Tuna Salad

Prep Time: 10 minutes / Cook Time: 0 minutes
Yield: 1 serving

Ingredients

- 1 can (5 ounces) water-packed tuna, drained
- 2 cups mixed salad greens (e.g., lettuce, spinach, and arugula)
- 1/4 cup cherry tomatoes, halved, 1 tablespoon extra-virgin olive oil
- 1/4 cup cucumber, sliced, 1/4 cup red bell pepper, diced
- 2 tablespoons red onion, finely chopped
- 2 tablespoons Kalamata olives, pitted and sliced
- 2 tablespoons reduced-fat feta cheese, crumbled
- 1 tablespoon lemon juice, 1/2 teaspoon Dijon mustard
- Salt and freshly ground black pepper, to taste

Directions

1. Begin by draining the canned tuna to remove excess water. In a large salad bowl, place the mixed salad greens as the base.
2. Flake the drained tuna over the greens. Halve the cherry tomatoes and scatter them over the salad.
3. Slice the cucumber, dice the red bell pepper, and finely chop the red onion. Add them to the salad.
4. Slice the Kalamata olives and crumble the reduced-fat feta cheese over the salad.
5. In a small bowl, whisk together the extra-virgin olive oil, lemon juice, Dijon mustard, salt, and freshly ground black pepper to create the dressing.
6. Drizzle the dressing over the salad ingredients.
7. Gently toss everything together to ensure the dressing is evenly distributed.

Nutritional Information (Approximate)

Calories	350	Dietary Fiber	4g
Protein	30g	Sodium	550mg
Carbohydrates	12g	Cholesterol	50mg
Total Fat	20g	Potassium	500mg
Saturated Fat	4g		

Waldorf Chicken Salad

Prep Time: 15 minutes / Yield: 1 serving / Cook Time: 10 minutes (for chicken, optional)

Ingredients

- 1 boneless, skinless chicken breast (4-5 ounces), cooked and diced (optional), 2 tablespoons chopped walnuts, toasted
- 2 cups mixed salad greens (e.g., lettuce, spinach, and arugula)
- 1/2 medium apple, cored and diced, 1/4 cup red grapes, halved
- 1/4 cup celery, chopped, 1 tablespoon raisins or dried cranberries
- 2 tablespoons plain Greek yogurt (reduced-fat if available)
- 1 tablespoon light mayonnaise, 1/2 tablespoon lemon juice
- 1/2 tablespoon honey, salt and freshly ground black pepper, to taste

Nutritional Information

Calories	400	Dietary Fiber	6g
Protein	25g	Sodium	350mg
Carbohydrates	35g	Cholesterol	50mg
Total Fat	18g	Potassium	450mg
Saturated Fat	2g		

Directions

1. If using chicken, cook it first. You can grill, bake, or pan-fry it until fully cooked, then dice it into bite-sized pieces.

2. In a large salad bowl, place the mixed salad greens as the base. Dice the cooked chicken (if using) and add it to the salad greens.

3. Core and dice the apple, halve the red grapes, and chop the celery. Scatter them over the salad.

4. Toast the chopped walnuts in a dry skillet over medium heat for a few minutes until they become golden and fragrant. Be careful not to burn them. Sprinkle the toasted walnuts over the salad. Add raisins or dried cranberries to the salad for a touch of sweetness.

5. In a small bowl, whisk together the plain Greek yogurt, light mayonnaise, honey, lemon juice, salt, and freshly ground black pepper to create the dressing. Drizzle the dressing over the salad ingredients. Gently toss everything together to ensure the dressing is evenly distributed.

chapter 5
SNACK & APPETIZERS

Avocado & Tomato Salsa 26

Baked Sweet Potato Fries
with Greek Yogurt Dip 26

Quinoa-Stuffed Bell Peppers 27

Hummus & Veggie Platter 27

Grilled Chicken Skewers 28
with Lemon Herb Marinade

Roasted Red Pepper & Walnut Dip 28

Spinach & Artichoke Dip (Lightened Up) 29

Cucumber & Greek Yogurt Tzatziki 29

Greek Salad Bites 29

Zucchini Chips with Garlic Parmesan 30

Caprese Salad Skewers 30

Edamame Guacamole 30

Whole Wheat Pita Chips
with Roasted Red Pepper Hummus 31

Beet & Goat Cheese Crostini 31

Baked Buffalo Cauliflower Bites 32

Smoked Salmon & Cucumber Rolls 32

Spicy Chickpea Popcorn 33

Stuffed Mushrooms with Spinach & Feta 33

Roasted Garlic & White Bean Dip 34

Mini Quinoa & Black Bean Stuffed Peppers 34

Greek Yogurt & Berry Parfait 35

Grilled Eggplant Bruschetta 35

Roasted Chickpeas with Herbs 35

Mango Salsa with Baked Tortilla Chips 36

Ceviche with Fresh Seafood and Citrus 36

Avocado and Tomato Salsa

Prep Time: 15 minutes / Cook Time: 0 minutes
Yield: 2 serving

Ingredients

- 2 ripe avocados, diced
- 1 cup cherry tomatoes, halved
- 1/4 cup red onion, finely chopped
- 1/4 cup fresh cilantro, chopped
- 1 small jalapeño pepper, seeded and minced (optional for heat)
- 2 cloves garlic, minced
- Juice of 1 lime
- Salt and pepper to taste

Directions

1. In a medium-sized bowl, combine the diced avocados, halved cherry tomatoes, finely chopped red onion, minced garlic, and chopped cilantro.

2. If you like a bit of heat, add the minced jalapeño pepper to the mixture.

3. Squeeze the juice of one lime over the ingredients. This not only adds flavor but also helps prevent the avocados from browning.

4. Gently toss all the ingredients together until well combined. Be careful not to mash the avocados; you want to maintain some chunks for texture.

5. Season with salt and pepper to taste. Start with a pinch of salt and a dash of pepper, then adjust according to your preference.

6. Allow the salsa to sit for a few minutes to let the flavors meld together.

7. Serve immediately as a dip with whole-grain tortilla chips or as a topping for grilled chicken or fish.

Nutritional Information

Calories	180	Dietary Fiber	6g
Protein	2g	Sodium	10mg
Carbohydrates	11g	Cholesterol	0mg
Total Fat	15g	Potassium	560mg
Saturated Fat	2g		

This heart-healthy Avocado and Tomato Salsa is not only delicious but also packed with nutrients, making it a perfect addition to your heart-healthy cookbook. Enjoy!

Baked Sweet Potato Fries with Greek Yogurt Dip

Prep Time: 15 minutes / Cook Time: 25 minutes
Yield: 1 serving

Ingredients

For Sweet Potato Fries:
- 2 medium sweet potatoes, washed and cut into fries
- 1 tablespoon olive oil, 1/2 teaspoon paprika
- 1/2 teaspoon garlic powder
- 1/2 teaspoon onion powder
- Salt and pepper to taste

For Greek Yogurt Dip:
- 1/2 cup plain Greek yogurt (low-fat or non-fat)
- 1 clove garlic, minced
- 1 tablespoon fresh lemon juice
- 1 tablespoon fresh dill, chopped
- Salt and pepper to taste

Directions

1. Preheat your oven to 425°F (220°C) and line a baking sheet with parchment paper or a silicone baking mat.

2. In a large mixing bowl, combine the sweet potato fries with olive oil, paprika, garlic powder, onion powder, salt, and pepper. Toss until the sweet potato fries are evenly coated.

3. Arrange the seasoned sweet potato fries in a single layer on the prepared baking sheet, ensuring they are not too crowded. This allows them to cook evenly and become crispy.

4. Bake in the preheated oven for 20-25 minutes, flipping the fries halfway through, or until they are golden brown and crispy on the outside and tender on the inside.

5. While the sweet potato fries are baking, prepare the Greek yogurt dip. In a small bowl, mix together Greek yogurt, minced garlic, fresh lemon juice, and chopped dill. Season with salt and pepper to taste.

6. Once the sweet potato fries are done, remove them from the oven and let them cool slightly before serving.

7. Serve the baked sweet potato fries with the creamy Greek yogurt dip on the side for dipping.

Nutritional Information

Calories	190	Dietary Fiber	5g
Protein	5g	Sodium	70mg
Carbohydrates	34g	Cholesterol	2mg
Total Fat	4g	Potassium	590mg
Saturated Fat	1g		

Quinoa-Stuffed Bell Peppers

Prep Time: 15 minutes / Cook Time: 30 minutes
Yield: 4 serving

Ingredients

- 4 large bell peppers, any color
- 1 cup quinoa, rinsed and drained
- 2 cups vegetable broth (low sodium)
- 1 can (15 oz) black beans, drained and rinsed
- 1 cup corn kernels (fresh or frozen)
- 1 cup diced tomatoes (canned or fresh)
- 1/2 cup diced red onion, 1/2 cup diced red bell pepper
- 1 teaspoon ground cumin, 1/2 teaspoon chili powder
- Salt and pepper to taste, 1/2 cup shredded low-fat cheddar cheese (optional for topping)
- Fresh cilantro leaves for garnish (optional)

Directions

1. Preheat your oven to 375°F (190°C).

2. Cut the tops off the bell peppers and remove the seeds and membranes. Rinse them under cold water and set aside.

3. In a medium saucepan, bring the vegetable broth to a boil. Add the quinoa, reduce the heat to low, cover, and simmer for about 15-20 minutes or until the quinoa is cooked and the liquid is absorbed. Fluff with a fork.

4. In a large mixing bowl, combine the cooked quinoa, black beans, corn, diced tomatoes, red onion, red bell pepper, ground cumin, and chili powder. Season with salt and pepper to taste. Mix until all the ingredients are well combined.

5. Stuff each bell pepper with the quinoa mixture, packing it tightly. Place the stuffed peppers upright in a baking dish.

6. If desired, top each stuffed pepper with a sprinkle of shredded low-fat cheddar cheese.

7. Cover the baking dish with aluminum foil and bake in the preheated oven for 20-25 minutes or until the peppers are tender.

8. Remove the foil and bake for an additional 5-10 minutes, or until the cheese is melted and bubbly (if using).

9. Garnish with fresh cilantro leaves before serving, if desired.

Nutritional Information

Calories	280	Dietary Fiber	11g
Protein	9g	Sodium	560mg
Carbohydrates	55g	Cholesterol	0mg
Total Fat	2g	Potassium	980mg
Saturated Fat	0g		

Hummus and Veggie Platter

Prep Time: 10 minutes / Cook Time: 0 minutes
Yield: 4 serving

Ingredients

For Hummus:
- 1 can (15 oz) chickpeas, drained and rinsed
- 2 cloves garlic, minced, 3 tablespoons tahini
- 2 tablespoons fresh lemon juice
- 2 tablespoons extra-virgin olive oil
- 1/2 teaspoon ground cumin, salt and pepper to taste
- 2-4 tablespoons water (for desired consistency)

For Veggie Platter:
- Assorted fresh vegetables (e.g., carrot sticks, cucumber slices, cherry tomatoes, bell pepper strips, celery sticks)
- Fresh parsley or cilantro leaves for garnish (optional)

Directions

1. To make the hummus, place the chickpeas, minced garlic, tahini, fresh lemon juice, extra-virgin olive oil, ground cumin, salt, and pepper in a food processor.

2. Process the ingredients until smooth, scraping down the sides of the bowl as needed. If the hummus is too thick, add water, one tablespoon at a time, until you achieve your desired creamy consistency.

3. Taste the hummus and adjust the seasonings if necessary by adding more lemon juice, salt, or pepper.

4. Transfer the hummus to a serving bowl and drizzle with a bit of extra-virgin olive oil. Garnish with fresh parsley or cilantro leaves if desired.

5. Prepare the fresh vegetables by washing and cutting them into bite-sized sticks or slices.

6. Arrange the vegetable sticks and slices around the hummus bowl on a serving platter.

7. Serve the hummus and veggie platter as a healthy and heart-healthy snack or appetizer.

Nutritional Information

Calories	200	Dietary Fiber	5g
Protein	7g	Sodium	220mg
Carbohydrates	18g	Cholesterol	0mg
Total Fat	12g	Potassium	280mg
Saturated Fat	2g		

This Hummus and Veggie Platter is a nutritious and satisfying option for a heart-healthy snack or appetizer. Enjoy the delicious, creamy hummus with a variety of fresh vegetables!

Grilled Chicken Skewers with Lemon Herb Marinade

Prep Time: 20 minutes / Cook Time: 15 minutes
Yield: 4 serving

Ingredients

For Lemon Herb Marinade:
- Juice of 2 lemons, Zest of 1 lemon
- 2 cloves garlic, minced, salt and pepper to taste
- 2 tablespoons extra-virgin olive oil
- 2 tablespoons fresh parsley, chopped
- 1 tablespoon fresh rosemary, chopped

For Chicken Skewers:
- 1.5 lbs boneless, skinless chicken breasts, cut into 1-inch cubes
- Wooden skewers, soaked in water for 30 minutes to prevent burning
- Assorted bell peppers, onions, and zucchini, cut into chunks for skewering
- Cooking spray for grilling

Directions

1. In a small bowl, whisk together the lemon juice, lemon zest, minced garlic, extra-virgin olive oil, chopped parsley, chopped rosemary, salt, and pepper. This is your lemon herb marinade.

2. Place the chicken cubes in a zip-top bag or a shallow dish and pour the marinade over them. Seal the bag or cover the dish and refrigerate for at least 15-20 minutes, or up to 2 hours. The longer you marinate, the more flavorful the chicken will be.

3. While the chicken is marinating, prepare your grill for medium-high heat. Preheat the grill to about 375°F (190°C).

4. Thread the marinated chicken cubes onto the soaked wooden skewers, alternating with chunks of bell peppers, onions, and zucchini.

5. Spray the grill grates with cooking spray to prevent sticking. Place the chicken skewers on the preheated grill.

6. Grill the skewers for about 5-7 minutes per side, or until the chicken is cooked through and has grill marks. The internal temperature of the chicken should reach 165°F (74°C).

7. Once cooked, remove the skewers from the grill and let them rest for a few minutes before serving.

8. Serve the grilled chicken skewers with your choice of whole grains or a fresh green salad for a heart-healthy meal.

Nutritional Information

Calories	250	Dietary Fiber	1g
Protein	30g	Sodium	150mg
Carbohydrates	4g	Cholesterol	85mg
Total Fat	11g	Potassium	380mg
Saturated Fat	2g		

Roasted Red Pepper and Walnut Dip

Prep Time: 10 minutes / Cook Time: 15 minutes
Yield: 8 serving

Ingredients

- 2 red bell peppers, 1/2 cup walnuts, toasted
- 2 cloves garlic, minced
- 2 tablespoons extra-virgin olive oil
- 2 tablespoons fresh lemon juice
- 1 teaspoon ground cumin, 1/2 teaspoon paprika
- Salt and pepper to taste
- Fresh parsley leaves for garnish (optional)

Directions

1. Preheat your broiler to high. Place the whole red bell peppers on a baking sheet and broil them, turning occasionally, until the skin is charred and blistered. This should take about 10-12 minutes.

2. Remove the peppers from the oven and immediately transfer them to a bowl. Cover the bowl with plastic wrap and let the peppers steam for about 5 minutes. This will make it easier to remove the skin.

3. After steaming, peel off the charred skin from the roasted red peppers. Cut off the tops, remove the seeds, and roughly chop the flesh.

4. In a food processor, combine the roasted red peppers, toasted walnuts, minced garlic, extra-virgin olive oil, fresh lemon juice, ground cumin, paprika, salt, and pepper.

5. Process the ingredients until smooth, scraping down the sides of the bowl as needed. If the dip is too thick, you can add a bit of water to reach your desired consistency.

6. Taste the dip and adjust the seasonings if necessary by adding more lemon juice, salt, or pepper.

7. Transfer the roasted red pepper and walnut dip to a serving bowl and garnish with fresh parsley leaves if desired.

8. Serve the heart-healthy dip with whole-grain pita bread, fresh vegetable sticks, or as a flavorful spread.

Nutritional Information
(per serving, approximately 2 tablespoons)

Calories	90	Dietary Fiber	1g
Protein	2g	Sodium	80mg
Carbohydrates	4g	Cholesterol	0mg
Total Fat	8g	Potassium	130mg
Saturated Fat	1g		

This Roasted Red Pepper and Walnut Dip is a nutritious and delicious option for a heart-healthy snack or appetizer. Enjoy the rich flavors and creamy texture!

Spinach and Artichoke Dip
(Lightened Up)

Prep Time: 15 minutes / Cook Time: 20 minutes
Yield: 8 serving

Ingredients

- 1 (10 oz) package frozen chopped spinach, thawed and drained
- 1 (14 oz) can artichoke hearts, drained and chopped
- 1 cup low-fat Greek yogurt, 1/2 cup light mayonnaise
- 1 cup shredded part-skim mozzarella cheese
- 2 cloves garlic, minced, 1/2 teaspoon onion powder
- 1 cup grated Parmesan cheese, salt and pepper to taste
- Whole-grain crackers or vegetable sticks for dipping

Directions

1. Preheat your oven to 375°F (190°C).

2. In a large mixing bowl, combine the thawed and drained chopped spinach, chopped artichoke hearts, low-fat Greek yogurt, light mayonnaise, grated Parmesan cheese, shredded part-skim mozzarella cheese, minced garlic, onion powder, salt, and pepper. Mix until all the ingredients are well combined.

3. Transfer the mixture to a baking dish, spreading it out evenly.

4. Bake in the preheated oven for about 20 minutes or until the dip is hot and bubbly, and the top is golden brown.

5. Remove the dip from the oven and let it cool slightly before serving.

6. Serve the lightened-up spinach and artichoke dip with whole-grain crackers or vegetable sticks for dipping.

Nutritional Information

Calories	170	Dietary Fiber	2g
Protein	11g	Sodium	480mg
Carbohydrates	6g	Cholesterol	20mg
Total Fat	11g	Potassium	240mg
Saturated Fat	4g		

Cucumber and Greek Yogurt Tzatziki

Prep Time: 15 minutes / Cook Time: 0 minutes
Yield: 4 serving

Ingredients

- 1 cucumber, grated and excess liquid squeezed out
- 1 1/2 cups Greek yogurt (low-fat or non-fat)
- 2 cloves garlic, minced, 1 tablespoon fresh dill, chopped
- 1 tablespoon fresh mint, chopped (optional)
- 1 tablespoon extra-virgin olive oil
- 1 tablespoon fresh lemon juice, salt and pepper to taste

Directions

1. Grate the cucumber using a box grater or a food processor with a grating attachment. Squeeze out any excess liquid from the grated cucumber using a clean kitchen towel or paper towels.

2. In a mixing bowl, combine the grated cucumber, Greek yogurt, minced garlic, chopped fresh dill, and, if desired, chopped fresh mint.

3. Add the fresh lemon juice and extra-virgin olive oil to the mixture. Mix all the ingredients together until well combined.

4. Season the tzatziki sauce with salt and pepper to taste. Start with a pinch of salt and a dash of pepper, then adjust according to your preference.

5. Refrigerate the tzatziki for at least 15-20 minutes before serving to allow the flavors to meld.

6. Serve the heart-healthy cucumber and Greek yogurt tzatziki as a dip for whole-grain pita bread, fresh vegetable sticks, or as a condiment for grilled chicken or fish.

Nutritional Information

Calories	70	Dietary Fiber	1g
Protein	6g	Sodium	30mg
Carbohydrates	6g	Cholesterol	4mg
Total Fat	3g	Potassium	190mg
Saturated Fat	0g		

Greek Salad Bites

Prep Time: 15 minutes / Cook Time: 0 minutes / Yield: 4 serving

Ingredients

- 1 cucumber, cut into 1-inch thick rounds
- 1 cup cherry tomatoes, halved, 1 cup Kalamata olives, pitted
- 1/2 cup feta cheese, crumbled (reduced-fat if preferred)
- 1/4 cup red onion, finely chopped, 2 tablespoons extra-virgin olive oil
- 1 tablespoon red wine vinegar, 1 teaspoon dried oregano
- Salt and pepper to taste, fresh parsley leaves for garnish (optional)

Nutritional Information

Calories	180	Dietary Fiber	2g
Protein	4g	Sodium	520mg
Carbohydrates	7g	Cholesterol	10mg
Total Fat	15g	Potassium	250mg
Saturated Fat	3.5g		

Directions

1. In a large mixing bowl, combine the cherry tomatoes, Kalamata olives, crumbled feta cheese, and finely chopped red onion.

2. In a small bowl, whisk together the extra-virgin olive oil, red wine vinegar, dried oregano, salt, and pepper to create the Greek salad dressing.

3. Pour the dressing over the tomato, olive, feta, and onion mixture. Toss until everything is well coated with the dressing.

4. To assemble the Greek Salad Bites, place a cucumber round on a serving platter or individual plates. Spoon a generous portion of the tomato, olive, feta, and onion mixture on top of each cucumber round. If desired, garnish with fresh parsley leaves for added color and flavor.

5. Serve these heart-healthy Greek Salad Bites as a refreshing and nutritious appetizer or snack.

(Zucchini Chips with Garlic Parmesan)

Prep Time: 15 minutes / Cook Time: 15 minutes
Yield: 4 serving

Ingredients

- 2 large zucchinis, sliced into thin rounds
- 2 tablespoons olive oil, 2 cloves garlic, minced
- 1/4 cup grated Parmesan cheese
- 1/2 teaspoon dried oregano, 1/2 teaspoon dried basil
- Salt and pepper to taste, cooking spray (optional)

Directions

1. Preheat your oven to 425°F (220°C). Line two baking sheets with parchment paper or use a non-stick baking mat. If desired, lightly coat the parchment paper with cooking spray to prevent sticking.

2. In a large mixing bowl, combine the zucchini rounds, olive oil, minced garlic, grated Parmesan cheese, dried oregano, dried basil, salt, and pepper. Toss until the zucchini slices are evenly coated with the seasoning mixture.

3. Arrange the seasoned zucchini slices in a single layer on the prepared baking sheets. Ensure they are not too crowded, allowing them to cook evenly and become crispy.

4. Place the baking sheets in the preheated oven and bake for about 12-15 minutes, flipping the zucchini slices halfway through, or until they are golden brown and crispy.

5. Remove the zucchini chips from the oven and let them cool slightly before serving.

6. Serve the heart-healthy zucchini chips with your choice of low-fat dip or enjoy them as a guilt-free snack on their own.

Nutritional Information

Calories	90	Dietary Fiber	2g
Protein	3g	Sodium	110mg
Carbohydrates	6g	Cholesterol	3mg
Total Fat	6g	Potassium	400mg
Saturated Fat	1g		

(Caprese Salad Skewers)

Prep Time: 15 minutes / Cook Time: 0 minutes
Yield: 4 serving

Ingredients

- 12 cherry tomatoes, 12 fresh basil leaves
- 12 small fresh mozzarella balls (bocconcini)
- 2 tablespoons extra-virgin olive oil, wooden skewers
- 2 tablespoons balsamic vinegar (reduced sodium)
- Salt and pepper to taste, balsamic glaze for drizzling (optional)

Directions

1. Wash and dry the cherry tomatoes and fresh basil leaves.

2. Assemble the Caprese Salad Skewers by threading a cherry tomato, a fresh basil leaf, and a mozzarella ball onto each wooden skewer. Repeat until you have 12 skewers.

3. Arrange the skewers on a serving platter.

4. In a small bowl, whisk together the extra-virgin olive oil and balsamic vinegar. Season with salt and pepper to taste.

5. Drizzle the olive oil and balsamic vinegar mixture over the Caprese Salad Skewers.

6. If desired, you can also drizzle a bit of balsamic glaze over the skewers for extra flavor and presentation.

7. Serve the heart-healthy Caprese Salad Skewers as an appetizer or a refreshing snack.

Nutritional Information

Calories	150	Dietary Fiber	1g
Protein	6g	Sodium	200mg
Carbohydrates	3g	Cholesterol	15mg
Total Fat	12g	Potassium	200mg
Saturated Fat	4g		

(Edamame Guacamole)

Cook Time: 5 minutes (for edamame) / Prep Time: 15 minutes / Yield: 1 serving

Ingredients

- 1 cup shelled edamame (frozen, thawed), juice of 1 lime
- 2 ripe avocados, peeled, pitted, and diced, 2 cloves garlic, minced
- 2 tablespoons fresh cilantro, chopped
- 1/2 teaspoon ground cumin, salt and pepper to taste
- Cherry tomatoes and cilantro leaves for garnish (optional)

Nutritional Information

Calories	130	Dietary Fiber	6g
Protein	6g	Sodium	110mg
Carbohydrates	9g	Cholesterol	0mg
Total Fat	9g	Potassium	480mg
Saturated Fat	1g		

Directions

1. Boil the shelled edamame in water for about 5 minutes or until tender. Drain and rinse them under cold water to stop the cooking process. Let them cool.

2. In a food processor, combine the cooked and cooled edamame, diced avocados, minced garlic, lime juice, chopped fresh cilantro, ground cumin, salt, and pepper. Process the ingredients until smooth, scraping down the sides of the bowl as needed.

3. Taste the guacamole and adjust the seasonings if necessary by adding more lime juice, salt, or pepper.

4. Transfer the Edamame Guacamole to a serving bowl. If desired, garnish with halved cherry tomatoes and cilantro leaves for a pop of color and extra flavor.

5. Serve the heart-healthy Edamame Guacamole with whole-grain tortilla chips or fresh vegetable sticks for dipping.

Whole Wheat Pita Chips with Roasted Red Pepper Hummus

Cook Time: 10 minutes (for pita chips)
Prep Time: 10 minutes / Yield: 4 serving

Ingredients

- 2 whole wheat pita bread rounds
- 2 tablespoons extra-virgin olive oil
- 1/2 teaspoon garlic powder
- 1/2 teaspoon dried oregano
- Salt and pepper to taste

For Roasted Red Pepper Hummus:
- 1 can (15 oz) chickpeas, drained and rinsed
- 1 roasted red pepper (store-bought or homemade)
- 2 cloves garlic, minced, 2 tablespoons tahini
- 2 tablespoons fresh lemon juice
- 2 tablespoons extra-virgin olive oil
- 1/2 teaspoon ground cumin, salt and pepper to taste

Directions

For Whole Wheat Pita Chips:

1. Preheat your oven to 375°F (190°C).

2. Split each whole wheat pita bread round into two rounds, creating four rounds in total.

3. Cut each round into triangles, similar to cutting a pizza.

4. In a mixing bowl, combine the extra-virgin olive oil, garlic powder, dried oregano, salt, and pepper.

5. Toss the pita triangles in the olive oil and spice mixture until they are evenly coated.

6. Place the seasoned pita triangles on a baking sheet in a single layer.

7. Bake in the preheated oven for about 10 minutes or until the pita chips are golden brown and crispy.

For Roasted Red Pepper Hummus:

8. In a food processor, combine the drained and rinsed chickpeas, roasted red pepper, minced garlic, tahini, fresh lemon juice, extra-virgin olive oil, ground cumin, salt, and pepper.

9. Process the ingredients until smooth, scraping down the sides of the bowl as needed. If the hummus is too thick, you can add a bit of water to reach your desired consistency.

To Serve:

10. Transfer the Roasted Red Pepper Hummus to a serving bowl.

11. Serve the heart-healthy Whole Wheat Pita Chips with the Roasted Red Pepper Hummus for dipping.

Nutritional Information

Calories	240	Dietary Fiber	6g
Protein	7g	Sodium	280mg
Carbohydrates	28g	Cholesterol	0mg
Total Fat	12g	Potassium	250mg
Saturated Fat	2g		

Beet and Goat Cheese Crostini

Cook Time: 20 minutes (for roasting beets)
Prep Time: 15 minutes / Yield: 4 serving

Ingredients

- 4 small whole-grain baguette slices
- 2 medium-sized beets, roasted, peeled, and sliced
- 4 oz goat cheese (reduced-fat if preferred)
- 1 tablespoon fresh thyme leaves
- 1 tablespoon honey (optional)
- Salt and pepper to taste
- Extra-virgin olive oil for drizzling

Directions

For Roasting Beets:

1. Preheat your oven to 400°F (200°C).

2. Wash the beets and trim off the tops and roots.

3. Wrap each beet individually in aluminum foil and place them on a baking sheet.

4. Roast the beets in the preheated oven for about 45 minutes to 1 hour, or until they are tender when pierced with a fork.

5. Let the roasted beets cool, then peel and slice them into thin rounds.

For Beet and Goat Cheese Crostini:

6. Preheat your oven's broiler.

7. Place the whole-grain baguette slices on a baking sheet and toast them under the broiler for about 1-2 minutes on each side, or until they are golden brown.

8. Spread a generous layer of goat cheese onto each toasted baguette slice.

9. Arrange the roasted beet slices on top of the goat cheese.

10. Sprinkle fresh thyme leaves over the beet and goat cheese.

11. If desired, drizzle a small amount of honey over the crostini for added sweetness.

12. Season the crostini with a pinch of salt and a dash of pepper.

13. Drizzle a touch of extra-virgin olive oil over the crostini for a final touch.

Nutritional Information

Calories	170	Dietary Fiber	3g
Protein	7g	Sodium	320mg
Carbohydrates	24g	Cholesterol	10mg
Total Fat	5g	Potassium	230mg
Saturated Fat	3g		

These Beet and Goat Cheese Crostini are a delightful and heart-healthy appetizer or snack that balances earthy beets with creamy goat cheese on a crispy baguette slice. Enjoy the vibrant colors and flavors!

Baked Buffalo Cauliflower Bites

Prep Time: 25 minutes / Cook Time: 15 minutes
Yield: 4 serving

Ingredients

- 1 head cauliflower, cut into florets
- 1/2 cup whole wheat flour, 1/2 cup water
- 1 teaspoon garlic powder, 1/2 teaspoon paprika
- 1/2 teaspoon salt, 1/4 teaspoon black pepper
- Cooking spray (olive oil or canola oil)
- 1/2 cup buffalo sauce (reduced sodium if preferred)
- 1 tablespoon melted butter
  (optional, for added richness)
- Ranch or blue cheese dressing for dipping (optional)

Directions

1. . Preheat your oven to 450°F (230°C). Line a baking sheet with parchment paper or use a non-stick baking mat.

2. In a mixing bowl, combine the whole wheat flour, water, garlic powder, paprika, salt, and black pepper to create a batter.

3. Dip each cauliflower floret into the batter, ensuring it's evenly coated, then place it on the prepared baking sheet.

4. Lightly coat the battered cauliflower with cooking spray. This will help them become crispy when baked.

5. Bake the cauliflower florets in the preheated oven for about 20-25 minutes, or until they are golden brown and crispy, turning them halfway through.

6. While the cauliflower is baking, mix the buffalo sauce and melted butter (if using) in a separate bowl.

7. Once the cauliflower bites are done, remove them from the oven and place them in a clean mixing bowl.

8. Pour the buffalo sauce mixture over the baked cauliflower and gently toss to coat all the pieces.

9. Return the coated cauliflower to the baking sheet and bake for an additional 5 minutes to set the sauce.

Nutritional Information (Approximate)

Calories	130	Dietary Fiber	4g
Protein	4g	Sodium	900mg
Carbohydrates	21g	Cholesterol	5mg
Total Fat	3g	Potassium	380mg
Saturated Fat	1g		

These Baked Buffalo Cauliflower Bites are a heart-healthy alternative to traditional buffalo wings. They're spicy, crispy, and perfect for snacking or serving as an appetizer. Enjoy with a side of ranch or blue cheese dressing if desired!

Smoked Salmon and Cucumber Rolls

Prep Time: 15 minutes / Cook Time: 0 minutes
Yield: 4 serving

Ingredients

- 2 large cucumbers, 4 oz smoked salmon
- 1/4 cup low-fat cream cheese
  (or Greek yogurt for a lighter option)
- 2 tablespoons fresh dill, chopped
- 1 tablespoon capers, drained and rinsed
- 1 lemon, zested and juiced, Salt and black pepper to taste
- Fresh dill sprigs for garnish (optional)

Directions

1. Wash and peel the cucumbers. Using a vegetable peeler, create long, thin cucumber ribbons by sliding the peeler along the length of the cucumber. Rotate the cucumber as you go to create even ribbons. You may discard the first and last slices if they are mostly skin.

2. Lay out the cucumber ribbons on a clean kitchen towel or paper towels to remove excess moisture. Pat them dry gently.

3. In a mixing bowl, combine the low-fat cream cheese (or Greek yogurt), chopped fresh dill, capers, lemon zest, and a squeeze of lemon juice. Mix until the ingredients are well incorporated.

4. Lay out a cucumber ribbon flat on a clean surface. Place a small amount of the cream cheese mixture at one end of the ribbon.

5. Lay a strip of smoked salmon on top of the cream cheese mixture.

6. Carefully roll up the cucumber ribbon, starting from the end with the cream cheese and smoked salmon. Continue rolling until you have a neat cucumber roll.

7. Repeat the process with the remaining cucumber ribbons, cream cheese mixture, and smoked salmon.

8. Place the finished rolls on a serving platter.

9. Season the Smoked Salmon and Cucumber Rolls with a pinch of salt and a dash of black pepper.

10. Garnish with fresh dill sprigs if desired.

11. Serve these heart-healthy rolls as an elegant appetizer or a light and refreshing snack.

Nutritional Information (Approximate)

Calories	80	Dietary Fiber	1g
Protein	7g	Sodium	60mg
Carbohydrates	4g	Cholesterol	15mg
Total Fat	380g	Potassium	250mg
Saturated Fat	2g		

These Smoked Salmon and Cucumber Rolls are a delightful and heart-healthy treat that's perfect for any occasion. Enjoy the combination of cool cucumber, creamy filling, and savory smoked salmon!

Spicy Chickpea Popcorn

Prep Time: 10 minutes / Cook Time: 25 minutes
Yield: 4 serving

Ingredients

- 2 (15 oz) cans chickpeas, drained, rinsed, and patted dry
- 2 tablespoons olive oil
- 1 teaspoon chili powder
- 1/2 teaspoon cayenne pepper (adjust to taste)
- 1/2 teaspoon garlic powder
- 1/2 teaspoon paprika
- Salt and black pepper to taste
- Cooking spray (olive oil or canola oil)

Directions

1. Preheat your oven to 425°F (220°C). Line a baking sheet with parchment paper or use a non-stick baking mat.

2. In a large mixing bowl, combine the chickpeas, olive oil, chili powder, cayenne pepper, garlic powder, paprika, salt, and black pepper. Toss until the chickpeas are evenly coated with the spices and oil.

3. Spread the seasoned chickpeas on the prepared baking sheet in a single layer. Ensure they are not too crowded for even roasting.

4. Lightly coat the chickpeas with cooking spray. This will help them become crispy.

5. Bake in the preheated oven for about 20-25 minutes, stirring or shaking the pan occasionally, until the chickpeas are golden brown and crispy.

6. Remove the Spicy Chickpea Popcorn from the oven and let them cool slightly.

Nutritional Information (Approximate)

Calories	180	Dietary Fiber	6g
Protein	7g	Sodium	350mg
Carbohydrates	25g	Cholesterol	0mg
Total Fat	6g	Potassium	240mg
Saturated Fat	1g		

These Spicy Chickpea Popcorn bites are a fantastic and heart-healthy snack option. Enjoy the crunchy texture and bold flavors as a satisfying snack or appetizer with a kick of spice!

Stuffed Mushrooms with Spinach and Feta

Prep Time: 20 minutes / Cook Time: 20 minutes
Yield: 4 serving

Ingredients

- 16 large white button mushrooms, cleaned and stems removed, 2 cloves garlic, minced
- 2 cups fresh spinach, chopped
- 1/2 cup crumbled feta cheese (reduced-fat if preferred)
- 1/4 cup finely chopped red onion
- 1/4 cup whole-wheat breadcrumbs
- 1 tablespoon olive oil, 1 teaspoon dried oregano
- Salt and black pepper to taste
- Cooking spray (olive oil or canola oil)

Directions

1. Preheat your oven to 375°F (190°C). Line a baking sheet with parchment paper or use a non-stick baking mat.

2. In a large skillet, heat the olive oil over medium heat. Add the minced garlic and chopped red onion. Sauté for 2-3 minutes until the onion is translucent.

3. Add the chopped spinach to the skillet and cook for another 2-3 minutes until wilted. Remove from heat and let it cool slightly.

4. In a mixing bowl, combine the cooked spinach mixture, crumbled feta cheese, whole-wheat breadcrumbs, dried oregano, salt, and black pepper. Mix until all the ingredients are well combined.

5. Fill each cleaned mushroom cap with a generous spoonful of the spinach and feta mixture, pressing it down gently.

6. Place the stuffed mushrooms on the prepared baking sheet.

7. Lightly coat the stuffed mushrooms with cooking spray to help them brown while baking.

8. Bake in the preheated oven for about 15-20 minutes, or until the mushrooms are tender and the stuffing is golden brown.

Nutritional Information
(per serving, approximately 4 stuffed mushrooms)

Calories	90	Dietary Fiber	2g
Protein	4g	Sodium	190mg
Carbohydrates	9g	Cholesterol	10mg
Total Fat	5g	Potassium	340mg
Saturated Fat	2g		

These Stuffed Mushrooms with Spinach and Feta are a delicious and heart-healthy appetizer option. Enjoy the savory combination of spinach and feta cheese in every bite!

Roasted Garlic and White Bean Dip

Cook Time: 30 minutes (for roasting garlic)
Prep Time: 10 minutes / Yield: 9 serving

Ingredients

- 1 (15 oz) can white beans
  (cannellini or great northern), drained and rinsed
- 1 whole head of garlic, 2 tablespoons olive oil
- 2 tablespoons lemon juice
- 1/4 cup fresh parsley, chopped
- 1/2 teaspoon dried rosemary
- Salt and black pepper to taste
- Carrot and cucumber sticks,
  and whole-grain pita bread for dipping

Directions

For Roasting Garlic:

1. Preheat your oven to 400°F (200°C).

2. Slice off the top 1/4 inch of the head of garlic to expose the cloves.

3. Place the garlic head on a piece of aluminum foil, drizzle with a tablespoon of olive oil, and wrap it tightly in the foil.

4. Roast the garlic in the preheated oven for about 30 minutes, or until the cloves are soft and golden brown. Let it cool.

For White Bean Dip:

5. Squeeze the roasted garlic cloves out of their skins into a food processor.

6. Add the drained and rinsed white beans, lemon juice, fresh parsley, dried rosemary, and a pinch of salt and black pepper.

7. Pulse the mixture in the food processor until smooth. If it's too thick, you can add a little water or more olive oil to reach your desired consistency.

8. Taste and adjust the seasoning if needed by adding more salt, black pepper, or lemon juice.

9. Transfer the Roasted Garlic and White Bean Dip to a serving bowl.

10. Drizzle with the remaining olive oil and garnish with additional chopped fresh parsley.

11. Serve with carrot and cucumber sticks, and whole-grain pita bread for dipping.

Nutritional Information

Calories	120	Dietary Fiber	4g
Protein	4g	Sodium	220mg
Carbohydrates	18g	Cholesterol	0mg
Total Fat	4.5g	Potassium	230mg
Saturated Fat	0.5g		

Mini Quinoa and Black Bean Stuffed Peppers

Prep Time: 15 minutes / Cook Time: 25 minutes
Yield: 4 serving

Ingredients

- 4 mini bell peppers, any color
- 1/2 cup quinoa, rinsed and drained
- 1 cup low-sodium vegetable broth or water
- 1 (15 oz) can black beans, drained and rinsed
- 1 cup diced tomatoes (canned or fresh)
- 1/2 cup frozen corn kernels, 1/2 teaspoon chili powder
- 1/2 teaspoon cumin, 1/4 teaspoon paprika
- Salt and black pepper to taste
- 1/4 cup shredded reduced-fat cheddar cheese (optional)
- Fresh cilantro leaves for garnish (optional)

Directions

1. Preheat your oven to 375°F (190°C).

2. Cut the tops off the mini bell peppers and remove the seeds and membranes. Set aside.

3. In a medium saucepan, combine the rinsed quinoa and low-sodium vegetable broth (or water). Bring to a boil, then reduce the heat to low, cover, and simmer for 15-20 minutes or until the quinoa is cooked and the liquid is absorbed.

4. In a large mixing bowl, combine the cooked quinoa, drained black beans, diced tomatoes, frozen corn kernels, chili powder, cumin, paprika, salt, and black pepper. Mix well to combine all the ingredients.

5. Stuff each mini bell pepper with the quinoa and black bean mixture, pressing it down gently to pack the peppers.

6. Place the stuffed peppers in a baking dish and cover with aluminum foil.

7. Bake in the preheated oven for 20-25 minutes or until the peppers are tender.

8. If desired, sprinkle shredded reduced-fat cheddar cheese on top of each stuffed pepper during the last 5 minutes of baking, then return to the oven until the cheese is melted and bubbly.

9. Garnish with fresh cilantro leaves if you like.

Nutritional Information
(per serving, 1 stuffed pepper)

Calories	170	Dietary Fiber	6g
Protein	7g	Sodium	310mg
Carbohydrates	30g	Cholesterol	0mg
Total Fat	2g	Potassium	390mg
Saturated Fat	0.5g		

Greek Yogurt and Berry Parfait

Prep Time: 5 minutes / Cook Time: 0 minutes
Yield: 1 serving

Ingredients

- 1/2 cup non-fat Greek yogurt, 1/4 cup granola (choose a low-sugar or sugar-free option for heart health)
- 1/2 cup mixed berries (strawberries, blueberries, raspberries, etc.)
- 1 teaspoon honey (optional, for drizzling)
- Fresh mint leaves for garnish (optional)

Directions

1. Start by assembling your parfait in a clear glass or bowl for a visually appealing presentation.

2. Begin with a layer of non-fat Greek yogurt at the bottom of the glass.

3. Add a layer of mixed berries on top of the yogurt.

4. Sprinkle a layer of granola over the berries.

5. Repeat the layers until you've used up all the ingredients, ending with a layer of berries and a sprinkle of granola on top.

6. If desired, drizzle a teaspoon of honey over the top for a touch of sweetness. You can skip this step if you prefer a lower sugar option.

7. Garnish with fresh mint leaves for an extra burst of flavor and a beautiful presentation.

8. Serve your heart-healthy Greek Yogurt and Berry Parfait immediately as a satisfying and nutritious breakfast, snack, or dessert.

Nutritional Information

Calories	250	Dietary Fiber	6g
Protein	14g	Sodium	60mg
Carbohydrates	45g	Cholesterol	5mg
Total Fat	2g	Potassium	320mg
Saturated Fat	0g		

Grilled Eggplant Bruschetta

Prep Time: 10 minutes / Cook Time: 10 minutes
Yield: 4 serving

Ingredients

- 1 large eggplant, sliced into 1/2-inch rounds
- 2 tablespoons olive oil, 2 cloves garlic, minced
- 2 medium tomatoes, diced, 1/4 cup fresh basil leaves, chopped
- 2 tablespoons balsamic vinegar, salt and black pepper to taste
- Whole-grain baguette slices for serving

Directions

1. Preheat your grill or grill pan to medium-high heat.

2. Brush both sides of the eggplant slices with olive oil and season with a pinch of salt and black pepper.

3. Grill the eggplant slices for about 3-4 minutes per side, or until they are tender and have grill marks. Remove from the grill and set aside.

4. In a mixing bowl, combine the minced garlic, diced tomatoes, chopped fresh basil, balsamic vinegar, and a pinch of salt and black pepper. Mix well to make the bruschetta topping.

5. To serve, place a grilled eggplant slice on each whole-grain baguette slice.

6. Spoon a generous amount of the bruschetta topping over each eggplant slice.

7. Drizzle a little extra balsamic vinegar over the top if desired.

8. Serve your heart-healthy Grilled Eggplant Bruschetta as an appetizer or light meal.

Nutritional Information
(per serving, 2 bruschetta slices)

Calories	150	Dietary Fiber	6g
Protein	3g	Sodium	10mg
Carbohydrates	17g	Cholesterol	0mg
Total Fat	9g	Potassium	400mg
Saturated Fat	1g		

Roasted Chickpeas with Herbs

Prep Time: 10 minutes / Cook Time: 25-30 minutes / Yield: 4 serving

Ingredients

- 2 (15 oz) cans chickpeas (garbanzo beans), drained and rinsed
- 2 tablespoons olive oil, 1 teaspoon garlic powder
- 1 teaspoon onion powder, 1 teaspoon dried oregano
- 1 teaspoon dried thyme, 1/2 teaspoon paprika
- Salt and black pepper to taste, fresh lemon zest (from 1 lemon)
- Fresh parsley, chopped, for garnish (optional)

Nutritional Information
(per serving, approximately 1/2 cup)

Calories	200	Dietary Fiber	7g
Protein	7g	Sodium	240mg
Carbohydrates	27g	Cholesterol	0mg
Total Fat	7g	Potassium	250mg
Saturated Fat	1g		

Directions

1. Preheat your oven to 400°F (200°C). Rinse and drain the canned chickpeas. Place them on a clean kitchen towel and pat them dry to remove excess moisture.

2. In a large mixing bowl, combine the dried chickpeas, olive oil, garlic powder, onion powder, dried oregano, dried thyme, paprika, salt, and black pepper. Toss to coat the chickpeas evenly with the seasonings and oil. Spread the seasoned chickpeas in a single layer on a baking sheet.

3. Roast in the preheated oven for 25-30 minutes, or until the chickpeas are crispy and golden brown.

4. Shake the pan or stir the chickpeas occasionally during roasting to ensure even cooking. Remove the roasted chickpeas from the oven and sprinkle fresh lemon zest over them while they are still hot.

5. Allow the roasted chickpeas to cool slightly before serving. If desired, garnish with fresh chopped parsley for added flavor and presentation.

Mango Salsa with Baked Tortilla Chips

Prep Time: 15 minutes / Cook Time: 10 minutes
Yield: 4 serving

Ingredients

For Mango Salsa:
- 2 ripe mangoes, peeled, pitted, and diced
- 1/2 red onion, finely chopped, juice of 2 limes
- 1 red bell pepper, diced
- 1 jalapeño pepper, seeded and finely chopped (adjust to taste)
- 1/4 cup fresh cilantro, chopped
- Salt and black pepper to taste

For Baked Tortilla Chips:
- 4 whole-grain tortillas, olive oil
- Cooking spray, salt to taste

Directions

For Mango Salsa:

1. In a large mixing bowl, combine the diced mangoes, finely chopped red onion, diced red bell pepper, finely chopped jalapeño pepper, and chopped fresh cilantro.

2. Squeeze the juice of 2 limes over the ingredients in the bowl.

3. Gently toss the mixture to combine all the ingredients.

4. Season the Mango Salsa with salt and black pepper to taste. Adjust the seasonings to your preference.

For Baked Tortilla Chips:

5. Preheat your oven to 375°F (190°C).

6. Brush both sides of each whole-grain tortilla lightly with olive oil or use olive oil cooking spray.

7. Stack the tortillas and cut them into wedges (like slicing a pizza).

8. Place the tortilla wedges on a baking sheet in a single layer.

9. Sprinkle a pinch of salt over the top.

10. Bake in the preheated oven for about 8-10 minutes or until the tortilla chips are crisp and golden brown.

To Serve:

11. Allow the baked tortilla chips to cool slightly.

12. Serve the Mango Salsa alongside the baked tortilla chips for dipping.

Nutritional Information (Approximate)

Calories	160	Dietary Fiber	5g
Protein	2g	Sodium	150mg
Carbohydrates	36g	Cholesterol	0mg
Total Fat	1g	Potassium	280mg
Saturated Fat	0g		

Ceviche with Fresh Seafood and Citrus

Prep Time: 20 minutes (plus marinating time)
Cook Time: 0 minutes / Yield: 4 serving

Ingredients

- 1 pound fresh white fish fillets (such as sea bass or snapper), diced into small cubes
- 1/2 pound fresh shrimp, peeled, deveined, and chopped
- 1/2 cup fresh lime juice (about 4-5 limes)
- 1/2 cup fresh lemon juice (about 2-3 lemons)
- 1/2 red onion, finely chopped, 2 cloves garlic, minced
- 1 red bell pepper, finely diced
- 1 jalapeño pepper, seeded and finely chopped
- 1 cup fresh cilantro leaves, chopped
- Salt and black pepper to taste
- 1 ripe avocado, diced (optional)
- Lettuce leaves for serving (optional)

Directions

1. In a large glass or stainless steel bowl, combine the diced white fish and chopped shrimp.

2. Pour the fresh lime juice and lemon juice over the seafood, making sure it's completely submerged. The citrus juice will "cook" the seafood by curing it. Cover the bowl and refrigerate for at least 30 minutes or until the seafood turns opaque and firm.

3. While the seafood is marinating, prepare the vegetables. Finely chop the red onion, red bell pepper, jalapeño pepper, and garlic.

4. After the seafood been marinated, drain the excess citrus juice. The seafood should be opaque and have a firmer texture.

5. Add the chopped red onion, red bell pepper, jalapeño pepper, minced garlic, and chopped cilantro to the seafood. Toss everything together gently.

6. Season the ceviche with salt and black pepper to taste. Adjust the seasonings to your preference.

7. If desired, add diced avocado to the ceviche and gently mix to combine.

8. Serve the ceviche with fresh lettuce leaves for wrapping or as a side dish. You can also enjoy it with tortilla chips or crackers.

Nutritional Information
(per serving, without avocado or lettuce)

Calories	120	Dietary Fiber	2g
Protein	20g	Sodium	35mg
Carbohydrates	8g	Cholesterol	90mg
Total Fat	1g	Potassium	450mg
Saturated Fat	0g		

chapter 6
SOUPS & STEWS

Chicken Noodle Soup 38

Tomato Basil Soup 38

Minestrone Soup 39

Beef Stew 39

Clam Chowder 40

French Onion Soup 40

Split Pea Soup 41

Chicken and Rice Soup 41

Butternut Squash Soup 42

Potato Leek Soup 42

Lentil Soup 43

Vegetable Curry Stew 43

Italian Wedding Soup 44

Chili 44

Thai Coconut Soup 45
(Tom Kha Gai)

Corn Chowder 45

Goulash 46

Gazpacho 46

Beef & Barley Soup 47

Moroccan Harira Soup 47

Chicken Noodle Soup

Prep Time: 25 minutes / Cook Time: 15 minutes
Yield: 4 serving

Ingredients

- 1 tablespoon olive oil, 1 small onion, finely chopped
- 2 carrots, sliced, 2 celery stalks, sliced
- 2 cloves garlic, minced, 2 cups water
- 4 cups low-sodium chicken broth
- 2 boneless, skinless chicken breasts
- 2 cups whole wheat egg noodles
- 1 teaspoon dried thyme, salt and pepper to taste
- 1 cup frozen peas
- Fresh parsley for garnish (optional)

Directions

1. In a large pot, heat olive oil over medium heat. Add the chopped onion, carrots, and celery. Sauté for about 5 minutes until the vegetables start to soften.

2. Add minced garlic and cook for another minute until fragrant.

3. Pour in the chicken broth and water. Bring the mixture to a boil.

4. Add the chicken breasts to the boiling broth. Reduce heat to low, cover, and simmer for about 15-20 minutes until the chicken is cooked through and no longer pink in the center. Remove the chicken from the pot and shred it using two forks.

5. Meanwhile, add the whole wheat egg noodles and dried thyme to the pot. Cook according to the package instructions until the noodles are al dente.

6. Return the shredded chicken to the pot and add frozen peas. Simmer for an additional 5 minutes until the peas are heated through.

7. Season with salt and pepper to taste. Serve hot, garnished with fresh parsley if desired.

Nutritional Information (Approximate)

Calories	250	Dietary Fiber	5g
Protein	20g	Sodium	400mg
Carbohydrates	24g	Cholesterol	35mg
Total Fat	6g	Potassium	450mg
Saturated Fat	1g		

Enjoy this heart-healthy chicken noodle soup that's low in saturated fat and sodium, packed with lean protein, and loaded with nutritious veggies!

Tomato Basil Soup

Prep Time: 30 minutes / Cook Time: 10 minutes
Yield: 4 serving

Ingredients

- 1 tablespoon olive oil
- 1 small onion, finely chopped
- 2 cloves garlic, minced
- 1 can (28 ounces) low-sodium crushed tomatoes
- 2 cups low-sodium vegetable broth
- 1 teaspoon dried basil, 1 teaspoon dried oregano
- Salt and pepper to taste
- 1/2 cup low-fat Greek yogurt
- Fresh basil leaves for garnish (optional)

Directions

1. In a large pot, heat olive oil over medium heat. Add the chopped onion and sauté for about 3-4 minutes until translucent.

2. Add the minced garlic and cook for another minute until fragrant.

3. Stir in the crushed tomatoes, vegetable broth, dried basil, and dried oregano. Season with salt and pepper to taste. Bring the mixture to a simmer.

4. Reduce heat to low, cover, and let the soup simmer for about 20-25 minutes, stirring occasionally.

5. Remove the pot from heat and let the soup cool slightly. Use an immersion blender to carefully blend the soup until smooth. Alternatively, you can transfer the soup in batches to a countertop blender and blend until smooth, then return it to the pot.

6. Return the pot to low heat and stir in the low-fat Greek yogurt until well incorporated. Heat the soup for an additional 5 minutes, but do not let it come to a boil.

7. Serve hot, garnished with fresh basil leaves if desired.

Nutritional Information (Approximate)

Calories	120	Dietary Fiber	4g
Protein	4g	Sodium	350mg
Carbohydrates	18g	Cholesterol	0mg
Total Fat	4g	Potassium	620mg
Saturated Fat	0,5g		

Enjoy this heart-healthy tomato basil soup that's low in calories, saturated fat, and sodium, and rich in flavor!

Minestrone Soup

Prep Time: 30 minutes / Cook Time: 15 minutes
Yield: 4 serving

Ingredients

- 1 tablespoon olive oil, 1 onion, chopped
- 2 cloves garlic, minced, 2 carrots, peeled and diced
- 2 celery stalks, diced, 1 zucchini, diced
- 1 yellow squash, diced, 1 teaspoon dried basil
- 1 cup green beans, cut into 1-inch pieces
- 1 can (14 ounces) diced tomatoes (no salt added)
- 1 can (14 ounces) kidney beans, drained and rinsed
- 1 can (14 ounces) cannellini beans, drained and rinsed
- 8 cups low-sodium vegetable broth
- 1 teaspoon dried oregano, salt and pepper to taste
- 1 cup whole wheat pasta (small shape)
- 2 cups fresh spinach leaves
- Grated Parmesan cheese for garnish (optional)
- Chopped fresh basil leaves for garnish (optional)

Directions

1. In a large pot, heat the olive oil over medium heat. Add the chopped onion and sauté for about 3-4 minutes until it becomes translucent.

2. Add the minced garlic and cook for an additional minute until fragrant.

3. Stir in the diced carrots, diced celery, diced zucchini, diced yellow squash, and cut green beans.

4. Add the diced tomatoes, drained kidney beans, drained cannellini beans, low-sodium vegetable broth, dried basil, dried oregano, salt, and pepper. Bring the mixture to a boil.

5. Reduce the heat to low, cover, and simmer for about 15 minutes, or until the vegetables are tender, stirring occasionally.

6. Stir in the whole wheat pasta and cook according to package instructions until al dente.

7. Just before serving, stir in the fresh spinach leaves and cook for an additional 2 minutes until wilted.

8. Taste and adjust the seasoning with additional salt and pepper if needed.

9. Optionally, garnish the minestrone soup with grated Parmesan cheese and chopped fresh basil leaves before serving.

Nutritional Information (Approximate)

Calories	200	Dietary Fiber	8g
Protein	8g	Sodium	360mg
Carbohydrates	38g	Cholesterol	0mg
Total Fat	2g	Potassium	580mg
Saturated Fat	0.5g		

Beef Stew

Prep Time: 15 minutes / Cook Time: 2 hours
Yield: 6 serving

Ingredients

- 1 pound lean beef stew meat, trimmed of excess fat and cut into 1-inch cubes
- 2 tablespoons whole wheat flour
- 1 tablespoon olive oil
- 1 onion, chopped, 2 cloves garlic, minced
- 4 cups low-sodium beef broth, 4 cups water
- 4 carrots, peeled and sliced into rounds
- 2 cups potatoes, diced, 1 cup celery, sliced
- 1 cup green beans, cut into 1-inch pieces
- 1 teaspoon dried thyme, salt and pepper to taste

Directions

1. In a large bowl, coat the beef stew meat with whole wheat flour, shaking off any excess.

2. Heat the olive oil in a large pot over medium-high heat. Add the beef cubes and cook until browned on all sides, about 5-7 minutes. Remove the beef from the pot and set it aside.

3. In the same pot, add the chopped onion and minced garlic. Sauté for 2-3 minutes until they become fragrant.

4. Return the browned beef to the pot and add the beef broth, water, carrots, potatoes, celery, green beans, dried thyme, salt, and pepper. Stir to combine.

5. Bring the stew to a boil, then reduce the heat to low, cover, and simmer for about 1.5 to 2 hours or until the beef is tender and the vegetables are cooked through.

6. Taste and adjust the seasoning with additional salt and pepper if needed.

7. Serve hot and enjoy your heart-healthy beef stew!

Nutritional Information (Approximate)

Calories	260	Dietary Fiber	4g
Protein	26g	Sodium	310mg
Carbohydrates	23g	Cholesterol	55mg
Total Fat	7g	Potassium	720mg
Saturated Fat	2g		

This heart-healthy beef stew is low in saturated fat and sodium, making it a delicious and nutritious option for a comforting meal.

Clam Chowder

Prep Time: 25 minutes / Cook Time: 10 minutes
Yield: 4 serving

Ingredients

- 2 (6.5-ounce) cans of chopped clams, drained,
- Juice reserved
- 1 cup low-sodium chicken or vegetable broth
- 1 cup low-fat milk, 1 tablespoon olive oil
- 1 onion, finely chopped
- 2 celery stalks, finely chopped
- 2 carrots, peeled and finely chopped
- 2 cloves garlic, minced, 2 cups diced potatoes
- 1/4 cup whole wheat flour, 1 bay leaf
- 1/2 teaspoon dried thyme, salt and pepper to taste
- Chopped fresh parsley for garnish (optional)

Directions

1. In a large pot, heat the olive oil over medium heat. Add the chopped onion, celery, carrots, and garlic. Sauté for about 5 minutes until the vegetables begin to soften.

2. Sprinkle the whole wheat flour over the vegetables and stir well to coat them evenly. Cook for an additional 2 minutes, stirring constantly.

3. Gradually add the reserved clam juice, chicken or vegetable broth, and low-fat milk to the pot while stirring continuously to prevent lumps from forming.

4. Stir in the diced potatoes, bay leaf, dried thyme, salt, and pepper. Bring the mixture to a boil.

5. Reduce the heat to low, cover, and simmer for about 15-20 minutes or until the potatoes are tender.

6. Add the drained chopped clams to the pot and cook for an additional 2-3 minutes until they are heated through.

7. Remove the bay leaf, and taste the chowder, adjusting the seasoning with salt and pepper if needed.

8. Serve hot, garnished with chopped fresh parsley if desired.

Nutritional Information (Approximate)

Calories	220	Dietary Fiber	4g
Protein	12g	Sodium	320mg
Carbohydrates	32g	Cholesterol	20mg
Total Fat	5g	Potassium	650mg
Saturated Fat	1g		

French Onion Soup

Prep Time: 40 minutes / Cook Time: 10 minutes
Yield: 4 serving

Ingredients

- 1 tablespoon olive oil, 4 large onions, thinly sliced
- 2 cloves garlic, minced
- 4 cups low-sodium beef broth
- 2 cups water, 1 teaspoon dried thyme
- Salt and pepper to taste
- 4 whole wheat bread slices, toasted
- 1/2 cup grated reduced-fat Swiss cheese

Directions

1. In a large pot, heat the olive oil over medium heat. Add the thinly sliced onions and cook, stirring occasionally, for about 20-25 minutes, or until the onions are caramelized and golden brown.

2. Stir in the minced garlic and cook for an additional 2 minutes until fragrant.

3. Pour in the low-sodium beef broth, water, dried thyme, salt, and pepper. Bring the mixture to a simmer.

4. Reduce the heat to low, cover the pot, and let the soup simmer for another 10-15 minutes to allow the flavors to meld.

5. Preheat your oven's broiler.

6. Ladle the hot soup into oven-safe bowls. Place a slice of toasted whole wheat bread on top of each bowl of soup.

7. Sprinkle the grated reduced-fat Swiss cheese evenly over the bread slices.

8. Place the bowls under the broiler for 2-3 minutes, or until the cheese is bubbly and lightly browned.

9. Carefully remove the bowls from the oven (they will be hot), garnish with chopped fresh chives if desired, and serve immediately.

Nutritional Information (Approximate)

Calories	180	Dietary Fiber	4g
Protein	8g	Sodium	450mg
Carbohydrates	27g	Cholesterol	10mg
Total Fat	5g	Potassium	550mg
Saturated Fat	2g		

Enjoy this heart-healthy French Onion Soup with reduced sodium and lower saturated fat, while still savoring the rich flavors of this classic soup!

Split Pea Soup

Prep Time: 45 minutes / Cook Time: 10 minutes
Yield: 6 serving

Ingredients

- 1 tablespoon olive oil, 1 onion, chopped
- 2 carrots, peeled and diced
- 2 celery stalks, diced
- 2 cloves garlic, minced
- 1 pound dried green split peas, rinsed and drained
- 8 cups low-sodium vegetable broth, 1 bay leaf
- 1 teaspoon dried thyme, salt and pepper to taste
- 1 cup chopped kale or spinach (optional)
- Fresh lemon juice (optional, for serving)

Directions

1. In a large pot, heat the olive oil over medium heat. Add the chopped onion, carrots, and celery. Sauté for about 5 minutes until the vegetables begin to soften.

2. Add the minced garlic and cook for an additional minute until fragrant.

3. Stir in the rinsed and drained green split peas, low-sodium vegetable broth, bay leaf, dried thyme, salt, and pepper.

4. Bring the mixture to a boil, then reduce the heat to low, cover, and simmer for about 35-40 minutes, or until the split peas are tender and the soup has thickened, stirring occasionally.

5. If using kale or spinach, add it to the soup during the last 5 minutes of cooking.

6. Taste and adjust the seasoning with additional salt and pepper if needed.

7. Remove the bay leaf before serving.

8. Optionally, drizzle fresh lemon juice over each serving for a burst of flavor.

Nutritional Information (Approximate)

Calories	240	Dietary Fiber	14g
Protein	14g	Sodium	300mg
Carbohydrates	42g	Cholesterol	0mg
Total Fat	3g	Potassium	730mg
Saturated Fat	0.5g		

Enjoy this heart-healthy split pea soup that's high in fiber, low in sodium, and packed with nutrients to nourish your body!

Chicken and Rice Soup

Prep Time: 30 minutes / Cook Time: 15 minutes
Yield: 6 serving

Ingredients

- 1 tablespoon olive oil, 1 onion, chopped
- 2 carrots, peeled and diced
- 2 celery stalks, diced
- 2 cloves garlic, minced
- 6 cups low-sodium chicken broth
- 1 cup uncooked brown rice
- 2 boneless, skinless chicken breasts, cut into small pieces
- 1 teaspoon dried thyme, salt and pepper to taste
- 2 cups chopped spinach or kale (optional)
- Fresh lemon juice (optional, for serving)

Directions

1. In a large pot, heat the olive oil over medium heat. Add the chopped onion, carrots, and celery. Sauté for about 5 minutes until the vegetables start to soften.

2. Add the minced garlic and cook for an additional minute until fragrant.

3. Pour in the low-sodium chicken broth and add the uncooked brown rice, chicken pieces, dried thyme, salt, and pepper.

4. Bring the mixture to a boil, then reduce the heat to low, cover, and simmer for about 20-25 minutes, or until the rice is tender and the chicken is cooked through, stirring occasionally.

5. If using spinach or kale, stir it into the soup during the last 5 minutes of cooking until wilted.

6. Taste and adjust the seasoning with additional salt and pepper if needed.

7. Optionally, drizzle fresh lemon juice over each serving for added brightness.

Nutritional Information (Approximate)

Calories	270	Dietary Fiber	3g
Protein	22g	Sodium	300mg
Carbohydrates	33g	Cholesterol	30mg
Total Fat	5g	Potassium	530mg
Saturated Fat	1g		

Enjoy this heart-healthy chicken and rice soup that's low in saturated fat and sodium, high in protein and fiber, and full of wholesome ingredients!

Butternut Squash Soup

Prep Time: 35 minutes / Cook Time: 15 minutes
Yield: 6 serving

Ingredients

- 1 tablespoon olive oil, 1 onion, chopped
- 2 cloves garlic, minced, 1 cup water
- 1 butternut squash (about 2 pounds), peeled, seeded, and diced
- 2 carrots, peeled and diced
- 2 apples, peeled, cored, and diced
- 4 cups low-sodium vegetable broth
- 1 teaspoon dried sage, salt and pepper to taste
- 1/2 cup low-fat plain Greek yogurt (optional, for garnish)
- Chopped fresh chives or parsley for garnish (optional)

Directions

1. In a large pot, heat the olive oil over medium heat. Add the chopped onion and sauté for about 3-4 minutes until it becomes translucent.

2. Add the minced garlic and cook for an additional minute until fragrant.

3. Stir in the diced butternut squash, carrots, and apples. Sauté for 5 minutes, allowing the vegetables and apples to soften slightly.

4. Pour in the low-sodium vegetable broth and water. Add the dried sage, salt, and pepper. Bring the mixture to a boil.

5. Reduce the heat to low, cover, and simmer for about 20-25 minutes or until the butternut squash is tender when pierced with a fork.

6. Use an immersion blender to carefully blend the soup until smooth. Alternatively, transfer the soup in batches to a countertop blender and blend until smooth, then return it to the pot.

7. Taste and adjust the seasoning with additional salt and pepper if needed.

8. Optionally, swirl in a spoonful of low-fat plain Greek yogurt into each serving for added creaminess and garnish with chopped fresh chives or parsley.

Nutritional Information (Approximate)

Calories	120	Dietary Fiber	1g
Protein	3g	Sodium	0mg
Carbohydrates	28g	Cholesterol	6mg
Total Fat	0g	Potassium	700mg
Saturated Fat	170g		

Enjoy this heart-healthy butternut squash soup that's low in calories, fat, and sodium, and packed with vitamins and fiber!

Potato Leek Soup

Prep Time: 25 minutes / Cook Time: 10 minutes
Yield: 4 serving

Ingredients

- 1 tablespoon olive oil, 2 cloves garlic, minced
- 2 leeks, white and light green parts, sliced`
- 4 cups low-sodium vegetable broth
- 4 cups diced potatoes, peeled (about 4 medium potatoes)
- 1 bay leaf, 1/2 teaspoon dried thyme
- Salt and pepper to taste
- 1 cup low-fat milk or unsweetened almond milk
- Fresh chives or parsley for garnish (optional)

Directions

1. In a large pot, heat the olive oil over medium heat. Add the sliced leeks and sauté for about 3-4 minutes until they become tender.

2. Stir in the minced garlic and cook for an additional minute until fragrant.

3. Add the low-sodium vegetable broth, diced potatoes, bay leaf, dried thyme, salt, and pepper. Bring the mixture to a boil.

4. Reduce the heat to low, cover, and simmer for about 15-20 minutes, or until the potatoes are soft when pierced with a fork.

5. Remove the bay leaf and discard it.

6. Use an immersion blender to carefully blend the soup until smooth. Alternatively, transfer the soup in batches to a countertop blender and blend until smooth, then return it to the pot.

7. Stir in the low-fat milk or unsweetened almond milk, and heat the soup for an additional 2-3 minutes until warmed through.

8. Taste and adjust the seasoning with additional salt and pepper if needed.

9. Optionally, garnish with fresh chives or parsley before serving.

Nutritional Information (Approximate)

Calories	180	Dietary Fiber	4g
Protein	4g	Sodium	480mg
Carbohydrates	36g	Cholesterol	0mg
Total Fat	2g	Potassium	900mg
Saturated Fat	0g		

Enjoy this heart-healthy potato leek soup that's low in fat and sodium, yet rich and satisfying in flavor!

Lentil Soup

Prep Time: 30 minutes / Cook Time: 15 minutes
Yield: 6 serving

Ingredients

- 1 tablespoon olive oil
- 1 onion, chopped
- 2 carrots, peeled and diced
- 2 celery stalks, diced
- 2 cloves garlic, minced
- Salt and pepper to taste
- 1 cup dried green or brown lentils, rinsed and drained
- 8 cups low-sodium vegetable broth
- 1 bay leaf
- 1 teaspoon ground cumin
- 1/2 teaspoon ground turmeric
- 2 cups chopped kale or spinach (optional)
- Fresh lemon wedges for serving (optional)

Directions

1. In a large pot, heat the olive oil over medium heat. Add the chopped onion, carrots, and celery. Sauté for about 5 minutes until the vegetables begin to soften.

2. Add the minced garlic and cook for an additional minute until fragrant.

3. Stir in the rinsed and drained lentils, low-sodium vegetable broth, bay leaf, ground cumin, ground turmeric, salt, and pepper.

4. Bring the mixture to a boil, then reduce the heat to low, cover, and simmer for about 25-30 minutes, or until the lentils are tender, stirring occasionally.

5. If using kale or spinach, stir it into the soup during the last 5 minutes of cooking until wilted.

6. Remove the bay leaf before serving.

7. Optionally, serve with fresh lemon wedges to squeeze over each serving for added brightness.

Nutritional Information (Approximate)

Calories	220	Dietary Fiber	11g
Protein	14g	Sodium	380mg
Carbohydrates	36g	Cholesterol	0mg
Total Fat	4g	Potassium	750mg
Saturated Fat	0.5g		

Enjoy this heart-healthy lentil soup that's high in fiber, low in saturated fat, and packed with plant-based protein and nutrients!

Vegetable Curry Stew

Prep Time: 30 minutes / Cook Time: 15 minutes
Yield: 4 serving

Ingredients

- 1 tablespoon olive oil, 1 onion, chopped
- 2 cloves garlic, minced, 1 tablespoon curry powder
- 1 teaspoon ground cumin, 1 cup diced zucchini
- 1 teaspoon ground coriander
- 1 teaspoon paprika, 1/2 teaspoon ground turmeric
- 1/4 teaspoon cayenne pepper (adjust to taste)
- 4 cups low-sodium vegetable broth
- 1 cup diced sweet potatoes, 1 cup diced carrots
- 1 cup diced bell peppers (assorted colors)
- 1 cup canned chickpeas, drained and rinsed
- 1 cup canned diced tomatoes (no salt added)
- Salt and pepper to taste, 1 cup light coconut milk
- Fresh cilantro leaves for garnish (optional)

Directions

1. In a large pot, heat the olive oil over medium heat. Add the chopped onion and sauté for about 3-4 minutes until it becomes translucent.

2. Add the minced garlic, curry powder, ground cumin, ground coriander, paprika, ground turmeric, and cayenne pepper. Cook for an additional 1-2 minutes until the spices become fragrant.

3. Pour in the low-sodium vegetable broth, diced sweet potatoes, carrots, zucchini, bell peppers, chickpeas, and diced tomatoes. Season with salt and pepper to taste.

4. Bring the mixture to a boil, then reduce the heat to low, cover, and simmer for about 20-25 minutes, or until the vegetables are tender, stirring occasionally.

5. Stir in the light coconut milk and heat the stew for an additional 5 minutes, but do not let it come to a boil.

6. Taste and adjust the seasoning with additional salt and pepper if needed.

7. Serve hot, garnished with fresh cilantro leaves if desired.

Nutritional Information (Approximate)

Calories	230	Dietary Fiber	8g
Protein	6g	Sodium	380mg
Carbohydrates	32g	Cholesterol	0mg
Total Fat	9g	Potassium	700mg
Saturated Fat	4g		

Enjoy this heart-healthy vegetable curry stew that's packed with flavor, fiber, and wholesome ingredients!

Italian Wedding Soup

Prep Time: 25 minutes / Cook Time: 15 minutes
Yield: 4 serving

Ingredients

- 1 tablespoon olive oil, 1 onion, finely chopped
- 2 cloves garlic, minced, 1 carrot, diced
- 1 celery stalk, diced, 4 cups water
- 4 cups low-sodium chicken broth
- 1 cup whole wheat orzo pasta
- 1 cup lean ground turkey, salt and pepper to taste
- 1/4 cup whole wheat breadcrumbs, 1 egg, beaten
- 1/4 cup grated Parmesan cheese
- 1/4 cup chopped fresh parsley
- 2 cups baby spinach leaves
- Fresh lemon wedges for serving (optional)

Directions

1. In a large pot, heat the olive oil over medium heat. Add the chopped onion, minced garlic, diced carrot, and diced celery. Sauté for about 3-4 minutes until the vegetables start to soften.

2. Pour in the low-sodium chicken broth and water. Bring the mixture to a boil.

3. Stir in the whole wheat orzo pasta and cook according to package instructions until al dente.

4. While the pasta is cooking, prepare the meatballs. In a bowl, combine the lean ground turkey, whole wheat breadcrumbs, grated Parmesan cheese, chopped fresh parsley, beaten egg, salt, and pepper. Mix well.

5. Form the mixture into small meatballs, about 1 inch in diameter.

6. Drop the meatballs into the boiling soup one by one. Reduce the heat to low, cover, and simmer for about 10 minutes, or until the meatballs are cooked through.

7. Stir in the baby spinach leaves and cook for an additional 2 minutes until wilted.

8. Taste and adjust the seasoning with additional salt and pepper if needed.

9. Optionally, serve with fresh lemon wedges to squeeze over each serving for added brightness.

Nutritional Information (Approximate)

Calories	280	Dietary Fiber	4g
Protein	18g	Sodium	520mg
Carbohydrates	31g	Cholesterol	85mg
Total Fat	9g	Potassium	470mg
Saturated Fat	2g		

Chili

Prep Time: 30 minutes / Cook Time: 15 minutes
Yield: 6 serving

Ingredients

- 1 tablespoon olive oil, 1 onion, chopped
- 2 cloves garlic, minced, 2 tablespoons chili powder
- 1 pound lean ground turkey or lean ground beef (93% lean)
- 1 bell pepper, chopped (red, green, or yellow)
- 1 jalapeño pepper, finely chopped (adjust to taste)
- 1 can (14 ounces) low-sodium diced tomatoes
- 1 can (14 ounces) low-sodium kidney beans, drained and rinsed
- 1 can (14 ounces) low-sodium black beans, drained and rinsed
- 1 cup low-sodium vegetable broth
- 1 teaspoon ground cumin
- 1/2 teaspoon smoked paprika
- Salt and pepper to taste, chopped fresh cilantro for garnish (optional)
- Reduced-fat shredded cheddar cheese for garnish (optional)
- Low-fat plain Greek yogurt for garnish (optional)

Directions

1. In a large pot, heat the olive oil over medium heat. Add the chopped onion and sauté for about 3-4 minutes until it becomes translucent.

2. Add the minced garlic and cook for an additional minute until fragrant.

3. Add the lean ground turkey or beef and cook, breaking it apart with a spoon, until browned and cooked through. Drain any excess fat if necessary.

4. Stir in the chopped bell pepper and jalapeño pepper. Cook for about 3-4 minutes until the peppers begin to soften.

5. Add the low-sodium diced tomatoes, drained kidney beans, drained black beans, low-sodium vegetable broth, chili powder, ground cumin, smoked paprika, salt, and pepper.

6. Bring the mixture to a boil, then reduce the heat to low, cover, and simmer for about 15-20 minutes, stirring occasionally.

7. Taste and adjust the seasoning with additional salt and pepper if needed.

8. Optionally, serve the chili garnished with chopped fresh cilantro, reduced-fat shredded cheddar cheese, and a dollop of low-fat plain Greek yogurt.

Nutritional Information (Approximate)

Calories	280	Dietary Fiber	9g
Protein	21g	Sodium	430mg
Carbohydrates	29g	Cholesterol	45mg
Total Fat	10g	Potassium	720mg
Saturated Fat	2g		

Thai Coconut Soup (Tom Kha Gai)

Prep Time: 20 minutes / Cook Time: 15 minutes
Yield: 4 serving

Ingredients

- 1 tablespoon olive oil, 1 onion, chopped
- 2 cloves garlic, minced, 8 ounces mushrooms, sliced
- 1-2 tablespoons Thai red curry paste (adjust to taste)
- 1 can (14 ounces) light coconut milk
- 4 cups low-sodium chicken or vegetable broth
- 2 boneless, skinless chicken breasts, cut into thin strips
- 1 red bell pepper, thinly sliced, juice of 2 limes
- 2 tablespoons fish sauce (or soy sauce for a vegetarian version)
- 2 teaspoons brown sugar, salt and pepper to taste
- 2-3 kaffir lime leaves (optional but highly recommended)
- Fresh cilantro leaves for garnish (optional)
- Sliced green onions for garnish (optional)
- Sliced red chili peppers for garnish (optional)

Directions

1. In a large pot, heat the olive oil over medium heat. Add the chopped onion and sauté for about 3-4 minutes until it becomes translucent.

2. Add the minced garlic and Thai red curry paste. Cook for an additional 1-2 minutes until fragrant.

3. Pour in the light coconut milk and low-sodium chicken or vegetable broth. Stir to combine.

4. Add the thinly sliced chicken breasts, sliced mushrooms, and thinly sliced red bell pepper. Bring the mixture to a simmer.

5. Stir in the fish sauce (or soy sauce), brown sugar, and kaffir lime leaves if using. Simmer for about 10-12 minutes, or until the chicken is cooked through and the vegetables are tender.

6. Remove and discard the kaffir lime leaves.

7. Stir in the lime juice, and season the soup with salt and pepper to taste.

8. Optionally, serve the Thai coconut soup garnished with fresh cilantro leaves, sliced green onions, and sliced red chili peppers for added flavor and color.

Nutritional Information (Approximate)

Calories	230	Dietary Fiber	2g
Protein	20g	Sodium	800mg
Carbohydrates	11g	Cholesterol	35mg
Total Fat	10g	Potassium	570mg
Saturated Fat	6g		

Corn Chowder

Prep Time: 25 minutes / Cook Time: 15 minutes
Yield: 4 serving

Ingredients

- 1 tablespoon olive oil, 1 onion, chopped
- 2 cloves garlic, minced, 1 teaspoon dried thyme
- 2 cups fresh or frozen corn kernels (about 4 ears of corn)
- 2 medium potatoes, peeled and diced
- 2 carrots, peeled and diced, salt and pepper to taste
- 4 cups low-sodium vegetable broth
- 1/2 teaspoon smoked paprika
- 1 cup low-fat milk or unsweetened almond milk
- 2 tablespoons whole wheat flour
- Chopped fresh chives or green onions for garnish (optional)

Directions

1. In a large pot, heat the olive oil over medium heat. Add the chopped onion and sauté for about 3-4 minutes until it becomes translucent.

2. Add the minced garlic and cook for an additional minute until fragrant.

3. Stir in the fresh or frozen corn kernels, diced potatoes, and diced carrots.

4. Pour in the low-sodium vegetable broth and add the dried thyme, smoked paprika, salt, and pepper. Bring the mixture to a boil.

5. Reduce the heat to low, cover, and simmer for about 15-20 minutes, or until the potatoes and carrots are tender, stirring occasionally.

6. In a separate small bowl, whisk together the low-fat milk and whole wheat flour until smooth.

7. Slowly pour the milk mixture into the soup, stirring constantly. Continue to cook for an additional 5 minutes until the soup thickens slightly.

8. Taste and adjust the seasoning with additional salt and pepper if needed.

9. Optionally, garnish the corn chowder with chopped fresh chives or green onions before serving.

Nutritional Information (Approximate)

Calories	190	Dietary Fiber	5g
Protein	5g	Sodium	460mg
Carbohydrates	36g	Cholesterol	2mg
Total Fat	4g	Potassium	580mg
Saturated Fat	1g		

Goulash

Prep Time: 15 minutes / Cook Time: 40 minutes
Yield: 4 serving

Ingredients

- 1 tablespoon olive oil, 1 onion, chopped
- 2 cloves garlic, minced, 2 tablespoons paprika
- 1 pound lean beef stew meat,
  cut into bite-sized pieces
- 2 tablespoons whole wheat flour
- 1 teaspoon caraway seeds
- 1 red bell pepper, chopped
- 1 green bell pepper, chopped
- 1 can (14 ounces) diced tomatoes (no salt added)
- 2 cups low-sodium beef broth
- 2 cups sliced mushrooms, salt and pepper to taste
- Chopped fresh parsley for garnish (optional)
- Whole wheat noodles or brown rice for serving
  (optional)

Directions

1. In a large pot, heat the olive oil over medium heat. Add the chopped onion and sauté for about 3-4 minutes until it becomes translucent.

2. Add the minced garlic and cook for an additional minute until fragrant.

3. Add the lean beef stew meat and cook until browned on all sides.

4. Sprinkle the whole wheat flour, paprika, and caraway seeds over the meat and stir well to coat.

5. Stir in the chopped red and green bell peppers and cook for another 2-3 minutes until they start to soften.

6. Add the diced tomatoes, low-sodium beef broth, and sliced mushrooms. Season with salt and pepper to taste.

7. Bring the mixture to a boil, then reduce the heat to low, cover, and simmer for about 30 minutes, or until the meat is tender and the sauce has thickened, stirring occasionally.

8. Optionally, serve the goulash over whole wheat noodles or brown rice and garnish with chopped fresh parsley for added flavor and color.

Nutritional Information (Approximate)

Calories	250	Dietary Fiber	3g
Protein	25g	Sodium	480mg
Carbohydrates	15g	Cholesterol	60mg
Total Fat	9g	Potassium	700mg
Saturated Fat	2g		

Enjoy this heart-healthy goulash that's rich in flavor, lean protein, and wholesome ingredients!

Gazpacho

Prep Time: 15 minutes / Cook Time: 0 minutes
Yield: 6 serving

Ingredients

- 6 ripe tomatoes, cored and roughly chopped
- 1 cucumber, peeled, seeded, and roughly chopped
- 1 red bell pepper, seeded and roughly chopped
- 1 small red onion, roughly chopped
- 2 cloves garlic, minced
- 1/4 cup red wine vinegar
- 4 cups low-sodium tomato juice
- 1/4 cup olive oil, 1 teaspoon salt
- 1/2 teaspoon black pepper
- 1/2 teaspoon ground cumin
- 1/4 teaspoon cayenne pepper (adjust to taste)
- Fresh basil leaves for garnish (optional)
- Croutons for garnish (optional)

Directions

1. In a large bowl, combine the chopped tomatoes, cucumber, red bell pepper, red onion, and minced garlic.

2. In a blender or food processor, working in batches if necessary, blend the tomato and vegetable mixture until smooth.

3. Pour the blended mixture back into the large bowl.

4. Stir in the low-sodium tomato juice, red wine vinegar, olive oil, salt, black pepper, ground cumin, and cayenne pepper. Mix well.

5. Taste and adjust the seasoning with additional salt, black pepper, or cayenne pepper if needed. If the gazpacho is too thick, you can add a bit more tomato juice to reach your desired consistency.

6. Chill the gazpacho in the refrigerator for at least 2 hours to allow the flavors to meld.

7. Serve the chilled gazpacho garnished with fresh basil leaves and croutons if desired.

Nutritional Information (Approximate)

Calories	140	Dietary Fiber	3g
Protein	3g	Sodium	380mg
Carbohydrates	18g	Cholesterol	0mg
Total Fat	7g	Potassium	700mg
Saturated Fat	1g		

Enjoy this heart-healthy Gazpacho as a refreshing and low-calorie summer soup that's packed with vitamins and antioxidants!

Beet and Barley Soup

Prep Time: 15 minutes / Cook Time: 40 minutes
Yield: 4 serving

Ingredients

- 2 medium beets, peeled and diced
- 1 cup pearled barley
- 1 onion, chopped
- 2 cloves garlic, minced
- 2 carrots, peeled and diced
- 2 celery stalks, diced
- 4 cups low-sodium vegetable broth
- 4 cups water, 1 teaspoon dried thyme
- 1 bay leaf
- Salt and pepper to taste
- 1 tablespoon fresh lemon juice (optional)
- Greek yogurt or sour cream for garnish (optional)
- Fresh dill for garnish (optional)

Directions

1. In a large pot, add the diced beets, pearled barley, chopped onion, and minced garlic.

2. Stir in the diced carrots, diced celery, low-sodium vegetable broth, water, dried thyme, bay leaf, salt, and pepper.

3. Bring the mixture to a boil over medium-high heat.

4. Reduce the heat to low, cover, and simmer for about 30-35 minutes, or until the beets and barley are tender, stirring occasionally.

5. Remove the bay leaf and discard.

6. If desired, stir in fresh lemon juice to brighten the flavors.

7. Taste and adjust the seasoning with additional salt and pepper if needed.

8. Optionally, garnish each bowl of beet and barley soup with a dollop of Greek yogurt or sour cream and a sprinkle of fresh dill.

Nutritional Information (Approximate)

Calories	200	Dietary Fiber	9g
Protein	6g	Sodium	300mg
Carbohydrates	45g	Cholesterol	0mg
Total Fat	1g	Potassium	580mg
Saturated Fat	0g		

Enjoy this heart-healthy Beet and Barley Soup, a vibrant and nutritious dish that's rich in flavor and packed with fiber!

Moroccan Harira Soup

Prep Time: 15 minutes / Cook Time: 30 minutes
Yield: 4 serving

Ingredients

- 1 tablespoon olive oil, 1 onion, chopped
- 2 cloves garlic, minced, 1 teaspoon ground cumin
- 1 teaspoon ground coriander
- 1/2 teaspoon ground cinnamon
- 1/4 teaspoon cayenne pepper (adjust to taste)
- 1 can (14 ounces) diced tomatoes (no salt added)
- 1/2 cup red lentils, rinsed and drained
- 1/4 cup brown rice, 2 carrots, peeled and diced
- 4 cups low-sodium vegetable broth
- 2 celery stalks, diced, 1 red bell pepper, diced
- 1/2 cup chopped fresh cilantro, juice of 1 lemon
- 1/4 cup chopped fresh parsley
- Salt and pepper to taste
- Lemon wedges for serving (optional)

Directions

1. In a large pot, heat the olive oil over medium heat. Add the chopped onion and sauté for about 3-4 minutes until it becomes translucent.

2. Add the minced garlic, ground cumin, ground coriander, ground cinnamon, and cayenne pepper. Cook for an additional 1-2 minutes until fragrant.

3. Stir in the diced tomatoes, red lentils, brown rice, and low-sodium vegetable broth. Bring the mixture to a boil.

4. Reduce the heat to low, cover, and simmer for about 10 minutes.

5. Add the diced carrots, diced celery, and diced red bell pepper. Continue to simmer for another 15-20 minutes, or until the vegetables are tender and the lentils and rice are cooked.

6. Stir in the chopped fresh cilantro, chopped fresh parsley, and lemon juice.

7. Taste and adjust the seasoning with additional salt, pepper, or lemon juice if needed.

8. Optionally, serve the Moroccan Harira Soup with lemon wedges for an extra burst of flavor.

Nutritional Information (Approximate)

Calories	180	Dietary Fiber	6g
Protein	7g	Sodium	480mg
Carbohydrates	33g	Cholesterol	0mg
Total Fat	3g	Potassium	620mg
Saturated Fat	0g		

Enjoy this heart-healthy Moroccan Harira Soup, a delicious and nutritious dish rich in spices and fresh ingredients!

chapter 7
LEAN MEATS & POULTRY

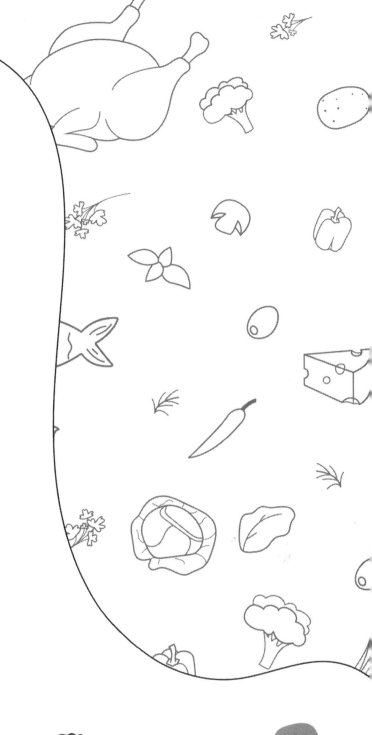

Grilled Chicken Breast
with Lemon-Herb Marinade 50

Turkey & Vegetable Stir-Fry 50

Herb-Crusted Cod Fillets 51

Lean Beef and Broccoli Stir-Fry 51

Lemon Garlic Shrimp Skewers 52

Honey Mustard Glazed Chicken Thighs 52

Chili-Lime Grilled Turkey Tenderloin 52

Teriyaki Salmon with Steamed Vegetables 53

Mediterranean Turkey & Quinoa Stuffed Peppers .. 53

Herb-Roasted Pork Tenderloin 53

Lemon Pepper Grilled Tilapia 54

Balsamic Glazed Grilled Pork Chops 54

Moroccan Spiced Chicken with Couscous 54

Garlic and Rosemary Grilled Lamb Chops 55

Pesto Baked Cod with Cherry Tomatoes 55

Thai Basil Ground Turkey Stir-Fry 55

Orange-Glazed Turkey Cutlets 56

Spicy Cajun Shrimp and Brown Rice 56

Lemon Garlic Herb Turkey Breast 57

Sesame Ginger Tofu Stir-Fry 57

Greek-Style Grilled Chicken Skewers 58

Paprika-Rubbed Grilled Pork Tenderloin 58

Cajun Blackened Salmon 59

Asian-inspired ground Chicken Lettuce Wraps 59

Grilled Chicken Breast with Lemon-Herb Marinade

Prep Time: 10 minutes / Cook Time: 12 minutes
Yield: 2 serving

Ingredients

- 1 boneless, skinless chicken breast
- 1 lemon, juiced and zested
- 2 cloves garlic, minced
- 1 tablespoon fresh basil, chopped
- 1 tablespoon fresh parsley, chopped
- 1 tablespoon olive oil
- Salt and pepper to taste

Directions

1. In a small bowl, combine the lemon juice, lemon zest, minced garlic, chopped basil, chopped parsley, and olive oil. Season with salt and pepper to taste. This mixture will be your marinade.

2. Place the chicken breast in a resealable plastic bag or a shallow dish. Pour the lemon-herb marinade over the chicken, ensuring it is evenly coated. Seal the bag or cover the dish and refrigerate for at least 30 minutes to marinate. You can leave it longer for more flavor, even overnight.

3. Preheat your grill to medium-high heat.

4. Remove the chicken from the marinade and let any excess drip off. Discard the marinade.

5. Grill the chicken breast for about 6 minutes per side or until the internal temperature reaches 165°F (74°C) and the juices run clear. Cooking time may vary depending on the thickness of the chicken breast.

6. Remove the chicken from the grill and let it rest for a few minutes before slicing it.

Nutritional Information (Approximate)

Calories	280	Dietary Fiber	1g
Protein	40g	Sodium	120mg
Carbohydrates	4g	Cholesterol	110mg
Total Fat	10g	Potassium	380mg
Saturated Fat	2g		

This heart-healthy Grilled Chicken Breast with Lemon-Herb Marinade is a delicious and low-calorie option that's perfect for a light and satisfying meal. Enjoy!

Turkey and Vegetable Stir-Fry

Prep Time: 15 minutes / Cook Time: 10 minutes
Yield: 1 serving

Ingredients

- 4 ounces lean ground turkey
- 1 cup broccoli florets
- 1/2 cup red bell pepper, sliced
- 1/2 cup snap peas, trimmed
- 1/2 cup carrots, thinly sliced
- 1 clove garlic, minced
- 1 tablespoon low-sodium soy sauce
- 1/2 tablespoon sesame oil
- 1/2 teaspoon ginger, minced
- 1/2 teaspoon honey
- Salt and pepper to taste
- Cooking spray

Directions

1. In a small bowl, whisk together the low-sodium soy sauce, sesame oil, minced garlic, minced ginger, honey, salt, and pepper. This will be your stir-fry sauce.

2. Heat a non-stick skillet or wok over medium-high heat and lightly coat it with cooking spray.

3. Add the ground turkey to the skillet and cook, breaking it apart with a spatula, until it's browned and cooked through. Remove the turkey from the skillet and set it aside.

4. In the same skillet, add a bit more cooking spray if needed, and then add the broccoli, red bell pepper, snap peas, and carrots. Stir-fry the vegetables for about 5-6 minutes or until they are tender-crisp.

5. Return the cooked turkey to the skillet with the vegetables.

6. Pour the stir-fry sauce over the turkey and vegetables. Stir-fry for an additional 2-3 minutes to heat everything through and coat it in the sauce.

7. Serve your heart-healthy turkey and vegetable stir-fry hot.

Nutritional Information (Approximate)

Calories	300	Dietary Fiber	5g
Protein	25g	Sodium	550mg
Carbohydrates	20g	Cholesterol	45mg
Total Fat	12g	Potassium	600mg
Saturated Fat	2g		

This heart-healthy Turkey and Vegetable Stir-Fry is a nutritious and satisfying meal with lean protein and a variety of colorful vegetables. Enjoy!

Herb-Crusted Cod Fillets

Prep Time: 10 minutes / Cook Time: 15 minutes
Yield: 1 serving

Ingredients

- 1 cod fillet (about 6 ounces)
- 1 tablespoon whole wheat breadcrumbs
- 1 tablespoon fresh parsley, chopped
- 1/2 teaspoon dried oregano
- 1/2 teaspoon dried thyme
- 1 clove garlic, minced
- 1/2 lemon, juiced and zested
- 1 teaspoon olive oil
- Salt and pepper to taste

Directions

1. Preheat your oven to 375°F (190°C). Line a baking sheet with parchment paper or lightly grease it to prevent sticking.

2. In a small bowl, combine the whole wheat breadcrumbs, chopped parsley, dried oregano, dried thyme, minced garlic, lemon juice, lemon zest, olive oil, salt, and pepper. This mixture will be your herb crust.

3. Place the cod fillet on the prepared baking sheet. Pat it dry with a paper towel if it's too moist.

4. Press the herb crust mixture onto the top of the cod fillet, ensuring it adheres evenly.

5. Bake the cod in the preheated oven for about 12-15 minutes, or until the fish flakes easily with a fork and is cooked to your desired level of doneness.

6. Carefully remove the cod from the oven and let it rest for a minute or two before serving.

Nutritional Information (Approximate)

Calories	250	Dietary Fiber	2g
Protein	30g	Sodium	350mg
Carbohydrates	12g	Cholesterol	65mg
Total Fat	8g	Potassium	400mg
Saturated Fat	1g		

This heart-healthy Herb-Crusted Cod Fillet is a flavorful and nutritious option that's low in saturated fat and high in protein. Enjoy this easy and delicious meal!

Lean Beef and Broccoli Stir-Fry

Prep Time: 15 minutes / Cook Time: 10 minutes
Yield: 1 serving

Ingredients

- 4 ounces lean beef (sirloin or flank steak), thinly sliced
- 1 cup broccoli florets
- 1/2 red bell pepper, sliced
- 1/2 cup snap peas, trimmed
- 1/2 cup carrots, thinly sliced
- 1 clove garlic, minced
- 1 tablespoon low-sodium soy sauce
- 1/2 tablespoon hoisin sauce
- 1/2 teaspoon ginger, minced
- 1/2 teaspoon cornstarch
- 1/2 teaspoon sesame oil
- Cooking spray, salt and pepper to taste

Directions

1. In a small bowl, mix together the low-sodium soy sauce, hoisin sauce, minced garlic, minced ginger, cornstarch, sesame oil, salt, and pepper. This will be your stir-fry sauce.

2. Heat a non-stick skillet or wok over medium-high heat and lightly coat it with cooking spray.

3. Add the thinly sliced beef to the skillet and stir-fry for about 2-3 minutes or until it's browned and cooked to your desired level of doneness. Remove the beef from the skillet and set it aside.

4. In the same skillet, add a bit more cooking spray if needed, and then add the broccoli, red bell pepper, snap peas, and carrots. Stir-fry the vegetables for about 4-5 minutes or until they are tender-crisp.

5. Return the cooked beef to the skillet with the vegetables.

6. Pour the stir-fry sauce over the beef and vegetables. Stir-fry for an additional 2-3 minutes to heat everything through and coat it in the sauce.

7. Serve your heart-healthy Lean Beef and Broccoli Stir-Fry hot.

Nutritional Information (Approximate)

Calories	300	Dietary Fiber	4g
Protein	28g	Sodium	650mg
Carbohydrates	18g	Cholesterol	60mg
Total Fat	12g	Potassium	620mg
Saturated Fat	3g		

This heart-healthy Lean Beef and Broccoli Stir-Fry is a delicious and nutritious meal option, offering lean protein and a variety of colorful vegetables. Enjoy!

Lemon Garlic Shrimp Skewers

Prep Time: 15 minutes / Cook Time: 6 minutes
Yield: 1 serving

Ingredients

- 6 large shrimp, peeled and deveined, 1 clove garlic, minced
- 1/2 lemon, juiced and zested
- 1 tablespoon fresh parsley, chopped
- 1 teaspoon olive oil, salt and pepper to taste

Directions

1. In a small bowl, combine the minced garlic, lemon juice, lemon zest, chopped parsley, olive oil, salt, and pepper. This mixture will be your marinade.

2. Thread the peeled and deveined shrimp onto a skewer.

3. Place the shrimp skewer in a shallow dish and pour the lemon garlic marinade over it. Make sure the shrimp are evenly coated. Let it marinate for about 10 minutes.

4. Preheat your grill or grill pan to medium-high heat.

5. Grill the shrimp skewer for about 2-3 minutes per side, or until they turn pink and are cooked through. Be careful not to overcook, as shrimp cook quickly.

6. Remove the shrimp skewer from the grill and let it rest for a minute before serving.

Nutritional Information (Approximate)

Calories	120	Dietary Fiber	0.5g
Protein	18g	Sodium	200mg
Carbohydrates	2g	Cholesterol	135mg
Total Fat	4g	Potassium	190mg
Saturated Fat	0.5g		

Honey Mustard Glazed Chicken Thighs

Prep Time: 10 minutes / Cook Time: 20 minutes
Yield: 1 serving

Ingredients

- 2 boneless, skinless chicken thighs, 1 tablespoon Dijon mustard
- 1 tablespoon honey, 1 clove garlic, minced
- 1/2 lemon, juiced and zested
- 1 teaspoon olive oil, salt and pepper to taste

Directions

1. In a small bowl, whisk together the Dijon mustard, honey, minced garlic, lemon juice, lemon zest, olive oil, salt, and pepper. This mixture will be your honey mustard glaze.

2. Preheat your oven to 375°F (190°C).

3. Place the chicken thighs in a baking dish or on a baking sheet lined with parchment paper.

4. Brush the honey mustard glaze generously over the chicken thighs, ensuring they are evenly coated.

5. Bake the chicken in the preheated oven for about 18-20 minutes, or until the internal temperature of the chicken reaches 165°F (74°C) and the glaze is caramelized and golden brown.

6. Remove the chicken thighs from the oven and let them rest for a few minutes before serving.

Nutritional Information (Approximate)

Calories	300	Dietary Fiber	0.5g
Protein	28g	Sodium	350mg
Carbohydrates	12g	Cholesterol	135mg
Total Fat	3.5g	Potassium	280mg
Saturated Fat	0,5g		

Chili-Lime Grilled Turkey Tenderloin

Prep Time: 15 minutes / Cook Time: 20 minutes / Yield: 1 serving

Ingredients

- 1 turkey tenderloin (about 6 ounces)
- Zest and juice of 1 lime
- 1 teaspoon chili powder
- 1/2 teaspoon ground cumin
- 1 clove garlic, minced
- 1 teaspoon olive oil
- Salt and pepper to taste

Nutritional Information (Approximate)

Calories	250	Dietary Fiber	1g
Protein	40g	Sodium	400mg
Carbohydrates	3g	Cholesterol	60mg
Total Fat	7g	Potassium	380mg
Saturated Fat	1g		

Directions

1. In a small bowl, combine the lime zest, lime juice, chili powder, ground cumin, minced garlic, olive oil, salt, and pepper. This mixture will be your marinade.

2. Place the turkey tenderloin in a resealable plastic bag or a shallow dish. Pour the chili-lime marinade over the turkey, ensuring it is evenly coated. Seal the bag or cover the dish and refrigerate for at least 30 minutes to marinate. You can leave it longer for more flavor, even overnight.

3. Preheat your grill to medium-high heat.

4. Remove the turkey tenderloin from the marinade and let any excess drip off. Discard the marinade.

5. Grill the turkey tenderloin for about 8-10 minutes per side or until the internal temperature reaches 165°F (74°C) and the juices run clear. Cooking time may vary depending on the thickness of the turkey tenderloin.

6. Remove the turkey from the grill and let it rest for a few minutes before slicing it.

Teriyaki Salmon with Steamed Vegetables

Prep Time: 15 minutes / Cook Time: 15 minutes
Yield: 1 serving

Ingredients

- 1 salmon fillet (about 6 ounces)
- 1 cup mixed vegetables (broccoli florets, carrots, snap peas)
- 2 tablespoons low-sodium teriyaki sauce
- 1/2 tablespoon honey, 1 clove garlic, minced
- 1/2 teaspoon ginger, minced, 1 teaspoon olive oil
- Salt and pepper to taste

Directions

1. In a small bowl, whisk together the low-sodium teriyaki sauce, honey, minced garlic, minced ginger, olive oil, salt, and pepper. This mixture will be your teriyaki sauce.

2. Preheat your oven to 375°F (190°C).

3. Place the salmon fillet on a baking sheet lined with parchment paper or lightly greased.

4. Brush the teriyaki sauce over the salmon fillet, ensuring it's evenly coated.

5. In a steamer basket or microwave-safe dish, steam the mixed vegetables until they are tender-crisp, about 5-6 minutes.

6. Place the salmon and steamed vegetables in the preheated oven and bake for about 10-12 minutes or until the salmon flakes easily with a fork and is cooked to your desired level of doneness.

7. Remove the salmon and vegetables from the oven.

Nutritional Information (Approximate)

Calories	350	Dietary Fiber	4g
Protein	30g	Sodium	600mg
Carbohydrates	30g	Cholesterol	70mg
Total Fat	12g	Potassium	600mg
Saturated Fat	2g		

Mediterranean Turkey and Quinoa Stuffed Pepper

Prep Time: 25 minutes / Cook Time: 35 minutes
Yield: 1 serving

Ingredients

- 1 large bell pepper (red, yellow, or green)
- 4 ounces lean ground turkey, 1/4 cup cooked quinoa
- 1/4 cup diced tomatoes (canned or fresh)
- 1/4 cup diced cucumber, 2 tablespoons diced red onion
- 2 tablespoons crumbled feta cheese
- 1/2 teaspoon dried oregano, 1/4 teaspoon garlic powder
- Salt and pepper to taste, cooking spray

Directions

1. Preheat your oven to 375°F (190°C). Cut the top off the bell pepper and remove the seeds and membranes. Rinse it under cold water.

2. In a skillet, cook the lean ground turkey over medium heat until it's browned and cooked through. Break it apart with a spatula as it cooks.

3. In a mixing bowl, combine the cooked quinoa, diced tomatoes, diced cucumber, diced red onion, crumbled feta cheese, dried oregano, garlic powder, salt, and pepper. Mix well.

4. Add the cooked ground turkey to the quinoa mixture and stir to combine.

5. Stuff the prepared bell pepper with the turkey and quinoa mixture, packing it in tightly.

6. Place the stuffed pepper in a baking dish or on a baking sheet, lightly coated with cooking spray.

7. Bake the stuffed pepper in the preheated oven for about 30-35 minutes, or until the pepper is tender and the filling is heated through.

Nutritional Information (Approximate)

Calories	350	Dietary Fiber	6g
Protein	30g	Sodium	650mg
Carbohydrates	35g	Cholesterol	65mg
Total Fat	10g	Potassium	800mg
Saturated Fat	3g		

Herb-Roasted Pork Tenderloin

Prep Time: 15 minutes / Cook Time: 25 minutes / Yield: 1 serving

Ingredients

- 1 pork tenderloin (about 6 ounces), 1 clove garlic, minced
- 1 tablespoon fresh rosemary, chopped
- 1 tablespoon fresh thyme, chopped
- 1 tablespoon fresh parsley, chopped
- 1 teaspoon olive oil, salt and pepper to taste

Nutritional Information (Approximate)

Calories	250	Dietary Fiber	1g
Protein	30g	Sodium	450mg
Carbohydrates	2g	Cholesterol	75mg
Total Fat	12g	Potassium	450mg
Saturated Fat	3g		

Directions

1. Preheat your oven to 375°F (190°C). In a small bowl, combine the chopped rosemary, thyme, parsley, minced garlic, olive oil, salt, and pepper. This mixture will be your herb rub. Rub the herb mixture evenly over the pork tenderloin, ensuring it's well coated.

2. Place the pork tenderloin in a baking dish or on a baking sheet. Roast the pork in the preheated oven for about 20-25 minutes, or until the internal temperature reaches 145°F (63°C) and the pork is cooked to your desired level of doneness.

3. Remove the pork tenderloin from the oven and let it rest for a few minutes before slicing it.

Lemon Pepper Grilled Tilapia

Prep Time: 10 minutes / Cook Time: 10 minutes
Yield: 1 serving

Ingredients

- 1 tilapia fillet (about 6 ounces)
- 1/2 lemon, juiced and zested
- 1/2 teaspoon lemon pepper seasoning
- 1 teaspoon olive oil
- Salt and pepper to taste

Directions

1. Preheat your grill to medium-high heat.

2. In a small bowl, combine the lemon juice, lemon zest, lemon pepper seasoning, olive oil, salt, and pepper. This mixture will be your marinade.

3. Place the tilapia fillet in a shallow dish and pour the lemon marinade over it. Ensure that both sides of the fillet are coated. Let it marinate for about 10 minutes.

4. Lightly oil the grill grates to prevent sticking.

5. Grill the tilapia fillet for about 4-5 minutes per side, or until it flakes easily with a fork and is cooked through. Cooking time may vary depending on the thickness of the fillet.

6. Remove the grilled tilapia from the grill and let it rest for a minute before serving.

Nutritional Information (Approximate)

Calories	200	Dietary Fiber	1g
Protein	30g	Sodium	200mg
Carbohydrates	3g	Cholesterol	75mg
Total Fat	7g	Potassium	400mg
Saturated Fat	1g		

Balsamic Glazed Grilled Pork Chops

Prep Time: 10 minutes / Cook Time: 15 minutes
Yield: 1 serving

Ingredients

- 1 boneless pork chop (about 6 ounces)
- 2 tablespoons balsamic vinegar
- 1 tablespoon honey, 1 clove garlic, minced
- 1/2 teaspoon dried rosemary, 1/2 teaspoon olive oil
- Salt and pepper to taste

Directions

1. In a small bowl, whisk together the balsamic vinegar, honey, minced garlic, dried rosemary, olive oil, salt, and pepper. This mixture will be your balsamic glaze.

2. Preheat your grill to medium-high heat. Season the pork chop with salt and pepper on both sides.

3. Place the pork chop on the preheated grill and cook for about 6-7 minutes per side, or until it reaches an internal temperature of 145°F (63°C) and is no longer pink in the center.

4. Brush the balsamic glaze over the pork chop during the last 2 minutes of grilling, turning it once to coat both sides. This will caramelize the glaze and add a flavorful crust to the pork.

5. Remove the grilled pork chop from the grill and let it rest for a few minutes before serving

Nutritional Information (Approximate)

Calories	350	Dietary Fiber	0g
Protein	30g	Sodium	300mg
Carbohydrates	20g	Cholesterol	75mg
Total Fat	12g	Potassium	450mg
Saturated Fat	3g		

Moroccan Spiced Chicken with Couscous

Prep Time: 15 minutes / Cook Time: 20 minutes / Yield: 1 serving

Ingredients

- 1 boneless, skinless chicken breast (about 6 ounces)
- 1/2 cup whole wheat couscous, 1/2 cup low-sodium chicken broth
- 1/4 cup diced tomatoes (canned or fresh)
- 1/4 cup diced bell peppers (red, green, or yellow)
- 2 tablespoons diced red onion, 1 clove garlic, minced
- 1 teaspoon ground cumin, 1/2 teaspoon ground coriander
- 1/4 teaspoon ground cinnamon, 1/4 teaspoon paprika
- 1 teaspoon olive oil, salt and pepper to taste

Nutritional Information (Approximate)

Calories	400	Dietary Fiber	6g
Protein	40g	Sodium	600mg
Carbohydrates	40g	Cholesterol	90mg
Total Fat	8g	Potassium	600mg
Saturated Fat	1,5g		

Directions

1. In a small bowl, mix together the ground cumin, ground coriander, ground cinnamon, paprika, salt, and pepper. This mixture will be your Moroccan spice blend. Season the chicken breast on both sides with the Moroccan spice blend.

2. Heat olive oil in a skillet over medium-high heat. Add the chicken breast and cook for about 4-5 minutes per side, or until it's cooked through and no longer pink in the center. Remove the chicken from the skillet and let it rest for a few minutes before slicing it.

3. In the same skillet, add the diced onion, minced garlic, and diced bell peppers. Sauté for about 2-3 minutes, or until the vegetables are slightly softened. Add the diced tomatoes and sauté for an additional 2 minutes.

4. In a separate saucepan, bring the low-sodium chicken broth to a boil. Remove it from heat and stir in the whole wheat couscous. Cover and let it sit for about 5 minutes, then fluff it with a fork. To serve, place the cooked couscous on a plate, top it with the sautéed vegetables, and arrange the sliced Moroccan-spiced chicken on top.

Garlic and Rosemary Grilled Lamb Chops

Prep Time: 15 minutes / Cook Time: 10 minutes
Yield: 1 serving

Ingredients

- 2 lamb chops (about 6 ounces each), 2 cloves garlic, minced
- 1 tablespoon fresh rosemary leaves, chopped
- 1 tablespoon olive oil, salt and black pepper to taste
- Lemon wedges for garnish (optional)

Directions

1. In a small bowl, combine the minced garlic, chopped fresh rosemary, olive oil, salt, and black pepper. This mixture will be your marinade.

2. Season the lamb chops with a bit of salt and black pepper on both sides.

3. Brush the garlic and rosemary marinade over the lamb chops, ensuring they are evenly coated. Let them marinate for about 10 minutes at room temperature.

4. Preheat your grill to medium-high heat.

5. Place the marinated lamb chops on the grill and cook for about 4-5 minutes per side for medium-rare, or adjust the cooking time to your preferred level of doneness.

6. Remove the grilled lamb chops from the heat and let them rest for a few minutes.

7. Garnish with lemon wedges if desired.

Nutritional Information (Approximate)

Calories	400	Dietary Fiber	0g
Protein	40g	Sodium	100mg
Carbohydrates	1g	Cholesterol	120mg
Total Fat	26g	Potassium	450mg
Saturated Fat	10g		

Pesto Baked Cod with Cherry Tomatoes

Prep Time: 10 minutes / Cook Time: 15 minutes
Yield: 1 serving

Ingredients

- 1 cod fillet (about 6 ounces), 1/4 cup cherry tomatoes, halved
- 2 tablespoons pesto sauce, 1 teaspoon olive oil
- 1 clove garlic, minced, 1/2 lemon, juiced, salt and pepper to taste
- Fresh basil leaves for garnish (optional)

Directions

1. Preheat your oven to 375°F (190°C).

2. In a small bowl, combine the pesto sauce, minced garlic, olive oil, lemon juice, salt, and pepper. This mixture will be your pesto marinade.

3. Place the cod fillet in a baking dish.

4. Pour the pesto marinade over the cod fillet, ensuring it's evenly coated.

5. Scatter the halved cherry tomatoes around the cod fillet in the baking dish.

6. Bake the cod and cherry tomatoes in the preheated oven for about 12-15 minutes, or until the cod flakes easily with a fork and is cooked through.

7. Remove the baked cod from the oven and garnish with fresh basil leaves if desired.

Nutritional Information (Approximate)

Calories	300	Dietary Fiber	1g
Protein	30g	Sodium	500mg
Carbohydrates	5g	Cholesterol	70mg
Total Fat	16g	Potassium	500mg
Saturated Fat	2g		

Thai Basil Ground Turkey Stir-Fry

Prep Time: 15 minutes / Cook Time: 15 minutes / Yield: 1 serving

Ingredients

- 4 ounces lean ground turkey, 1 cup broccoli florets
- 1/2 red bell pepper, sliced, 1/2 yellow bell pepper, sliced
- 1/4 cup sliced carrots, 1 clove garlic, minced
- 1 tablespoon low-sodium soy sauce, 1 teaspoon fish sauce
- 1/2 teaspoon honey or brown sugar
- 1/2 teaspoon Sriracha sauce (adjust to taste)
- 1/4 cup fresh Thai basil leaves (or regular basil)
- 1/2 tablespoon vegetable oil, salt and pepper to taste

Nutritional Information (Approximate)

Calories	350	Dietary Fiber	5g
Protein	30g	Sodium	800mg
Carbohydrates	20g	Cholesterol	70mg
Total Fat	16g	Potassium	600mg
Saturated Fat	3g		

Directions

1. Heat vegetable oil in a skillet or wok over medium-high heat. Add the minced garlic and sauté for about 30 seconds until fragrant.

2. Add the lean ground turkey and cook, breaking it apart with a spatula, until it's no longer pink and starts to brown, about 5-6 minutes.

3. Stir in the broccoli florets, sliced red bell pepper, sliced yellow bell pepper, and sliced carrots. Cook for another 5-6 minutes or until the vegetables are tender-crisp and the turkey is fully cooked. In a small bowl, whisk together the low-sodium soy sauce, fish sauce, honey (or brown sugar), and Sriracha sauce. Pour this sauce mixture over the turkey and vegetables. Stir well to coat.

4. Add the fresh Thai basil leaves to the stir-fry and cook for an additional 1-2 minutes until the basil wilts. Season with salt and pepper to taste.

5. Serve the Thai Basil Ground Turkey Stir-Fry hot over steamed rice or cauliflower rice if desired.

Orange-Glazed Turkey Cutlets

Prep Time: 10 minutes / Cook Time: 15 minutes
Yield: 1 serving

Ingredients

- 1 turkey cutlet (about 4-6 ounces)
- 1/4 cup fresh orange juice
- 1 teaspoon orange zest
- 1 teaspoon honey
- 1/2 teaspoon low-sodium soy sauce
- 1/4 teaspoon ground ginger
- 1/4 teaspoon garlic powder
- 1/2 tablespoon olive oil
- Salt and pepper to taste
- Orange slices for garnish (optional)

Directions

1. In a small bowl, whisk together the fresh orange juice, orange zest, honey, low-sodium soy sauce, ground ginger, garlic powder, salt, and pepper. This mixture will be your orange glaze.

2. Season the turkey cutlet with a bit of salt and pepper on both sides.

3. Heat olive oil in a skillet over medium-high heat.

4. Place the turkey cutlet in the skillet and cook for about 3-4 minutes per side, or until it's cooked through and no longer pink in the center.

5. Pour the orange glaze over the turkey cutlet and let it simmer for an additional 2-3 minutes, allowing the glaze to thicken and coat the turkey.

6. Remove the orange-glazed turkey cutlet from the skillet.

7. Garnish with orange slices if desired.

Nutritional Information (Approximate)

Calories	250	Dietary Fiber	1g
Protein	30g	Sodium	300mg
Carbohydrates	12g	Cholesterol	70mg
Total Fat	8g	Potassium	350mg
Saturated Fat	1.5g		

This heart-healthy Orange-Glazed Turkey Cutlets recipe brings a burst of citrusy flavor to tender turkey cutlets. Enjoy the zesty and savory combination!

Spicy Cajun Shrimp and Brown Rice

Prep Time: 10 minutes / Cook Time: 20 minutes
Yield: 1 serving

Ingredients

- 6 large shrimp, peeled and deveined
- 1/2 cup cooked brown rice, salt and pepper to taste
- 1/4 cup diced bell peppers (red, green, or yellow)
- 1/4 cup diced onion, 1/4 cup diced tomatoes
- 1 clove garlic, minced, 1/2 teaspoon Cajun seasoning
- 1/2 teaspoon paprika, 1/2 tablespoon olive oil
- 1/4 teaspoon cayenne pepper (adjust to taste)
- Fresh parsley for garnish (optional)
- Lemon wedges for garnish (optional)

Directions

1. In a small bowl, combine the Cajun seasoning, paprika, cayenne pepper, salt, and pepper. This mixture will be your Cajun spice blend.

2. Season the shrimp with the Cajun spice blend on both sides.

3. Heat olive oil in a skillet over medium-high heat.

4. Add the diced onion and diced bell peppers to the skillet and sauté for about 2-3 minutes until they start to soften.

5. Add the minced garlic and diced tomatoes to the skillet and continue to cook for an additional 2 minutes.

6. Push the vegetable mixture to one side of the skillet and add the seasoned shrimp to the other side. Cook the shrimp for about 2-3 minutes per side or until they turn pink and opaque.

7. Add the cooked brown rice to the skillet and stir it into the vegetable mixture.

8. Continue to cook for an additional 2-3 minutes, allowing the rice to heat through and absorb the flavors.

9. Remove from heat and garnish with fresh parsley and lemon wedges if desired.

Nutritional Information (Approximate)

Calories	300	Dietary Fiber	4g
Protein	25g	Sodium	400mg
Carbohydrates	30g	Cholesterol	150mg
Total Fat	10g	Potassium	350mg
Saturated Fat	1,5g		

This heart-healthy Spicy Cajun Shrimp and Brown Rice recipe is a flavorful and satisfying dish with a spicy kick. Enjoy the bold flavors of Cajun seasoning and the wholesome goodness of brown rice!

Lemon Garlic Herb Turkey Breast

Prep Time: 10 minutes / Cook Time: 30 minutes
Yield: 1 serving

Ingredients

- 1 turkey breast fillet (about 6 ounces)
- 1 lemon, juiced and zested, 2 cloves garlic, minced
- 1 tablespoon fresh rosemary, chopped
- 1 tablespoon fresh thyme leaves, chopped
- 1/2 tablespoon olive oil, salt and pepper to taste
- Lemon slices for garnish (optional)
- Fresh herbs for garnish (optional)

Directions

1. Preheat your oven to 375°F (190°C).

2. In a small bowl, combine the minced garlic, lemon juice, lemon zest, chopped rosemary, chopped thyme, olive oil, salt, and pepper. This mixture will be your herb and lemon marinade.

3. Season the turkey breast fillet with a bit of salt and pepper on both sides.

4. Brush the herb and lemon marinade over the turkey breast, ensuring it's evenly coated.

5. Heat an oven-safe skillet over medium-high heat.

6. Place the turkey breast in the skillet and sear it for about 2-3 minutes per side, until it's nicely browned.

7. Transfer the skillet to the preheated oven and roast for about 20-25 minutes, or until the turkey reaches an internal temperature of 165°F (74°C) and is no longer pink in the center.

8. Remove the skillet from the oven and let the turkey breast rest for a few minutes.

9. Slice the lemon garlic herb turkey breast and garnish with lemon slices and fresh herbs if desired.

Nutritional Information (Approximate)

Calories	300	Dietary Fiber	2g
Protein	40g	Sodium	300mg
Carbohydrates	6g	Cholesterol	90mg
Total Fat	10g	Potassium	400mg
Saturated Fat	2g		

This heart-healthy Lemon Garlic Herb Turkey Breast is a delightful and aromatic dish that's bursting with flavor. Enjoy the zesty combination of lemon, garlic, and fresh herbs with tender turkey!

Sesame Ginger Tofu Stir-Fry

Prep Time: 15 minutes / Cook Time: 15 minutes
Yield: 1 serving

Ingredients

- 6 ounces extra-firm tofu, cubed
- 1 cup mixedvegetables (bell peppers, broccoli, snap peas, carrots, etc.), sliced
- 1/2 cup cooked brown rice or quinoa
- 2 cloves garlic, minced, 1 teaspoon sesame oil
- 1 teaspoon fresh ginger, grated
- 1 tablespoon low-sodium soy sauce
- 1/2 teaspoon honey or maple syrup
- 1/2 teaspoon sesame seeds (optional)
- Salt and pepper to taste
- Chopped green onions for garnish (optional)

Directions

1. Press the tofu: Place the tofu between two paper towels and set a heavy object (like a can or a cast-iron skillet) on top to press out excess water. Leave it for about 15 minutes, then cut the tofu into cubes.

2. In a small bowl, whisk together the minced garlic, grated ginger, low-sodium soy sauce, sesame oil, honey (or maple syrup), and a pinch of salt and pepper. This mixture will be your stir-fry sauce.

3. Heat a non-stick skillet or wok over medium-high heat.

4. Add the cubed tofu to the skillet and cook for about 5-6 minutes, turning occasionally, until it's lightly browned on all sides. Remove the tofu from the skillet and set it aside.

5. In the same skillet, add the sliced mixed vegetables and stir-fry for about 3-4 minutes until they start to become tender-crisp.

6. Return the tofu to the skillet with the vegetables and pour the stir-fry sauce over them. Stir well to coat everything evenly.

7. Cook for an additional 2-3 minutes, allowing the sauce to thicken and coat the tofu and vegetables.

8. Serve the sesame ginger tofu stir-fry hot over cooked brown rice or quinoa.

Nutritional Information (Approximate)

Calories	350	Dietary Fiber	7g
Protein	18g	Sodium	500mg
Carbohydrates	45g	Cholesterol	0mg
Total Fat	12g	Potassium	600mg
Saturated Fat	1,5g		

Greek-Style Grilled Chicken Skewers

Prep Time: 20 minutes / Cook Time: 12 minutes
Yield: 1 serving

Ingredients

- 6 ounces boneless, skinless chicken breast, cut into 1-inch cubes
- 1/4 cup plain Greek yogurt, 1 tablespoon olive oil
- 1 tablespoon lemon juice, 1 clove garlic, minced
- 1 teaspoon dried oregano
- 1/2 teaspoon dried thyme
- 1/2 teaspoon paprika
- Salt and black pepper to taste
- 1/4 red onion, cut into chunks
- 1/4 bell pepper (any color), cut into chunks
- 1/4 zucchini, sliced, cherry tomatoes for skewering (optional)
- Lemon wedges for garnish (optional)
- Fresh parsley for garnish (optional)

Directions

1. In a bowl, combine the Greek yogurt, olive oil, lemon juice, minced garlic, dried oregano, dried thyme, paprika, salt, and black pepper. This mixture will be your marinade.

2. Place the chicken cubes in the marinade and toss to coat evenly. Cover and refrigerate for at least 15 minutes to marinate.

3. While the chicken is marinating, soak wooden skewers in water for about 15 minutes to prevent them from burning on the grill.

4. Preheat your grill to medium-high heat.

5. Thread the marinated chicken, red onion chunks, bell pepper chunks, zucchini slices, and cherry tomatoes onto the skewers, alternating between the ingredients.

6. Grill the chicken skewers for about 10-12 minutes, turning occasionally, until the chicken is cooked through and has grill marks.

7. Remove the chicken skewers from the grill.

8. Garnish with lemon wedges and fresh parsley if desired.

Nutritional Information (Approximate)

Calories	300	Dietary Fiber	2g
Protein	35g	Sodium	300mg
Carbohydrates	10g	Cholesterol	90mg
Total Fat	13g	Potassium	450mg
Saturated Fat	2g		

These heart-healthy Greek-Style Grilled Chicken Skewers are packed with Mediterranean flavors. Enjoy the tender and flavorful chicken with a refreshing yogurt-based marinade!

Paprika-Rubbed Grilled Pork Tenderloin

Prep Time: 10 minutes / Cook Time: 20 minutes
Yield: 1 serving

Ingredients

- 6 ounces pork tenderloin
- 1 teaspoon smoked paprika
- 1/2 teaspoon garlic powder
- 1/2 teaspoon onion powder
- 1/2 teaspoon dried thyme
- 1/4 teaspoon cayenne pepper (adjust to taste)
- Salt and black pepper to taste
- 1/2 tablespoon olive oil
- Lemon wedges for garnish (optional)
- Fresh parsley for garnish (optional)

Directions

1. Preheat your grill to medium-high heat.

2. In a small bowl, combine the smoked paprika, garlic powder, onion powder, dried thyme, cayenne pepper, salt, and black pepper. This mixture will be your paprika rub.

3. Rub the paprika mixture all over the pork tenderloin, ensuring it's evenly coated.

4. Drizzle the olive oil over the pork tenderloin.

5. Place the pork tenderloin on the grill and cook for about 10-12 minutes per side, turning occasionally, until it's cooked through and has grill marks. The internal temperature of the pork should reach 145°F (63°C).

6. Remove the grilled pork tenderloin from the grill and let it rest for a few minutes.

7. Slice the pork into medallions and garnish with lemon wedges and fresh parsley if desired.

Nutritional Information (Approximate)

Calories	250	Dietary Fiber	1g
Protein	35g	Sodium	300mg
Carbohydrates	2g	Cholesterol	90mg
Total Fat	13g	Potassium	450mg
Saturated Fat	3g		

This heart-healthy Paprika-Rubbed Grilled Pork Tenderloin recipe delivers smoky and savory flavors with a touch of spice. Enjoy this tender and delicious dish!

Cajun Blackened Salmon

Prep Time: 10 minutes / Cook Time: 10 minutes
Yield: 1 serving

Ingredients

- 6 ounces salmon fillet
- 1 teaspoon smoked paprika
- 1/2 teaspoon dried thyme
- 1/2 teaspoon dried oregano
- 1/2 teaspoon garlic powder
- 1/4 teaspoon cayenne pepper (adjust to taste)
- 1/4 teaspoon black pepper
- 1/4 teaspoon salt
- 1/2 tablespoon olive oil
- Lemon wedges for garnish (optional)
- Fresh parsley for garnish (optional)

Directions

1. In a small bowl, combine the smoked paprika, dried thyme, dried oregano, garlic powder, cayenne pepper, black pepper, and salt. This mixture will be your Cajun seasoning.

2. Rub the Cajun seasoning evenly over both sides of the salmon fillet.

3. Heat olive oil in a skillet over medium-high heat.

4. Once the skillet is hot, carefully place the seasoned salmon fillet in the pan.

5. Cook the salmon for about 3-5 minutes per side, or until it's blackened on the outside and flakes easily with a fork. Adjust cooking time based on the thickness of the salmon.

6. Remove the Cajun blackened salmon from the skillet.

7. Garnish with lemon wedges and fresh parsley if desired.

Nutritional Information (Approximate)

Calories	300	Dietary Fiber	1g
Protein	35g	Sodium	400mg
Carbohydrates	2g	Cholesterol	90mg
Total Fat	15g	Potassium	500mg
Saturated Fat	2,5g		

This heart-healthy Cajun Blackened Salmon recipe offers a burst of spicy and smoky flavors, perfect for seafood lovers. Enjoy the bold and satisfying taste of blackened salmon!

Asian-Inspired Ground Chicken Lettuce Wraps

Prep Time: 15 minutes / Cook Time: 10 minutes
Yield: 1 serving

Ingredients

- 6 ounces ground chicken, 1 clove garlic, minced
- 1/2 tablespoon vegetable oil
- 1/2 teaspoon fresh ginger, minced
- 1/4 cup diced water chestnuts
- 2 tablespoons low-sodium soy sauce
- 1 teaspoon rice vinegar, 1/2 teaspoon sesame oil
- 1/2 teaspoon honey or maple syrup
- 1/2 teaspoon cornstarch (optional, for thickening)
- Salt and black pepper to taste
- 4 large lettuce leaves
  (such as iceberg or butter lettuce)
- Thinly sliced green onions for garnish (optional)
- Crushed red pepper flakes for garnish (optional)
- Lime wedges for garnish (optional)

Directions

1. In a small bowl, whisk together the low-sodium soy sauce, rice vinegar, sesame oil, honey (or maple syrup), and cornstarch (if using). Set this mixture aside; it will be your sauce.

2. Heat the vegetable oil in a skillet over medium-high heat.

3. Add the ground chicken to the skillet and cook, breaking it apart with a spatula, until it's no longer pink and has started to brown, about 5-7 minutes.

4. Stir in the minced garlic and ginger and cook for an additional 1-2 minutes until fragrant.

5. Add the diced water chestnuts to the skillet and stir to combine.

6. Pour the sauce over the chicken mixture and stir well. Cook for another 2-3 minutes, allowing the sauce to thicken and coat the chicken.

7. Season with salt and black pepper to taste.

8. Spoon the Asian-inspired ground chicken mixture into the lettuce leaves, creating wraps.

9. Garnish with thinly sliced green onions, crushed red pepper flakes, and lime wedges if desired.

Nutritional Information (Approximate)

Calories	300	Dietary Fiber	2g
Protein	27g	Sodium	800mg
Carbohydrates	10g	Cholesterol	70mg
Total Fat	18g	Potassium	450mg
Saturated Fat	3g		

chapter 8
SEAFOOD

Grilled Lemon Garlic Shrimp 60

Spicy Cajun Seafood Boil 60

Garlic Butter Lobster Tails 60

Baked Salmon with Dill Sauce 61

Tuna Poke Bowl 61

Crispy Fried Calamari 61

Coconut Shrimp with Mango Salsa... 62

Clam Linguine in White Wine Sauce.. 62

Blackened Catfish Tacos 63

Thai Red Curry Shrimp 63

Seafood Paella 64

Crab Stuffed Mushrooms.................. 64

Lemon Butter Scallops 64

Grilled Swordfish Steaks 65

Smoked Trout Pate 65

Teriyaki Glazed Salmon 65

Garlic Parmesan Baked Mussels 66

Shrimp & Grits 66

Lobster Bisque 67

Pan-Seared Mahi-Mahi with
Pineapple Salsa 67

Grilled Lemon Garlic Shrimp

Prep Time: 15 minutes / Cook Time: 6-8 minutes
Yield: 4 serving

Ingredients

- 1 pound large shrimp, peeled and deveined
- 2 cloves garlic, minced, 2 tablespoons olive oil
- Zest and juice of 1 lemon, 1 teaspoon dried oregano
- Salt and pepper to taste
- Wooden skewers, soaked in water for 30 minutes

Directions

1. In a mixing bowl, combine the minced garlic, olive oil, lemon zest, lemon juice, dried oregano, salt, and pepper. This will be your marinade.

2. Add the peeled and deveined shrimp to the marinade, making sure they are evenly coated. Allow the shrimp to marinate in the refrigerator for at least 10 minutes, but no more than 30 minutes.

3. Preheat your grill to medium-high heat.

4. Thread the marinated shrimp onto the soaked wooden skewers, ensuring they are evenly spaced.

5. Place the shrimp skewers on the preheated grill and cook for about 2-4 minutes on each side, or until they turn pink and opaque. Be careful not to overcook them, as shrimp can become rubbery if cooked for too long.

6. Remove the grilled shrimp from the skewers and serve hot. You can garnish them with additional lemon wedges and fresh herbs if desired.

Nutritional Information (Approximate)

Calories	180	Dietary Fiber	0g
Protein	24g	Sodium	290mg
Carbohydrates	2g	Cholesterol	172mg
Total Fat	8g	Potassium	190mg
Saturated Fat	1g		

Spicy Cajun Seafood Boil

Prep Time: 20 minutes / Cook Time: 30 minutes
Yield: 4 serving

Ingredients

- 1 pound large shrimp, shell-on, 2 ears of corn, cut into thirds
- 1 pound mussels, scrubbed and debearded
- 1 pound clams, scrubbed, 1 pound red potatoes, halved
- 1 andouille sausage, sliced into rounds
- 1 onion, quartered, 4 cloves garlic, minced
- 2 lemons, halved, 4 bay leaves, 4 quarts water
- 4 tablespoons Cajun seasoning, salt to taste
- Fresh parsley for garnish (optional)

Directions

1. In a large stockpot, bring 4 quarts of water to a boil. Add the Cajun seasoning, minced garlic, bay leaves, and a pinch of salt. Stir to combine.

2. Once the water is boiling and the seasonings are well mixed, add the halved potatoes and cook for 10-12 minutes, or until they are just tender when pierced with a fork. Add the andouille sausage, quartered onion, and corn to the pot. Continue to boil for another 5 minutes.

3. Add the clams and mussels to the pot, cover with a lid, and cook for 5-7 minutes, or until the shells have opened. Discard any unopened shells.

4. Finally, add the shrimp to the pot and cook for an additional 3-4 minutes, or until they turn pink and opaque.

5. Using a slotted spoon or strainer, transfer all the cooked ingredients to a large serving platter or a clean table lined with newspaper. Squeeze the lemon halves over the seafood boil and garnish with fresh parsley, if desired.

Nutritional Information (Approximate)

Calories	450	Dietary Fiber	4g
Protein	35g	Sodium	1350mg
Carbohydrates	32g	Cholesterol	175mg
Total Fat	20g	Potassium	810mg
Saturated Fat	6g		

Garlic Butter Lobster Tails

Prep Time: 10 minutes / Cook Time: 12-15 minutes / Yield: 2 serving

Ingredients

- 2 lobster tails, 4 tablespoons unsalted butter, melted
- 4 cloves garlic, minced, 2 tablespoons fresh parsley, chopped
- 1 lemon, juiced and zested
- Salt and pepper to taste
- Lemon wedges for garnish (optional)

Nutritional Information (Approximate)

Calories	260	Dietary Fiber	0g
Protein	24g	Sodium	360mg
Carbohydrates	2g	Cholesterol	170mg
Total Fat	17g	Potassium	310mg
Saturated Fat	10g		

Directions

1. Preheat your oven to 425°F (220°C) and set the top rack in the middle position. Using kitchen shears, carefully cut along the top of each lobster tail shell, stopping at the tail fan. Gently lift the lobster meat, leaving it attached at the base, and lay it on top of the shell.

2. In a small bowl, combine the melted butter, minced garlic, chopped parsley, lemon juice, lemon zest, salt, and pepper. Mix well to make the garlic butter sauce. Brush the garlic butter sauce generously over the exposed lobster meat, making sure to coat it evenly.

3. Place the prepared lobster tails on a baking sheet or in an ovenproof dish. Roast the lobster tails in the preheated oven for 12-15 minutes or until the lobster meat is opaque and the shells have turned bright red. Serve the garlic butter lobster tails hot, garnished with lemon wedges if desired.

Baked Salmon with Dill Sauce

Prep Time: 10 minutes / Cook Time: 15-20 minutes
Yield: 4 serving

Ingredients

- 4 salmon fillets (about 6 ounces each), skinless
- 1 tablespoon olive oil, 1 teaspoon garlic powder
- 1 teaspoon onion powder, 1 teaspoon dried dill
- Salt and pepper to taste, 1 lemon, thinly sliced

For the Dill Sauce:
- 1 tablespoon fresh dill, finely chopped
- 1 tablespoon lemon juice, 1 teaspoon Dijon mustard
- 1/2 cup Greek yogurt, salt and pepper to taste

Directions

1. Preheat your oven to 375°F (190°C). Line a baking sheet with parchment paper or lightly grease it with cooking spray.

2. In a small bowl, mix together the olive oil, garlic powder, onion powder, dried dill, salt, and pepper.

3. Place the salmon fillets on the prepared baking sheet. Brush each fillet with the olive oil and spice mixture.

4. Arrange lemon slices over the top of each salmon fillet.

5. Bake the salmon in the preheated oven for 15-20 minutes or until the salmon flakes easily with a fork and reaches an internal temperature of 145°F (63°C).

6. While the salmon is baking, prepare the dill sauce. In a small bowl, combine the Greek yogurt, fresh dill, lemon juice, Dijon mustard, salt, and pepper. Mix until well combined.

7. Once the salmon is done, remove it from the oven and serve hot, drizzled with the dill sauce.

Nutritional Information
(per serving, including dill sauce)

Calories	300	Dietary Fiber	0g
Protein	34g	Sodium	150mg
Carbohydrates	4g	Cholesterol	80mg
Total Fat	16g	Potassium	690mg
Saturated Fat	3g		

Tuna Poke Bowl

Prep Time: 15 minutes / Cook Time: 0 minutes
Yield: 1 serving

Ingredients

- 4 ounces sushi-grade tuna, cubed
- 1 cup cooked brown rice or sushi rice, cooled
- 1/2 cup cucumber, diced, 1/2 cup avocado, diced
- 1/4 cup red onion, finely chopped
- 1/4 cup edamame, shelled and cooked
- 1/4 cup shredded carrots, 1 teaspoon sesame seeds
- 1 tablespoon low-sodium soy sauce
- 1 teaspoon sesame oil, 1 teaspoon rice vinegar
- Sriracha or chili garlic sauce (optional, for heat)
- Fresh cilantro or green onions for garnish (optional)

Directions

1. In a small bowl, whisk together the low-sodium soy sauce, sesame oil, rice vinegar, and sesame seeds to create the poke sauce. Add Sriracha or chili garlic sauce if you like it spicy.

2. Place the cooked rice in a serving bowl as the base.

3. Arrange the cubed tuna, diced cucumber, diced avocado, finely chopped red onion, edamame, and shredded carrots on top of the rice in an organized manner.

4. Drizzle the prepared poke sauce evenly over the ingredients in the bowl.

5. Garnish your tuna poke bowl with fresh cilantro or green onions, if desired.

6. Serve your heart-healthy tuna poke bowl immediately, and mix everything together just before eating.

Nutritional Information

Calories	450	Dietary Fiber	7g
Protein	35g	Sodium	570mg
Carbohydrates	40g	Cholesterol	45mg
Total Fat	17g	Potassium	930mg
Saturated Fat	2,5g		

Crispy Fried Calamari

Prep Time: 20 minutes / Cook Time: 5 minutes / Yield: 4 serving

Ingredients

- 1 pound squid (calamari), cleaned and sliced into rings
- 1 cup buttermilk, 1 cup all-purpose flour
- 1 teaspoon paprika, 1/2 teaspoon garlic powder
- 1/2 teaspoon onion powder, salt and pepper to taste
- Vegetable oil for frying, Lemon wedges for serving (optional)
- Marinara sauce or aioli for dipping (optional)

Nutritional Information (Approximate)

Calories	250	Dietary Fiber	1g
Protein	14g	Sodium	300mg
Carbohydrates	23g	Cholesterol	150mg
Total Fat	10g	Potassium	300mg
Saturated Fat	1,5g		

Directions

1. Place the cleaned and sliced squid rings in a large bowl. Pour the buttermilk over them and let them soak for about 10 minutes. This helps tenderize the calamari.

2. In a separate bowl, combine the all-purpose flour, paprika, garlic powder, onion powder, salt, and pepper. Mix well to create the seasoned flour mixture. Heat vegetable oil in a deep fryer or large, heavy-bottomed pot to 350°F (175°C).

3. Remove the calamari rings from the buttermilk, allowing any excess liquid to drip off. Dredge the squid rings in the seasoned flour mixture, making sure to coat them thoroughly and shake off any excess flour.

4. Carefully lower the coated calamari rings into the hot oil in batches, making sure not to overcrowd the frying pan. Fry for about 2-3 minutes or until they are golden brown and crispy.

5. Use a slotted spoon to remove the fried calamari and place them on a plate lined with paper towels to drain any excess oil. Serve the crispy fried calamari hot with lemon wedges and your choice of dipping sauce, such as marinara or aioli.

Coconut Shrimp with Mango Salsa

Prep Time: 20 minutes / Cook Time: 10 minutes
Yield: 4 serving

Ingredients

For the Coconut Shrimp:
- 1 pound large shrimp, peeled and deveined
- 1 cup unsweetened shredded coconut
- 1 cup whole wheat breadcrumbs, 2 egg whites, beaten
- 1/2 teaspoon garlic powder, 1/2 teaspoon paprika
- Cooking spray, salt and pepper to taste

For the Mango Salsa:
- 2 ripe mangoes, peeled and diced
- 1/2 red onion, finely chopped, 1/2 red bell pepper, diced
- 1/4 cup fresh cilantro, chopped, Juice of 2 limes
- Salt and pepper to taste

Directions

For the Coconut Shrimp:

1. Preheat your oven to 425°F (220°C). Place a wire rack on a baking sheet and lightly coat it with cooking spray.

2. In a shallow bowl, combine the shredded coconut, whole wheat breadcrumbs, garlic powder, paprika, salt, and pepper.

3. Dip each shrimp into the beaten egg whites, allowing any excess to drip off.

4. Roll the egg-coated shrimp in the coconut breadcrumb mixture, pressing gently to adhere the coating.

5. Place the coated shrimp on the prepared wire rack.

6. Bake the shrimp in the preheated oven for 10-12 minutes or until they are golden brown and cooked through. Flip them over halfway through the cooking time to ensure even browning.

For the Mango Salsa:

7. In a mixing bowl, combine the diced mangoes, finely chopped red onion, diced red bell pepper, chopped cilantro, lime juice, salt, and pepper. Mix well.

8. Refrigerate the mango salsa until you're ready to serve.

Nutritional Information
(per serving, including mango salsa)

Calories	270	Dietary Fiber	6g
Protein	21g	Sodium	390mg
Carbohydrates	31g	Cholesterol	110mg
Total Fat	6g	Potassium	470mg
Saturated Fat	4g		

This heart-healthy Coconut Shrimp with Mango Salsa recipe combines the crispy goodness of coconut shrimp with the fresh and tangy flavors of mango salsa. It's a delicious and nutritious dish that's perfect for a light and satisfying meal. Enjoy!

Clam Linguine in White Wine Sauce

Prep Time: 15 minutes / Cook Time: 20 minutes
Yield: 4 serving

Ingredients

- 12 ounces whole wheat linguine or your preferred pasta
- 2 pounds littleneck clams, scrubbed and cleaned
- 2 tablespoons olive oil, 4 cloves garlic, minced
- 1/2 cup dry white wine
- 1 cup low-sodium chicken or vegetable broth
- 1/2 cup fresh parsley, chopped
- Zest and juice of 1 lemon, salt and pepper to taste
- Red pepper flakes (optional, for added heat)

Directions

1. Cook the linguine according to the package instructions until al dente. Drain and set aside.

2. In a large skillet or saucepan, heat the olive oil over medium heat. Add the minced garlic and sauté for about 1 minute, or until fragrant.

3. Pour in the dry white wine and bring it to a simmer. Allow it to cook for 2-3 minutes to reduce slightly.

4. Add the cleaned clams to the skillet and cover with a lid. Cook for 5-7 minutes, shaking the pan occasionally, until the clams open. Discard any clams that do not open.

5. Remove the cooked clams from the skillet and set them aside. Leave the cooking liquid in the pan.

6. Add the chicken or vegetable broth to the skillet with the cooking liquid and bring it to a simmer. Cook for another 5 minutes to reduce and concentrate the flavors.

7. Stir in the chopped parsley, lemon zest, lemon juice, salt, and pepper. Add red pepper flakes if you like a bit of heat.

8. Return the cooked clams to the skillet and stir gently to combine.

9. To serve, divide the cooked linguine among plates and spoon the clam and white wine sauce over the top.

Nutritional Information

Calories	350	Dietary Fiber	6g
Protein	20g	Sodium	380mg
Carbohydrates	47g	Cholesterol	65mg
Total Fat	7g	Potassium	370mg
Saturated Fat	1g		

This heart-healthy Clam Linguine in White Wine Sauce is a delightful seafood pasta dish. It's rich in flavor, low in saturated fat, and packed with lean protein. Enjoy the taste of the sea with a white wine-infused sauce, balanced by the freshness of lemon and parsley.

Blackened Catfish Tacos

Prep Time: 10 minutes / Cook Time: 10 minutes
Yield: 4 serving

Ingredients

For the Blackened Catfish:
- 4 catfish fillets (about 4-6 ounces each)
- 2 tablespoons olive oil, 2 teaspoons paprika
- 1 teaspoon dried thyme, 1 teaspoon garlic powder
- 1/2 teaspoon onion powder, 1/2 teaspoon cayenne pepper (adjust to your preferred spice level)
- 1/2 teaspoon black pepper, 1/2 teaspoon salt

For the Tacos:
- 8 small whole wheat or corn tortillas
- 2 cups shredded cabbage or coleslaw mix
- 1 cup cherry tomatoes, halved
- 1/2 cup plain Greek yogurt or low-fat sour cream
- 1 lime, cut into wedges
- Fresh cilantro leaves for garnish (optional)

Directions

For the Blackened Catfish:

1. In a small bowl, mix together the paprika, dried thyme, garlic powder, onion powder, cayenne pepper, black pepper, and salt to create the blackening seasoning.

2. Pat the catfish fillets dry with a paper towel. Rub each fillet with the olive oil, ensuring they are coated evenly.

3. Sprinkle the blackening seasoning generously over both sides of the catfish fillets, pressing it onto the fish to adhere.

4. Heat a non-stick skillet over medium-high heat. Once hot, add the catfish fillets and cook for about 4-5 minutes on each side, or until they are opaque and flake easily with a fork.

For the Tacos:

5. Warm the tortillas according to the package instructions.

6. To assemble each taco, place a warmed tortilla on a plate. Add a portion of shredded cabbage or coleslaw mix.

7. Top the cabbage with a blackened catfish fillet.

8. Add cherry tomato halves and a dollop of Greek yogurt or low-fat sour cream.

9. Squeeze a lime wedge over the top and garnish with fresh cilantro leaves if desired.

10. Serve your heart-healthy Blackened Catfish Tacos immediately.

Nutritional Information
(per serving, including 2 tacos)

Calories	450	Dietary Fiber	6g
Protein	32g	Sodium	550mg
Carbohydrates	35g	Cholesterol	70mg
Total Fat	18g	Potassium	720mg
Saturated Fat	3g		

These heart-healthy Blackened Catfish Tacos are a flavorful and satisfying meal option. They're rich in protein and packed with fresh vegetables, making them a nutritious choice for lunch or dinner. Enjoy the bold flavors and a touch of spice in this delicious dish!

Thai Red Curry Shrimp

Prep Time: 15 minutes / Cook Time: 15 minutes
Yield: 4 serving

Ingredients

- 1 pound large shrimp, peeled and deveined
- 1 can (14 ounces) light coconut milk
- 2 tablespoons Thai red curry paste
- 1 red bell pepper, thinly sliced
- 1 yellow bell pepper, thinly sliced
- 1 cup snap peas, trimmed
- 1 carrot, julienned
- 1 tablespoon fresh ginger, minced
- 2 cloves garlic, minced
- 1 tablespoon fish sauce (optional, for added flavor)
- 1 tablespoon brown sugar or honey, juice of 1 lime
- Fresh cilantro leaves for garnish
- Cooked brown rice or whole wheat noodles for serving

Directions

1. In a large skillet or wok, heat a small amount of the coconut milk over medium-high heat. Add the Thai red curry paste and stir well to combine. Cook for about 2 minutes, or until fragrant.

2. Add the minced ginger and garlic to the skillet and sauté for another minute.

3. Add the shrimp to the skillet and cook for about 2-3 minutes on each side, or until they turn pink and opaque. Remove the cooked shrimp from the skillet and set them aside.

4. In the same skillet, add the sliced red and yellow peppers, snap peas, and julienned carrot. Stir-fry for about 3-4 minutes, or until the vegetables start to soften.

5. Pour in the remaining coconut milk, fish sauce (if using), and brown sugar or honey. Stir well and bring the mixture to a simmer.

6. Return the cooked shrimp to the skillet and add the lime juice. Cook for an additional 2 minutes, or until everything is heated through.

Nutritional Information
(per serving, without rice or noodles)

Calories	220	Dietary Fiber	3g
Protein	20g	Sodium	450mg
Carbohydrates	15g	Cholesterol	150mg
Total Fat	8g	Potassium	370mg
Saturated Fat	6g		

This heart-healthy Thai Red Curry Shrimp is a flavorful and aromatic dish that's packed with protein and a variety of colorful vegetables. Serve it with brown rice or whole wheat noodles for a satisfying meal that's as nutritious as it is delicious. Enjoy the bold flavors of Thai cuisine!

Seafood Paella

Prep Time: 15 minutes / Cook Time: 30 minutes
Yield: 4 serving

Ingredients

- 1 cup brown rice, salt and pepper to taste
- 1 pound mixed seafood (shrimp, mussels, squid, etc.)
- 2 tablespoons olive oil, 1 onion, finely chopped
- 2 cloves garlic, minced, 1 red bell pepper, diced
- 1 yellow bell pepper, diced, 1 teaspoon paprika
- 1/2 teaspoon saffron threads (optional, for color and flavor)
- 2 cups low-sodium chicken or vegetable broth
- 1 cup canned diced tomatoes, 1 cup frozen green peas
- 1 lemon, cut into wedges, fresh parsley for garnish

Directions

1. Rinse the brown rice thoroughly and cook it according to package instructions. Set aside.

2. In a large skillet or paella pan, heat the olive oil over medium heat. Add the chopped onion and garlic, and sauté for 2-3 minutes, or until they become fragrant and translucent.

3. Add the diced red and yellow bell peppers to the skillet and cook for another 2-3 minutes until they start to soften.

4. Stir in the paprika and saffron threads (if using) to infuse the flavors.

5. Add the mixed seafood to the pan and cook for about 2-3 minutes, or until they start to turn opaque.

6. Pour in the low-sodium chicken or vegetable broth and canned diced tomatoes. Bring the mixture to a simmer.

7. Stir in the cooked brown rice and frozen green peas. Cook for an additional 5-7 minutes, or until the peas are heated through.

Nutritional Information

Calories	350	Dietary Fiber	6g
Protein	25g	Sodium	450mg
Carbohydrates	50g	Cholesterol	120mg
Total Fat	7g	Potassium	570mg
Saturated Fat	1g		

Crab Stuffed Mushrooms

Prep Time: 20 minutes / Cook Time: 20 minutes
Yield: 4 serving (approximately 16 stuffed mushrooms)

Ingredients

- 16 large white or cremini mushrooms, cleaned and stems removed
- 1/2 pound lump crabmeat, picked over for shells
- 1/4 cup whole wheat breadcrumbs
- 1/4 cup grated Parmesan cheese, 2 cloves garlic, minced
- 2 tablespoons fresh parsley, chopped
- 2 tablespoons low-fat mayonnaise
- 1 tablespoon lemon juice, 1 teaspoon Dijon mustard
- 1/4 teaspoon black pepper, cooking spray
- Lemon wedges for garnish (optional)

Directions

1. Preheat your oven to 375°F (190°C).

2. In a mixing bowl, combine the lump crabmeat, whole wheat breadcrumbs, grated Parmesan cheese, minced garlic, chopped fresh parsley, low-fat mayonnaise, lemon juice, Dijon mustard, and black pepper. Mix well until all ingredients are evenly incorporated.

3. Fill each mushroom cap with a generous spoonful of the crab mixture, pressing it gently to pack the filling into the mushroom.

4. Place the stuffed mushrooms on a baking sheet that has been lightly coated with cooking spray.

5. Bake the stuffed mushrooms in the preheated oven for about 15-20 minutes, or until the mushrooms are tender and the filling is heated through and lightly browned on top.

Nutritional Information
(per serving, 4 stuffed mushrooms)

Calories	150	Dietary Fiber	2g
Protein	12g	Sodium	350mg
Carbohydrates	9g	Cholesterol	40mg
Total Fat	6g	Potassium	440mg
Saturated Fat	1.5g		

Lemon Butter Scallops

Prep Time: 10 minutes / Cook Time: 10 minutes / Yield: 2 serving

Ingredients

- 8 large sea scallops, 2 tablespoons olive oil
- 1/4 cup low-sodium chicken or vegetable broth
- Juice of 1 lemon, 2 tablespoons unsalted butter
- 1 tablespoon fresh parsley, chopped, salt and pepper to taste
- 2 cloves garlic, minced, lemon slices for garnish (optional)

Nutritional Information

Calories	250	Dietary Fiber	0g
Protein	16g	Sodium	350mg
Carbohydrates	5g	Cholesterol	60mg
Total Fat	18g	Potassium	290mg
Saturated Fat	6g		

Directions

1. Pat the scallops dry with a paper towel and season them with salt and pepper. Heat the olive oil in a large skillet over medium-high heat.

2. Add the scallops to the skillet and sear for about 2-3 minutes on each side, or until they are golden brown and have a caramelized crust. Remove the scallops from the skillet and set them aside.

3. In the same skillet, add the minced garlic and sauté for about 1 minute until fragrant.Pour in the low-sodium chicken or vegetable broth and lemon juice. Stir to deglaze the pan, scraping up any browned bits from the bottom.

4. Reduce the heat to low and add the unsalted butter to the skillet.Stir continuously until the butter has melted and the sauce has thickened slightly.

5. Return the seared scallops to the skillet and simmer for an additional 2 minutes, or until the scallops are heated through.

Grilled Swordfish Steaks

Prep Time: 10 minutes / Cook Time: 10 minutes
Yield: 4 serving

Ingredients

- 4 swordfish steaks (about 6 ounces each)
- 2 tablespoons olive oil, 2 cloves garlic, minced
- Zest and juice of 1 lemon, 1 teaspoon dried oregano
- 1/2 teaspoon black pepper, 1/2 teaspoon salt
- Lemon wedges for garnish (optional)
- Fresh parsley for garnish (optional)

Directions

1. Preheat your grill to medium-high heat.

2. In a small bowl, whisk together the olive oil, minced garlic, lemon zest, lemon juice, dried oregano, black pepper, and salt to create a marinade.

3. Brush both sides of the swordfish steaks generously with the marinade.

4. Place the swordfish steaks on the preheated grill and cook for about 4-5 minutes on each side, or until they are opaque and easily flake with a fork. The internal temperature should reach 145°F (63°C).

5. Once cooked, remove the swordfish steaks from the grill and let them rest for a few minutes.

6. Garnish with lemon wedges and fresh parsley if desired.

Nutritional Information (Approximate)

Calories	220	Dietary Fiber	0g
Protein	35g	Sodium	350mg
Carbohydrates	2g	Cholesterol	7mg
Total Fat	8g	Potassium	620mg
Saturated Fat	1,5g		

Smoked Trout Pate

Prep Time: 10 minutes / Cook Time: 0 minutes
Yield: 4 serving

Ingredients

- 8 ounces smoked trout, skin and bones removed
- 1/2 cup low-fat cream cheese, 1 tablespoon fresh lemon juice
- 2 tablespoons low-fat Greek yogurt
- 1 tablespoon fresh dill, chopped
- 1 green onion, chopped, salt and black pepper to taste
- Whole-grain crackers or sliced vegetables for serving

Directions

1. In a food processor, combine the smoked trout, low-fat cream cheese, low-fat Greek yogurt, fresh lemon juice, and chopped fresh dill.

2. Pulse the mixture until it becomes smooth and well combined.

3. Transfer the smoked trout pate to a mixing bowl and fold in the chopped green onion.

4. Season the pate with salt and black pepper to taste. Adjust the seasoning as needed.

5. Cover the bowl and refrigerate the pate for at least 30 minutes to allow the flavors to meld.

6. Serve the smoked trout pate with whole-grain crackers or sliced vegetables.

Nutritional Information

Calories	120	Dietary Fiber	0g
Protein	16g	Sodium	300mg
Carbohydrates	2g	Cholesterol	60mg
Total Fat	5g	Potassium	200mg
Saturated Fat	2g		

Teriyaki Glazed Salmon

Prep Time: 10 minutes / Cook Time: 15 minutes / Yield: 4 serving

Ingredients

- 4 salmon fillets (about 6 ounces each), 1 tablespoon cornstarch
- 1/4 cup reduced sodium soy sauce, 1 tablespoon fresh ginger, grated
- 2 tablespoons honey, 2 tablespoons rice vinegar
- 2 cloves garlic, minced, 2 tablespoons water, cooking spray
- Sesame seeds and chopped green onions for garnish (optional)

Nutritional Information

Calories	280	Dietary Fiber	0g
Protein	34g	Sodium	540mg
Carbohydrates	12g	Cholesterol	80mg
Total Fat	10g	Potassium	680mg
Saturated Fat	2g		

Directions

1. In a small saucepan, combine the reduced sodium soy sauce, honey, rice vinegar, grated fresh ginger, and minced garlic. Heat over medium heat and bring to a simmer.

2. In a separate small bowl, mix the cornstarch and water until smooth to create a slurry. Stir the slurry into the simmering sauce and continue to cook for another 2-3 minutes until the sauce thickens. Remove from heat.

3. Preheat your grill or oven to medium-high heat. If using a grill, lightly grease the grates with cooking spray to prevent sticking.

4. Brush both sides of the salmon fillets with the teriyaki glaze. Grill or bake the salmon for about 4-5 minutes on each side, or until the salmon flakes easily with a fork and reaches an internal temperature of 145°F (63°C).

5. While cooking, brush the salmon with additional glaze for extra flavor. Once cooked, remove the salmon from the grill or oven.

Garlic Parmesan Baked Mussels

Prep Time: 10 minutes / Cook Time: 10 minutes
Yield: 4 serving

Ingredients

- 24 fresh mussels, cleaned and debearded
- 3 tablespoons olive oil
- 3 cloves garlic, minced
- 1/4 cup grated Parmesan cheese
- 2 tablespoons fresh parsley, chopped
- 1 tablespoon whole wheat breadcrumbs (optional, for added crunch)
- Salt and black pepper to taste
- Lemon wedges for garnish (optional)

Directions

1. Preheat your oven to 425°F (220°C).

2. In a large skillet, heat 2 tablespoons of olive oil over medium heat. Add the minced garlic and sauté for about 1-2 minutes until fragrant. Remove the skillet from the heat and set it aside.

3. Scrub the mussels under cold running water to remove any dirt or debris. Remove the beards by firmly pulling them towards the hinge of the shell. Discard any mussels that are cracked or open.

4. In a mixing bowl, combine the cleaned mussels, sautéed garlic, grated Parmesan cheese, chopped fresh parsley, whole wheat breadcrumbs (if using), salt, and black pepper. Toss to coat the mussels evenly.

5. Arrange the coated mussels on a baking sheet or in a baking dish.

6. Drizzle the remaining 1 tablespoon of olive oil over the mussels.

7. Bake in the preheated oven for about 10 minutes, or until the mussels have opened, and the topping is golden brown.

Nutritional Information (Approximate)

Calories	130	Dietary Fiber	0g
Protein	11g	Sodium	300mg
Carbohydrates	4g	Cholesterol	30mg
Total Fat	8g	Potassium	240mg
Saturated Fat	2g		

These heart-healthy Garlic Parmesan Baked Mussels are a delectable seafood appetizer or snack. With a flavorful garlic and Parmesan topping, they are a great source of protein and low in carbohydrates. Enjoy them as an elegant and satisfying treat!

Shrimp and Grits

Prep Time: 15 minutes / Cook Time: 25 minutes
Yield: 4 serving

Ingredients

For the Grits:
- 1 cup stone-ground grits
- 4 cups low-sodium chicken broth
- 1 cup water, 1/2 cup low-fat milk
- 2 tablespoons unsalted butter
- Salt and black pepper to taste
- 1/2 cup shredded reduced-fat cheddar cheese (optional)

For the Shrimp:
- 1 pound large shrimp, peeled and deveined
- 2 tablespoons olive oil
- 1 small onion, finely chopped
- 1 bell pepper, diced, 2 cloves garlic, minced
- 1/2 cup low-sodium chicken broth
- 1 can (14.5 ounces) diced tomatoes, undrained
- 1 teaspoon Cajun seasoning
- 1/4 teaspoon red pepper flakes (adjust to taste)
- Fresh parsley for garnish (optional)

Directions

For the Grits

1. In a large saucepan, bring the chicken broth and water to a boil. Slowly whisk in the grits and reduce the heat to low. Cover and simmer, stirring occasionally, for about 15-20 minutes, or until the grits are tender and have absorbed most of the liquid.

2. Stir in the low-fat milk, unsalted butter, and shredded cheddar cheese (if using). Season with salt and black pepper to taste. Cover and keep warm.

For the Shrimp

3. In a large skillet, heat the olive oil over medium-high heat. Add the finely chopped onion and diced bell pepper. Sauté for about 3-4 minutes, or until the vegetables are softened.

4. Add the minced garlic and cook for another 1 minute until fragrant.

5. Add the peeled and deveined shrimp to the skillet. Cook for about 2-3 minutes on each side, or until they turn pink and opaque. Remove the shrimp from the skillet and set them aside.

6. In the same skillet, pour in the low-sodium chicken broth and diced tomatoes (with their juices). Stir in the Cajun seasoning and red pepper flakes. Simmer for about 5 minutes, or until the sauce has thickened slightly. Return the cooked shrimp to the skillet and cook for an additional 2 minutes, or until everything is heated through.

Nutritional Information
(per serving, without optional cheese)

Calories	300	Dietary Fiber	3g
Protein	20g	Sodium	600mg
Carbohydrates	35g	Cholesterol	140mg
Total Fat	10g	Potassium	480mg
Saturated Fat	3g		

Lobster Bisque

Prep Time: 25 minutes / Cook Time: 35 minutes
Yield: 4 serving

Ingredients

- 2 lobsters (about 1 1/2 pounds each), cooked and meat removed
- 4 cups low-sodium chicken broth, 1 cup water
- 1/2 cup dry white wine, 1 onion, chopped
- 2 carrots, chopped, 2 celery stalks, chopped
- 2 cloves garlic, minced, 2 tablespoons olive oil
- 2 tablespoons tomato paste
- 1/4 cup brandy or cognac
- 1/4 cup all-purpose flour, 1 cup low-fat milk
- 1/2 cup plain Greek yogurt
- 1 bay leaf, 1/4 teaspoon paprika
- Salt and black pepper to taste
- chopped fresh chives for garnish (optional)

Directions

1. In a large pot, heat the olive oil over medium-high heat. Add the chopped onion, carrots, celery, and minced garlic. Sauté for about 5 minutes, or until the vegetables are softened.
2. Stir in the tomato paste and cook for an additional 2 minutes, stirring constantly.
3. Add the brandy or cognac to the pot and let it simmer for about 2 minutes, allowing the alcohol to cook off.
4. Sprinkle the all-purpose flour over the mixture and stir well to combine. Cook for another 2 minutes to remove the raw flour taste.
5. Pour in the dry white wine, scraping up any browned bits from the bottom of the pot.
6. Add the chicken broth, water, and bay leaf to the pot. Bring the mixture to a simmer, then reduce the heat to low, cover, and let it cook for 15 minutes.
7. Remove the bay leaf and carefully transfer the mixture to a blender or use an immersion blender to puree until smooth.
8. Return the pureed mixture to the pot and place it over low heat. Stir in the low-fat milk, plain Greek yogurt, and paprika. Cook for an additional 5 minutes, or until the bisque is heated through.
9. Chop the lobster meat into bite-sized pieces and add it to the bisque. Cook for 2-3 minutes to heat the lobster.
10. Season the bisque with salt and black pepper to taste.
11. Serve hot, garnished with chopped fresh chives if desired.

Nutritional Information

Calories	280	Dietary Fiber	2g
Protein	28g	Sodium	610mg
Carbohydrates	14g	Cholesterol	130mg
Total Fat	10g	Potassium	480mg
Saturated Fat	2g		

Pan-Seared Mahi-Mahi with Pineapple Salsa

Prep Time: 15 minutes / Cook Time: 10 minutes
Yield: 4 serving

Ingredients

For the Mahi-Mahi:
- 4 Mahi-Mahi fillets (about 6 ounces each)
- 2 tablespoons olive oil, 1 teaspoon paprika
- 1/2 teaspoon ground cumin, 1/2 teaspoon ground coriander, salt and black pepper to taste
- 1 lime, cut into wedges (for garnish, optional)

For the Pineapple Salsa:
- 2 cups fresh pineapple, diced, 1/2 red onion, finely chopped, 1 red bell pepper, diced, salt to taste
- 1 jalapeño pepper, seeded and finely chopped
- 1/4 cup fresh cilantro, chopped, juice of 1 lime

Directions

For the Pineapple Salsa

1. In a mixing bowl, combine the diced pineapple, finely chopped red onion, diced red bell pepper, finely chopped jalapeño pepper, chopped fresh cilantro, and the juice of 1 lime. Toss to mix well.

2. Season the salsa with salt to taste. Cover and refrigerate while you prepare the Mahi-Mahi.

For the Mahi-Mahi

3. In a small bowl, mix together the paprika, ground cumin, ground coriander, salt, and black pepper.

4. Pat the Mahi-Mahi fillets dry with paper towels and rub them with the spice mixture on both sides.

5. In a large skillet, heat the olive oil over medium-high heat.

6. Add the seasoned Mahi-Mahi fillets to the skillet and cook for about 4-5 minutes on each side, or until they are opaque and easily flake with a fork. The internal temperature should reach 145°F (63°C).

7. Once cooked, remove the Mahi-Mahi fillets from the skillet and let them rest for a few minutes.

Nutritional Information

Calories	250	Dietary Fiber	3g
Protein	35g	Sodium	350mg
Carbohydrates	18g	Cholesterol	115mg
Total Fat	6g	Potassium	820mg
Saturated Fat	1g		

This heart-healthy Pan-Seared Mahi-Mahi with Pineapple Salsa is a delightful and flavorful seafood dish that's rich in protein and low in saturated fat. The vibrant pineapple salsa adds a refreshing and tangy twist to the dish, making it a perfect choice for a healthy and delicious meal!

chapter 9
SMOOTHIE RECIPES
(fruits, vegetables)

Green Goddess Smoothie 69

Berry Blast Smoothie 69

Tropical Paradise Smoothie 69

Spinach and Pineapple Delight 70

Mango Tango Smoothie 70

Strawberry Spinach Surprise 70

Blueberry Kale Crush 71

Carrot Cake Smoothie 71

Cucumber Melon Cooler 71

Peachy Green Smoothie 72

Kiwi Berry Bliss 72

Avocado Banana Smoothie 72

Raspberry Spinach Splash 73

Pineapple Coconut Dream 73

Beet and Berry Burst 73

Orange Creamsicle Smoothie 74

Papaya Passion Smoothie 74

Sweet Potato Pie Smoothie 74

Pomegranate Power Punch 75

Apple Cinnamon Delight 75

Green Goddess Smoothie

Prep Time: 5 minutes / Cook Time: 0 minutes
Yield: 2 serving

Ingredients

- 2 cups fresh spinach leaves, 1 cup chopped cucumber
- 1 ripe avocado, pitted and peeled, 1/2 cup fresh parsley leaves
- 1 green apple, cored and chopped, 1 tablespoon fresh lemon juice
- 1 1/2 cups unsweetened almond milk (or any milk of your choice)
- 1 tablespoon honey (optional, for sweetness)
- Ice cubes (optional, for extra chill)

Directions

1. In a blender, combine the fresh spinach, chopped cucumber, ripe avocado, fresh parsley leaves, chopped green apple, and fresh lemon juice.

2. Pour in the unsweetened almond milk and add honey if desired for a touch of sweetness.

3. If you prefer a colder smoothie, you can also add a handful of ice cubes.

4. Blend all the ingredients until smooth and creamy, ensuring there are no visible chunks.

5. Pour the Green Goddess Smoothie into two glasses and serve immediately.

Nutritional Information

Calories	230	Dietary Fiber	9g
Protein	4g	Sodium	200mg
Carbohydrates	19g	Cholesterol	0mg
Total Fat	16g	Potassium	760mg
Saturated Fat	2g		

Berry Blast Smoothie

Prep Time: 5 minutes / Cook Time: 0 minutes
Yield: 1 serving

Ingredients

- 1/2 cup frozen mixed berries (strawberries, blueberries, raspberries)
- 1/2 ripe banana, 1/2 cup low-fat Greek yogurt
- 1/2 cup unsweetened almond milk (or any milk of your choice)
- 1 tablespoon honey (optional, for sweetness)
- 1/2 teaspoon chia seeds (optional, for added fiber and omega-3)
- Ice cubes (optional, for extra chill)

Directions

1. Place the frozen mixed berries, ripe banana, low-fat Greek yogurt, and unsweetened almond milk in a blender.

2. If you prefer a sweeter smoothie, add honey at this stage.

3. Optionally, add chia seeds for extra fiber and omega-3 fatty acids.

4. If you like your smoothie extra cold, toss in a few ice cubes.

5. Blend all the ingredients until you achieve a smooth and creamy consistency.

6. Pour the Berry Blast Smoothie into a glass and serve immediately.

Nutritional Information

Calories	230	Dietary Fiber	7g
Protein	10g	Sodium	125mg
Carbohydrates	44g	Cholesterol	5mg
Total Fat	3g	Potassium	480mg
Saturated Fat	0g		

Tropical Paradise Smoothie

Prep Time: 5 minutes / Cook Time: 0 minutes / Yield: 1 serving

Ingredients

- 1/2 cup frozen mango chunks
- 1/2 cup frozen pineapple chunks
- 1/2 ripe banana, 1/2 cup low-fat coconut milk
- 1/2 cup unsweetened almond milk
  (or any milk of your choice)
- 1 tablespoon honey (optional, for sweetness)
- 1/2 teaspoon grated fresh ginger
  (optional, for added flavor)
- Ice cubes (optional, for extra chill)

Nutritional Information

Calories	280	Dietary Fiber	6g
Protein	3g	Sodium	85mg
Carbohydrates	59g	Cholesterol	0mg
Total Fat	5g	Potassium	630mg
Saturated Fat	2g		

Directions

1. Place the frozen mango chunks, frozen pineapple chunks, ripe banana, low-fat coconut milk, and unsweetened almond milk in a blender.

2. If you prefer a sweeter smoothie, add honey at this stage.

3. Optionally, add grated fresh ginger for a delightful tropical flavor twist.

4. If you like your smoothie extra cold, toss in a few ice cubes.

5. Blend all the ingredients until you achieve a smooth and creamy consistency.

6. Pour the Tropical Paradise Smoothie into a glass and serve immediately.

Spinach and Pineapple Delight

Prep Time: 5 minutes / Cook Time: 0 minutes
Yield: 1 serving

Ingredients

- 1 cup fresh spinach leaves, 1/2 cup frozen pineapple chunks
- 1/2 banana, 1/2 cup low-fat Greek yogurt
- 1/2 cup unsweetened almond milk (or any milk of your choice)
- 1 tablespoon honey (optional, for sweetness)
- Ice cubes (optional, for extra chill)

Directions

1. Place the fresh spinach leaves, frozen pineapple chunks, banana, low-fat Greek yogurt, and unsweetened almond milk in a blender.

2. If you prefer a sweeter smoothie, add honey at this stage. If you like your smoothie extra cold, toss in a few ice cubes.

3. Blend all the ingredients until you achieve a smooth and creamy consistency.

4. Pour the Spinach and Pineapple Delight Smoothie into a glass and serve immediately.

Nutritional Information

Calories	240	Dietary Fiber	5g
Protein	9g	Sodium	135mg
Carbohydrates	49g	Cholesterol	5mg
Total Fat	2g	Potassium	710mg
Saturated Fat	0,5g		

Mango Tango Smoothie

Prep Time: 5 minutes / Cook Time: 0 minutes
Yield: 1 serving

Ingredients

- 1 cup ripe mango chunks (fresh or frozen), 1/2 ripe banana
- 1/2 cup low-fat Greek yogurt, ice cubes (optional, for extra chill)
- 1/2 cup unsweetened almond milk (or any milk of your choice)
- 1/2 tablespoon honey (optional, for sweetness)
- 1/2 teaspoon vanilla extract (optional, for flavor)

Directions

1. Place the ripe mango chunks, low-fat Greek yogurt, unsweetened almond milk, banana, honey (if using), and vanilla extract (if using) in a blender.

2. If you prefer a sweeter smoothie, add honey at this stage.

3. If you like your smoothie extra cold, toss in a few ice cubes.

4. Blend all the ingredients until you achieve a smooth and creamy consistency.Pour the Mango Tango Smoothie into a glass and serve immediately.

Nutritional Information (Approximate)

Calories	280	Dietary Fiber	6g
Protein	12g	Sodium	145mg
Carbohydrates	56g	Cholesterol	5mg
Total Fat	2g	Potassium	680mg
Saturated Fat	1g		

Strawberry Spinach Surprise

Prep Time: 5 minutes / Cook Time: 0 minutes / Yield: 1 serving

Ingredients

- 1 cup fresh spinach leaves
- 1/2 cup fresh strawberries, hulled and halved
- 1/2 ripe banana
- 1/2 cup low-fat Greek yogurt
- 1/2 cup unsweetened almond milk
  (or any milk of your choice)
- 1 tablespoon honey (optional, for sweetness)
- 1/2 teaspoon vanilla extract (optional, for flavor)
- Ice cubes (optional, for extra chill)

Nutritional Information (Approximate)

Calories	250	Dietary Fiber	6g
Protein	11g	Sodium	155mg
Carbohydrates	51g	Cholesterol	5mg
Total Fat	2g	Potassium	710mg
Saturated Fat	0g		

Directions

1. Place the fresh spinach leaves, fresh strawberries, ripe banana, low-fat Greek yogurt, unsweetened almond milk, honey (if using), and vanilla extract (if using) in a blender.

2. If you prefer a sweeter smoothie, add honey at this stage.

3. If you like your smoothie extra cold, toss in a few ice cubes.

4. Blend all the ingredients until you achieve a smooth and creamy consistency.

5. Pour the Strawberry Spinach Surprise Smoothie into a glass and serve immediately.

Blueberry Kale Crush

Prep Time: 5 minutes / Cook Time: 0 minutes
Yield: 1 serving

Ingredients

- 1/2 cup fresh blueberries
- 1 cup fresh kale leaves, stems removed
- 1/2 banana, 1/2 cup low-fat Greek yogurt
- 1/2 cup unsweetened almond milk (or any milk of your choice)
- 1 tablespoon honey (optional, for sweetness)
- Ice cubes (optional, for extra chill)

Directions

1. Place the fresh blueberries, fresh kale leaves, banana, low-fat Greek yogurt, unsweetened almond milk, honey (if using), and ice cubes (if desired) in a blender.

2. If you prefer a sweeter smoothie, add honey at this stage.

3. If you like your smoothie extra cold, toss in a few ice cubes.

4. Blend all the ingredients until you achieve a smooth and creamy consistency.

5. Pour the Blueberry Kale Crush Smoothie into a glass and serve immediately.

Nutritional Information

Calories	270	Dietary Fiber	7g
Protein	11g	Sodium	150mg
Carbohydrates	55g	Cholesterol	5mg
Total Fat	3g	Potassium	750mg
Saturated Fat	1g		

Carrot Cake Smoothie

Prep Time: 5 minutes / Cook Time: 0 minutes
Yield: 1 serving

Ingredients

- 1 medium carrot, peeled and chopped
- 1/2 cup rolled oats, 1/2 cup low-fat Greek yogurt
- 1/2 cup unsweetened almond milk (or any milk of your choice)
- 1/2 banana, 1/2 teaspoon ground cinnamon
- 1/4 teaspoon ground nutmeg, 1/4 teaspoon vanilla extract
- 1 tablespoon honey (optional, for sweetness)
- Ice cubes (optional, for extra chill)

Directions

1. Place the chopped carrot, rolled oats, low-fat Greek yogurt, unsweetened almond milk, banana, ground cinnamon, ground nutmeg, vanilla extract, honey (if using), and ice cubes (if desired) in a blender.

2. If you prefer a sweeter smoothie, add honey at this stage.

3. If you like your smoothie extra cold, toss in a few ice cubes.

4. Blend all the ingredients until you achieve a smooth and creamy consistency.

5. Pour the Carrot Cake Smoothie into a glass and serve immediately.

Nutritional Information

Calories	340	Dietary Fiber	8g
Protein	14g	Sodium	175mg
Carbohydrates	65g	Cholesterol	5mg
Total Fat	5g	Potassium	5700mg
Saturated Fat	1g		

Cucumber Melon Cooler

Prep Time: 5 minutes / Cook Time: 0 minutes / Yield: 1 serving

Ingredients

- 1 cup cucumber, peeled and chopped
- 1 cup honeydew melon, chopped
- 1/2 lime, juiced, 1/2 cup fresh mint leaves, 1/2 cup cold water
- 1 tablespoon honey (optional, for sweetness)
- Ice cubes (optional, for extra chill)

Nutritional Information (Approximate)

Calories	90	Dietary Fiber	2g
Protein	1g	Sodium	15mg
Carbohydrates	23g	Cholesterol	0mg
Total Fat	0g	Potassium	440mg
Saturated Fat	0g		

Directions

1. Place the chopped cucumber, honeydew melon, fresh mint leaves, lime juice, cold water, honey (if using), and ice cubes (if desired) in a blender.

2. If you prefer a sweeter drink, add honey at this stage.

3. If you like your cooler extra cold, toss in a few ice cubes.

4. Blend all the ingredients until you achieve a smooth and refreshing consistency.

5. Pour the Cucumber Melon Cooler into a glass and serve immediately.

Peachy Green Smoothie

Prep Time: 5 minutes / Cook Time: 0 minutes
Yield: 1 serving

Ingredients

- 1 cup fresh spinach leaves
- 1 ripe peach, pitted and chopped
- 1/2 banana, 1/2 cup low-fat Greek yogurt
- 1/2 cup unsweetened almond milk (or any milk of your choice)
- 1 tablespoon honey (optional, for sweetness)
- Ice cubes (optional, for extra chill)

Directions

1. Place the fresh spinach leaves, ripe peach chunks, banana, low-fat Greek yogurt, unsweetened almond milk, honey (if using), and ice cubes (if desired) in a blender.

2. If you prefer a sweeter smoothie, add honey at this stage.

3. If you like your smoothie extra cold, toss in a few ice cubes.

4. Blend all the ingredients until you achieve a smooth and creamy consistency.

5. Pour the Peachy Green Smoothie into a glass and serve immediately.

Nutritional Information (Approximate)

Calories	250	Dietary Fiber	6g
Protein	11g	Sodium	180mg
Carbohydrates	50g	Cholesterol	5mg
Total Fat	3g	Potassium	730mg
Saturated Fat	0g		

Kiwi Berry Bliss

Prep Time: 5 minutes / Cook Time: 0 minutes
Yield: 1 serving

Ingredients

- 2 ripe kiwis, peeled and chopped
- 1/2 cup fresh strawberries, hulled and halved
- 1/2 banana, 1/2 cup low-fat Greek yogurt
- 1/2 cup unsweetened almond milk (or any milk of your choice)
- 1 tablespoon honey (optional, for sweetness)
- Ice cubes (optional, for extra chill)

Directions

1. Place the chopped kiwis, fresh strawberries, banana, low-fat Greek yogurt, unsweetened almond milk, honey (if using), and ice cubes (if desired) in a blender.

2. If you prefer a sweeter smoothie, add honey at this stage.

3. If you like your smoothie extra cold, toss in a few ice cubes.

4. Blend all the ingredients until you achieve a smooth and creamy consistency.

5. Pour the Kiwi Berry Bliss Smoothie into a glass and serve immediately.

Nutritional Information

Calories	260	Dietary Fiber	7g
Protein	11g	Sodium	135mg
Carbohydrates	54g	Cholesterol	5mg
Total Fat	2g	Potassium	860mg
Saturated Fat	0g		

Avocado Banana Smoothie

Prep Time: 5 minutes / Cook Time: 0 minutes / Yield: 1 serving

Ingredients

- 1/2 ripe avocado, pitted and peeled
- 1 ripe banana, 1/2 cup low-fat Greek yogurt
- 1/2 cup unsweetened almond milk
  (or any milk of your choice)
- 1 tablespoon honey (optional, for sweetness)
- 1/2 teaspoon vanilla extract (optional, for flavor)
- Ice cubes (optional, for extra chill)

Nutritional Information

Calories	320	Dietary Fiber	9g
Protein	8g	Sodium	180mg
Carbohydrates	50g	Cholesterol	5mg
Total Fat	12g	Potassium	900mg
Saturated Fat	2g		

Directions

1. Place the ripe avocado, banana, low-fat Greek yogurt, unsweetened almond milk, honey (if using), and ice cubes (if desired) in a blender.

2. If you prefer a sweeter smoothie, add honey at this stage.

3. If you like your smoothie extra cold, toss in a few ice cubes.

4. Blend all the ingredients until you achieve a smooth and creamy consistency.

5. Pour the Avocado Banana Smoothie into a glass and serve immediately.

Raspberry Spinach Splash

Prep Time: 5 minutes / Cook Time: 0 minutes
Yield: 1 serving

Ingredients

- 1 cup fresh spinach leaves
- 1/2 cup fresh raspberries
- 1/2 banana, 1/2 cup low-fat Greek yogurt
- 1/2 cup unsweetened almond milk (or any milk of your choice)
- 1 tablespoon honey (optional, for sweetness)
- Ice cubes (optional, for extra chill)

Directions

1. Place the fresh spinach leaves, fresh raspberries, banana, low-fat Greek yogurt, unsweetened almond milk, honey (if using), and ice cubes (if desired) in a blender.

2. If you prefer a sweeter smoothie, add honey at this stage.

3. If you like your smoothie extra cold, toss in a few ice cubes.

4. Blend all the ingredients until you achieve a smooth and vibrant consistency.

5. Pour the Raspberry Spinach Splash Smoothie into a glass and serve immediately.

Nutritional Information (Approximate)

Calories	240	Dietary Fiber	8g
Protein	9g	Sodium	170mg
Carbohydrates	48g	Cholesterol	5mg
Total Fat	3g	Potassium	710mg
Saturated Fat	0g		

Pineapple Coconut Dream

Prep Time: 5 minutes / Cook Time: 0 minutes
Yield: 1 serving

Ingredients

- 1/2 cup fresh pineapple chunks
- 1/2 ripe banana, 1/2 cup low-fat Greek yogurt
- 1/2 cup unsweetened coconut milk
- 1 tablespoon honey (optional, for sweetness)
- 1/2 teaspoon coconut extract (optional, for flavor)
- Ice cubes (optional, for extra chill)

Directions

1. Place the fresh pineapple chunks, ripe banana, low-fat Greek yogurt, unsweetened coconut milk, honey (if using), coconut extract (if using), and ice cubes (if desired) in a blender.

2. If you prefer a sweeter smoothie, add honey at this stage.

3. If you like your smoothie extra cold, toss in a few ice cubes.

4. Blend all the ingredients until you achieve a smooth and creamy tropical delight.

5. Pour the Pineapple Coconut Dream Smoothie into a glass and serve immediately.

Nutritional Information (Approximate)

Calories	250	Dietary Fiber	4g
Protein	9g	Sodium	95mg
Carbohydrates	50g	Cholesterol	5mg
Total Fat	3g	Potassium	480mg
Saturated Fat	1g		

Beet and Berry Burst

Prep Time: 5 minutes / Cook Time: 0 minutes / Yield: 1 serving

Ingredients

- 1/2 small beet, peeled and chopped
- 1/2 cup fresh mixed berries
  (such as strawberries, blueberries, and raspberries)
- 1/2 banana, 1/2 cup low-fat Greek yogurt
- 1/2 cup unsweetened almond milk (or any milk of your choice)
- 1 tablespoon honey (optional, for sweetness)
- Ice cubes (optional, for extra chill)

Nutritional Information (Approximate)

Calories	250	Dietary Fiber	8g
Protein	10g	Sodium	175mg
Carbohydrates	52g	Cholesterol	5mg
Total Fat	2g	Potassium	740mg
Saturated Fat	0g		

Directions

1. Place the chopped beet, mixed berries, banana, low-fat Greek yogurt, unsweetened almond milk, honey (if using), and ice cubes (if desired) in a blender. If you prefer a sweeter smoothie, add honey at this stage.

2. If you like your smoothie extra cold, toss in a few ice cubes.

3. Blend all the ingredients until you achieve a smooth and vibrant consistency.

4. Pour the Beet and Berry Burst Smoothie into a glass and serve immediately.

Orange Creamsicle Smoothie

Prep Time: 5 minutes / Cook Time: 0 minutes
Yield: 1 serving

Ingredients

- 1 large orange, peeled and segmented
- 1/2 cup low-fat Greek yogurt
- 1/2 cup unsweetened almond milk (or any milk of your choice)
- 1/2 banana, 1 tablespoon honey (optional, for sweetness)
- 1/2 teaspoon vanilla extract (optional, for flavor)
- Ice cubes (optional, for extra chill)

Directions

1. Place the orange segments, low-fat Greek yogurt, unsweetened almond milk, banana, honey (if using), and ice cubes (if desired) in a blender.

2. If you prefer a sweeter smoothie, add honey at this stage.

3. If you like your smoothie extra cold, toss in a few ice cubes.

4. Blend all the ingredients until you achieve a smooth and creamy consistency.

5. Pour the Orange Creamsicle Smoothie into a glass and serve immediately.

Nutritional Information (Approximate)

Calories	250	Dietary Fiber	6g
Protein	9g	Sodium	180mg
Carbohydrates	50g	Cholesterol	5mg
Total Fat	2g	Potassium	660mg
Saturated Fat	0g		

Papaya Passion Smoothie

Prep Time: 5 minutes / Cook Time: 0 minutes
Yield: 1 serving

Ingredients

- 1 cup fresh papaya chunks
- 1/2 cup fresh pineapple chunks
- 1/2 banana, 1/2 cup low-fat Greek yogurt
- 1/2 cup unsweetened almond milk (or any milk of your choice)
- 1 tablespoon honey (optional, for sweetness)
- Ice cubes (optional, for extra chill)

Directions

1. Place the fresh papaya chunks, fresh pineapple chunks, banana, low-fat Greek yogurt, unsweetened almond milk, honey (if using), and ice cubes (if desired) in a blender.

2. If you prefer a sweeter smoothie, add honey at this stage.

3. If you like your smoothie extra cold, toss in a few ice cubes.

4. Blend all the ingredients until you achieve a smooth and tropical perfection.

5. Pour the Papaya Passion Smoothie into a glass and serve immediately.

Nutritional Information (Approximate)

Calories	240	Dietary Fiber	4g
Protein	10g	Sodium	130mg
Carbohydrates	48g	Cholesterol	5mg
Total Fat	2g	Potassium	710mg
Saturated Fat	0g		

Sweet Potato Pie Smoothie

Prep Time: 5 minutes / Cook Time: 0 minutes / Yield: 1 serving

Ingredients

- 1/2 cup cooked sweet potato, cooled
- 1/2 ripe banana, 1/2 cup low-fat Greek yogurt
- 1/2 cup unsweetened almond milk (or any milk of your choice)
- 1 tablespoon honey (optional, for sweetness)
- 1/2 teaspoon ground cinnamon
- 1/4 teaspoon ground nutmeg
- Ice cubes (optional, for extra chill)

Nutritional Information (Approximate)

Calories	250	Dietary Fiber	6g
Protein	9g	Sodium	170mg
Carbohydrates	52g	Cholesterol	5mg
Total Fat	2g	Potassium	610mg
Saturated Fat	0g		

Directions

1. In a blender, combine the cooked sweet potato, ripe banana, low-fat Greek yogurt, unsweetened almond milk, honey (if using), ground cinnamon, ground nutmeg, and ice cubes (if desired).

2. If you prefer a sweeter smoothie, add honey at this stage. If you like your smoothie extra cold, toss in a few ice cubes.

3. Blend all the ingredients until you achieve a smooth and creamy consistency.

4. Pour the Sweet Potato Pie Smoothie into a glass and serve immediately.

Pomegranate Power Punch

Prep Time: 5 minutes / Cook Time: 0 minutes
Yield: 1 serving

Ingredients

- 1 cup pomegranate seeds
  (from about 1 large pomegranate)
- 1/2 cup plain low-fat Greek yogurt
- 1/2 cup unsweetened pomegranate juice
- 1/2 ripe banana
- 1 tablespoon honey (optional, for sweetness)
- Ice cubes (optional, for extra chill)

Directions

1. Remove the seeds from the pomegranate by cutting it in half and gently tapping the back of the fruit with a wooden spoon to release the seeds. Collect 1 cup of pomegranate seeds.

2. In a blender, combine the pomegranate seeds, plain low-fat Greek yogurt, unsweetened pomegranate juice, ripe banana, honey (if using), and ice cubes (if desired).

3. If you prefer a sweeter smoothie, add honey at this stage.

4. If you like your smoothie extra cold, toss in a few ice cubes.

5. Blend all the ingredients until you achieve a smooth and vibrant consistency.

6. Pour the Pomegranate Power Punch Smoothie into a glass and serve immediately.

Nutritional Information

Calories	240	Dietary Fiber	8g
Protein	9g	Sodium	50mg
Carbohydrates	54g	Cholesterol	5mg
Total Fat	2g	Potassium	550mg
Saturated Fat	0g		

This single-serving Pomegranate Power Punch Smoothie is a heart-healthy and antioxidant-rich choice, showcasing the vibrant flavor of pomegranates. Enjoy this nutritious and energizing drink to kickstart your day!

Apple Cinnamon Delight

Prep Time: 5 minutes / Cook Time: 0 minutes
Yield: 1 serving

Ingredients

- 1 medium apple, peeled, cored, and chopped
- 1/2 cup low-fat plain yogurt
- 1/2 cup unsweetened almond milk
  (or any milk of your choice)
- 1/2 teaspoon ground cinnamon
- 1/4 teaspoon vanilla extract
- 1 tablespoon honey (optional, for sweetness)
- Ice cubes (optional, for extra chill)

Directions

1. In a blender, combine the chopped apple, low-fat plain yogurt, unsweetened almond milk, ground cinnamon, vanilla extract, honey (if using), and ice cubes (if desired).

2. If you prefer a sweeter smoothie, add honey at this stage.

3. If you like your smoothie extra cold, toss in a few ice cubes.

4. Blend all the ingredients until you achieve a smooth and aromatic mixture.

5. Pour the Apple Cinnamon Delight Smoothie into a glass and serve immediately.

Nutritional Information

Calories	190	Dietary Fiber	5g
Protein	6g	Sodium	150mg
Carbohydrates	40g	Cholesterol	5mg
Total Fat	2g	Potassium	400mg
Saturated Fat	0g		

This single-serving Apple Cinnamon Delight Smoothie is a heart-healthy and comforting choice, combining the natural sweetness of apples with warm cinnamon spice. Enjoy this nutritious and cozy drink as a wholesome treat!

chapter 10
VEGETABLE

Mediterranean Stuffed Bell Peppers 77

Spinach & Feta Stuffed Mushrooms 77

Kale & White Bean Soup 78

Grilled Vegetable Platter
with Balsamic Glaze 78

Quinoa & Roasted Vegetable Salad 78

Cauliflower Rice Stir-Fry 79

Brussels Sprouts
with Pomegranate Seeds 79

Zucchini Noodles with Pesto 80

Roasted Beet & Citrus Salad 80

Sweet Potato & Black Bean Chili 81

Asparagus & Lemon Risotto 81

Baked Eggplant Parmesan 82

Garlic Roasted Broccoli 82

Rainbow Chard
with Garlic & Pine Nuts 83

Cucumber Avocado Gazpacho 83

Sautéed Spinach
with Garlic & Lemon 83

Spaghetti Squash
with Tomato & Basil Sauce 84

Green Bean Almondine 84

Stuffed Acorn Squash
with Quinoa & Cranberries 85

Creamy Cauliflower & Leek Soup 85

Mediterranean Stuffed Bell Peppers

Prep Time: 20 minutes / Cook Time: 35 minutes
Yield: 4 serving

Ingredients

- 4 large bell peppers, any color
- 1 cup cooked quinoa
- 1 cup canned chickpeas, drained and rinsed
- 1 cup diced tomatoes (canned or fresh)
- 1/2 cup diced cucumber, 1/2 cup diced red onion
- 1/4 cup chopped fresh parsley
- 1/4 cup crumbled feta cheese (optional)
- 2 tablespoons olive oil, 2 cloves garlic, minced
- 1 teaspoon dried oregano, salt and pepper to taste
- Lemon wedges, for serving

Directions

1. Preheat your oven to 375°F (190°C).

2. Cut the tops off the bell peppers and remove the seeds and membranes. Rinse them under cold water and set aside.

3. In a large bowl, combine the cooked quinoa, chickpeas, diced tomatoes, cucumber, red onion, parsley, and feta cheese (if using).

4. In a small bowl, whisk together the olive oil, minced garlic, dried oregano, salt, and pepper. Pour this dressing over the quinoa mixture and toss to combine.

5. Stuff each bell pepper with the quinoa mixture, pressing it down gently as you go.

6. Place the stuffed bell peppers in a baking dish and cover with foil.

7. Bake in the preheated oven for about 30-35 minutes, or until the peppers are tender.

8. Remove the foil during the last 10 minutes of baking to allow the tops to brown slightly.

9. Serve the Mediterranean Stuffed Bell Peppers with lemon wedges for a burst of citrusy flavor.

Nutritional Information

Calories	285	Dietary Fiber	8g
Protein	9g	Sodium	394mg
Carbohydrates	39g	Cholesterol	0mg
Total Fat	10g	Potassium	698mg
Saturated Fat	2g		

Enjoy your heart-healthy Mediterranean Stuffed Bell Peppers!

Spinach and Feta Stuffed Mushrooms

Prep Time: 15 minutes / Cook Time: 20 minutes
Yield: 4 serving

Ingredients

- 16 large button mushrooms, cleaned and stems removed
- 1 cup fresh spinach, chopped
- 1/2 cup crumbled feta cheese
- 1/4 cup finely diced red onion
- 2 cloves garlic, minced
- 1 tablespoon olive oil
- 1/2 teaspoon dried oregano
- Salt and pepper to taste
- Cooking spray

Directions

1. Preheat your oven to 375°F (190°C). Lightly grease a baking sheet with cooking spray.

2. Heat olive oil in a skillet over medium heat. Add the diced red onion and minced garlic. Sauté for about 2-3 minutes, or until the onion becomes translucent.

3. Add the chopped spinach to the skillet and cook for an additional 2-3 minutes, or until the spinach is wilted. Remove from heat and let it cool slightly.

4. In a mixing bowl, combine the sautéed spinach mixture with the crumbled feta cheese and dried oregano. Season with salt and pepper to taste.

5. Fill each mushroom cap with the spinach and feta mixture, pressing it in gently.

6. Place the stuffed mushrooms on the prepared baking sheet.

7. Bake in the preheated oven for approximately 15-20 minutes, or until the mushrooms are tender and the filling is golden brown.

8. Serve hot and enjoy your heart-healthy Spinach and Feta Stuffed Mushrooms!

Nutritional Information

Calories	65	Dietary Fiber	1g
Protein	4g	Sodium	187mg
Carbohydrates	5g	Cholesterol	8mg
Total Fat	4g	Potassium	295mg
Saturated Fat	2g		

These delicious stuffed mushrooms are a great heart-healthy appetizer or side dish.

Kale and White Bean Soup

Prep Time: 15 minutes / Cook Time: 30 minutes
Yield: 6 serving

Ingredients

- 1 tablespoon olive oil, 1 onion, chopped, 2 carrots, diced
- 2 cloves garlic, minced, 6 cups low-sodium vegetable broth
- 2 celery stalks, diced, 1 potato, peeled and diced
- 2 (15-ounce) cans white beans, drained and rinsed
- 4 cups kale, stems removed and chopped
- 1 teaspoon dried thyme, salt and pepper to taste
- Juice of 1 lemon, grated Parmesan cheese (optional, for garnish)

Directions

1. In a large pot, heat the olive oil over medium heat. Add the chopped onion and sauté for 3-4 minutes, or until it becomes translucent.

2. Add the minced garlic, diced carrots, celery, and potato to the pot. Sauté for another 5 minutes, stirring occasionally.

3. Pour in the low-sodium vegetable broth and bring the mixture to a boil. Reduce the heat to low, cover, and simmer for 15-20 minutes, or until the vegetables are tender.

4. Add the white beans, chopped kale, and dried thyme to the pot. Stir well and continue to simmer for an additional 5-7 minutes, or until the kale is wilted.

5. Season the soup with salt and pepper to taste. Remove the soup from heat and stir in the lemon juice. Serve hot, optionally garnished with a sprinkle of grated Parmesan cheese.

Nutritional Information

Calories	220	Dietary Fiber	9g
Protein	10g	Sodium	480mg
Carbohydrates	40g	Cholesterol	0mg
Total Fat	3g	Potassium	802mg
Saturated Fat	0g		

Grilled Vegetable Platter with Balsamic Glaze

Prep Time: 15 minutes / Cook Time: 15 minutes
Yield: 4 serving

Ingredients

- 2 zucchini, sliced lengthwise, 2 yellow squash, sliced lengthwise
- 1 red bell pepper, quartered and seeded
- 1 yellow bell pepper, quartered and seeded
- 1 red onion, sliced into thick rings
- 8 asparagus spears, trimmed, 2 tablespoons olive oil
- Salt and pepper to taste, 2 tablespoons balsamic vinegar
- 1 teaspoon honey (optional), fresh basil leaves, for garnish

Directions

1. Preheat your grill to medium-high heat.

2. In a large bowl, toss the zucchini, yellow squash, red bell pepper, yellow bell pepper, red onion, and asparagus with olive oil. Season with salt and pepper.

3. Place the vegetables on the preheated grill and cook for about 5-7 minutes per side, or until they are tender and have grill marks.

4. While grilling, in a small saucepan, combine balsamic vinegar and honey (if using). Heat over low heat, stirring occasionally, until the mixture thickens slightly. Remove from heat.

5. Transfer the grilled vegetables to a serving platter. Drizzle the balsamic glaze over the grilled vegetables. Garnish with fresh basil leaves.

Nutritional Information

Calories	105	Dietary Fiber	4g
Protein	2g	Sodium	9mg
Carbohydrates	14g	Cholesterol	0mg
Total Fat	6g	Potassium	456mg
Saturated Fat	1g		

Quinoa and Roasted Vegetable Salad

Prep Time: 15 minutes / Cook Time: 25 minutes / Yield: 4 serving

Ingredients

- 1 cup quinoa, rinsed, 2 cups water or vegetable broth
- 2 cups mixed vegetables (e.g., bell peppers, zucchini, cherry tomatoes, red onion), chopped, lemon zest, for garnish
- 2 tablespoons olive oil, 1 teaspoon dried thyme
- Salt and pepper to taste, 1/4 cup fresh basil leaves, chopped
- 1/4 cup crumbled feta cheese (optional)
- 2 tablespoons balsamic vinegar, 1 tablespoon honey (optional)

Nutritional Information (Approximate)

Calories	240	Dietary Fiber	5g
Protein	6g	Sodium	80mg
Carbohydrates	36g	Cholesterol	0mg
Total Fat	8g	Potassium	347mg
Saturated Fat	2g		

Directions

1. Preheat your oven to 425°F (220°C).

2. In a medium saucepan, combine the quinoa and water or vegetable broth. Bring to a boil, then reduce the heat to low, cover, and simmer for 15-20 minutes, or until the quinoa is cooked and the liquid is absorbed. Fluff the cooked quinoa with a fork and let it cool.

3. While the quinoa is cooking, place the chopped mixed vegetables on a baking sheet. Drizzle with olive oil and sprinkle with dried thyme, salt, and pepper. Toss to coat.

4. Roast the vegetables in the preheated oven for about 15 minutes, or until they are tender and slightly caramelized. Remove from the oven and let them cool.

5. In a large mixing bowl, combine the cooked quinoa, roasted vegetables, chopped basil, and crumbled feta cheese (if using).

6. In a small bowl, whisk together the balsamic vinegar and honey (if using). Drizzle this dressing over the salad and toss to combine. Garnish with lemon zest.

Cauliflower Rice Stir-Fry

Prep Time: 15 minutes / Cook Time: 15 minutes
Yield: 4 serving

Ingredients

- 1 medium head of cauliflower
- 2 tablespoons low-sodium soy sauce
- 1 tablespoon sesame oil, 1 tablespoon olive oil
- 1 cup diced mixed vegetables
  (e.g., bell peppers, broccoli, carrots)
- 1 cup diced tofu or skinless chicken breast
  (optional for added protein)
- 2 cloves garlic, minced, 1 teaspoon grated ginger
- 1/4 cup chopped green onions
- Salt and pepper to taste, sesame seeds, for garnish
- Crushed red pepper flakes (optional, for heat)

Directions

1. Remove the leaves and stem from the cauliflower and cut it into florets. Place the cauliflower florets in a food processor and pulse until it resembles rice-sized pieces. Set aside.

2. In a small bowl, whisk together the low-sodium soy sauce and sesame oil. Set the sauce aside.

3. In a large skillet or wok, heat the olive oil over medium-high heat.

4. Add the diced mixed vegetables to the skillet and stir-fry for about 3-4 minutes, or until they begin to soften.

5. If using tofu or chicken, add it to the skillet and cook until it's lightly browned and cooked through, about 5-7 minutes.

6. Push the cooked vegetables (and protein if added) to one side of the skillet and add the minced garlic and grated ginger to the other side. Sauté for about 30 seconds, or until fragrant.

7. Add the cauliflower rice to the skillet and pour the sauce over it. Stir-fry for 3-4 minutes, or until the cauliflower rice is tender but still slightly crisp.

8. Stir in the chopped green onions and season with salt, pepper, and crushed red pepper flakes (if desired). Cook for an additional 1-2 minutes to heat everything through.

9. Garnish with sesame seeds.

Nutritional Information
(per serving, without added protein)

Calories	70	Dietary Fiber	3g
Protein	2g	Sodium	60mg
Carbohydrates	7g	Cholesterol	0mg
Total Fat	4g	Potassium	321mg
Saturated Fat	0,5g		

Brussels Sprouts with Pomegranate Seeds

Prep Time: 10 minutes / Cook Time: 20 minutes
Yield: 4 serving

Ingredients

- 1 pound Brussels sprouts, trimmed and halved
- 1 tablespoon olive oil, salt and pepper to taste
- 1/2 cup pomegranate seeds
- 1/4 cup chopped walnuts
- 1 tablespoon balsamic vinegar
- 1 teaspoon honey (optional)
- Fresh thyme leaves, for garnish

Directions

1. Preheat your oven to 400°F (200°C).

2. In a large mixing bowl, toss the Brussels sprouts with olive oil, salt, and pepper until they are evenly coated.

3. Spread the Brussels sprouts in a single layer on a baking sheet.

4. Roast in the preheated oven for about 15-20 minutes, or until the Brussels sprouts are tender and slightly crispy, stirring once or twice during cooking.

5. While the Brussels sprouts are roasting, in a small bowl, whisk together the balsamic vinegar and honey (if using).

6. Once the Brussels sprouts are done, transfer them to a serving platter.

7. Drizzle the balsamic vinegar mixture over the roasted Brussels sprouts.

8. Sprinkle with pomegranate seeds and chopped walnuts.

9. Garnish with fresh thyme leaves.

Nutritional Information

Calories	125	Dietary Fiber	5g
Protein	3g	Sodium	18mg
Carbohydrates	17g	Cholesterol	0mg
Total Fat	6g	Potassium	395mg
Saturated Fat	1g		

This heart-healthy Brussels Sprouts with Pomegranate Seeds recipe combines the earthy flavor of roasted Brussels sprouts with the sweetness of pomegranate seeds and the crunch of walnuts. Enjoy!

Zucchini Noodles with Pesto

Prep Time: 15 minutes / Cook Time: 5 minutes
Yield: 2 serving

Ingredients

- 4 medium zucchinis, spiralized into noodles
- 1 cup fresh basil leaves
- 1/4 cup grated Parmesan cheese
- 1/4 cup pine nuts, 2 cloves garlic
- 1/4 cup extra-virgin olive oil
- Juice of 1 lemon
- Salt and pepper to taste
- Cherry tomatoes, halved (for garnish)
- Fresh basil leaves (for garnish)

Directions

1. Place the spiralized zucchini noodles in a colander and sprinkle with a pinch of salt. Let them sit for about 10 minutes to release excess moisture. Then, gently squeeze out any excess liquid and set aside.

2. In a food processor, combine the fresh basil, grated Parmesan cheese, pine nuts, and garlic. Pulse until the ingredients are finely chopped.

3. With the food processor running, slowly drizzle in the extra-virgin olive oil until the pesto becomes smooth and well combined.

4. Add the lemon juice and continue to blend until incorporated. Season with salt and pepper to taste.

5. In a large skillet, heat a drizzle of olive oil over medium-high heat. Add the zucchini noodles and sauté for 2-3 minutes, or until they are just tender but still slightly crisp.

6. Remove the skillet from heat and add the prepared pesto. Toss the noodles until they are evenly coated with the pesto sauce.

7. Serve the Zucchini Noodles with Pesto garnished with halved cherry tomatoes and fresh basil leaves.

Nutritional Information (Approximate)

Calories	340	Dietary Fiber	4g
Protein	7g	Sodium	160mg
Carbohydrates	14g	Cholesterol	5mg
Total Fat	30g	Potassium	550mg
Saturated Fat	5g		

This heart-healthy Zucchini Noodles with Pesto recipe is a flavorful and low-carb alternative to traditional pasta dishes. Enjoy!

Roasted Beet and Citrus Salad

Prep Time: 15 minutes / Cook Time: 45 minutes
Yield: 4 serving

Ingredients

- 4 medium-sized beets, trimmed and peeled
- 2 oranges, segmented
- 2 grapefruits, segmented
- 1/4 red onion, thinly sliced
- 1/4 cup fresh mint leaves, chopped
- 1/4 cup chopped walnuts (optional)
- 2 tablespoons extra-virgin olive oil
- 1 tablespoon balsamic vinegar
- 1 teaspoon honey (optional)
- Salt and pepper to taste
- Crumbled goat cheese (optional, for garnish)

Directions

1. Preheat your oven to 400°F (200°C).

2. Wrap each beet individually in aluminum foil and place them on a baking sheet.

3. Roast the beets in the preheated oven for about 45 minutes, or until they are tender when pierced with a fork.

4. Remove the beets from the oven and let them cool. Once cooled, cut the beets into bite-sized pieces.

5. In a large salad bowl, combine the roasted beet pieces, orange segments, grapefruit segments, thinly sliced red onion, and chopped fresh mint.

6. If using, add the chopped walnuts to the salad.

7. In a small bowl, whisk together the extra-virgin olive oil, balsamic vinegar, and honey (if using). Season the dressing with salt and pepper to taste.

8. Drizzle the dressing over the salad and toss to combine.

9. If desired, garnish with crumbled goat cheese.

Nutritional Information
(per serving, without optional goat cheese and walnuts)

Calories	140	Dietary Fiber	5g
Protein	2g	Sodium	95mg
Carbohydrates	23g	Cholesterol	0mg
Total Fat	6g	Potassium	430mg
Saturated Fat	1g		

This heart-healthy Roasted Beet and Citrus Salad is a colorful and refreshing dish that's perfect for any season. Enjoy the combination of earthy beets with the bright, citrusy flavors!

Sweet Potato and Black Bean Chili

Prep Time: 15 minutes / Cook Time: 30 minutes
Yield: 6 serving

Ingredients

- 1 tablespoon olive oil, 1 onion, chopped
- 2 cloves garlic, minced
- 2 medium sweet potatoes, peeled and diced
- 1 red bell pepper, diced, 1 green bell pepper, diced
- 1 (15-ounce) can black beans, drained and rinsed
- 1 (15-ounce) can diced tomatoes, undrained
- 3 cups low-sodium vegetable broth
- 2 teaspoons chili powder, 1 teaspoon ground cumin
- 1/2 teaspoon smoked paprika, salt and pepper to taste
- 1 cup frozen corn kernels, juice of 1 lime
- Fresh cilantro leaves, for garnish, avocado slices, for garnish

Directions

1. In a large pot, heat the olive oil over medium heat. Add the chopped onion and sauté for 3-4 minutes, or until it becomes translucent.

2. Add the minced garlic, diced sweet potatoes, red bell pepper, and green bell pepper to the pot. Sauté for about 5 minutes, stirring occasionally.

3. Stir in the black beans, diced tomatoes, low-sodium vegetable broth, chili powder, ground cumin, smoked paprika, salt, and pepper.

4. Bring the mixture to a boil, then reduce the heat to low, cover, and simmer for 15-20 minutes, or until the sweet potatoes are tender.

5. Add the frozen corn kernels to the chili and cook for an additional 5 minutes.

6. Remove the pot from heat and stir in the lime juice.

7. Serve the Sweet Potato and Black Bean Chili hot, garnished with fresh cilantro leaves and avocado slices.

Nutritional Information

Calories	210	Dietary Fiber	8g
Protein	6g	Sodium	470mg
Carbohydrates	41g	Cholesterol	0mg
Total Fat	3g	Potassium	694mg
Saturated Fat	0,5g		

This heart-healthy Sweet Potato and Black Bean Chili is a flavorful and nutritious dish that's perfect for a satisfying and warming meal. Enjoy!

Asparagus and Lemon Risotto

Prep Time: 10 minutes / Cook Time: 25 minutes
Yield: 4 serving

Ingredients

- 1 bunch (about 1 pound) asparagus, trimmed and cut into bite-sized pieces
- 4 cups low-sodium vegetable broth
- 1 small onion, finely chopped
- 2 cloves garlic, minced, 1 lemon, zest and juice
- 1/2 cup dry white wine (optional)
- 2 tablespoons olive oil, 1 cup Arborio rice
- 2 tablespoons grated Parmesan cheese
- Salt and pepper to taste
- Fresh parsley, chopped (for garnish)

Directions

1. In a medium saucepan, bring the vegetable broth to a simmer. Reduce the heat to low and keep it warm.

2. In a large skillet, heat the olive oil over medium heat. Add the chopped onion and sauté for 3-4 minutes until it becomes translucent.

3. Add the minced garlic and Arborio rice to the skillet. Sauté for another 2-3 minutes, stirring constantly until the rice is lightly toasted.

4. If using wine, pour it into the skillet and cook until it's mostly absorbed by the rice, stirring frequently.

5. Begin adding the warm vegetable broth to the rice mixture one ladle at a time, stirring constantly. Allow the liquid to be mostly absorbed before adding more broth. Continue this process until the rice is creamy and cooked to your desired level of doneness, usually about 18-20 minutes.

6. In the last 5 minutes of cooking, add the asparagus pieces to the risotto. They will cook with the residual heat.

7. Stir in the lemon zest and juice, grated Parmesan cheese, salt, and pepper. Adjust the seasoning to taste.

8. Serve the Asparagus and Lemon Risotto hot, garnished with chopped fresh parsley.

Nutritional Information

Calories	285	Dietary Fiber	4g
Protein	6g	Sodium	420mg
Carbohydrates	48g	Cholesterol	1mg
Total Fat	6g	Potassium	365mg
Saturated Fat	1g		

This heart-healthy Asparagus and Lemon Risotto is a creamy and zesty dish that's perfect for springtime or any time you want a comforting meal. Enjoy!

Baked Eggplant Parmesan

Prep Time: 20 minutes / Cook Time: 40 minutes
Yield: 4 serving

Ingredients

- 2 large eggplants, peeled and sliced into 1/2-inch thick rounds
- 1 1/2 cups whole-wheat breadcrumbs
- 1 cup grated Parmesan cheese
- 1 1/2 cups low-sodium marinara sauce
- 2 cups part-skim mozzarella cheese, shredded
- 1/4 cup fresh basil leaves, chopped
- 2 tablespoons olive oil, 2 eggs
- 1 teaspoon dried oregano
- Salt and pepper to taste, cooking spray

Directions

1. Preheat your oven to 375°F (190°C). Line a baking sheet with parchment paper and lightly grease it with cooking spray.

2. In a shallow dish, combine the whole-wheat breadcrumbs, grated Parmesan cheese, dried oregano, salt, and pepper.

3. In another shallow dish, beat the eggs.

4. Dip each eggplant slice first into the beaten eggs and then into the breadcrumb mixture, pressing the breadcrumbs onto both sides of the eggplant to adhere.

5. Place the breaded eggplant slices on the prepared baking sheet in a single layer.

6. Drizzle olive oil over the tops of the breaded eggplant slices.

7. Bake in the preheated oven for 20-25 minutes, or until the eggplant is tender and the breadcrumbs are golden brown.

8. In a separate saucepan, heat the low-sodium marinara sauce over low heat.

9. In a 9x13-inch baking dish, spread a thin layer of the marinara sauce.

10. Arrange half of the baked eggplant slices over the sauce.

11. Sprinkle half of the shredded mozzarella cheese and half of the chopped fresh basil over the eggplant.

12. Repeat with another layer of marinara sauce, remaining eggplant slices, mozzarella cheese, and fresh basil.

13. Bake in the oven for an additional 15-20 minutes, or until the cheese is melted and bubbly.

14. Serve the Baked Eggplant Parmesan hot and enjoy!

Nutritional Information

Calories	350	Dietary Fiber	10g
Protein	18g	Sodium	60mg
Carbohydrates	37g	Cholesterol	0mg
Total Fat	15g	Potassium	874mg
Saturated Fat	7g		

Cucumber Avocado Gazpacho

Prep Time: 15 minutes / Cook Time: 0 minutes
Yield: 4 serving

Ingredients

- 3 cucumbers, peeled, seeded, and chopped
- 2 ripe avocados, peeled and pitted
- 2 cloves garlic, minced
- 1/2 red onion, chopped
- 1/4 cup fresh cilantro leaves
- 1/4 cup fresh mint leaves
- 2 cups low-sodium vegetable broth
- 2 tablespoons fresh lime juice
- Salt and pepper to taste
- Greek yogurt or sour cream (optional, for garnish)
- Fresh cilantro leaves (for garnish)

Directions

1. In a blender or food processor, combine the chopped cucumbers, ripe avocados, minced garlic, chopped red onion, fresh cilantro leaves, and fresh mint leaves.

2. Add the low-sodium vegetable broth and fresh lime juice to the blender.

3. Blend the mixture until it's smooth and creamy. You may need to do this in batches depending on the size of your blender.

4. Season the Cucumber Avocado Gazpacho with salt and pepper to taste. Blend briefly to incorporate the seasoning.

5. If the gazpacho is too thick for your liking, you can add a bit more vegetable broth and blend until you reach your desired consistency.

6. Chill the gazpacho in the refrigerator for at least 2 hours before serving to allow the flavors to meld.

7. Serve the Cucumber Avocado Gazpacho cold, garnished with a dollop of Greek yogurt or sour cream (if desired) and fresh cilantro leaves.

Nutritional Information
(per serving, without optional garnishes)

Calories	180	Dietary Fiber	7g
Protein	4g	Sodium	150mg
Carbohydrates	17g	Cholesterol	0mg
Total Fat	13g	Potassium	740mg
Saturated Fat	2g		

This heart-healthy Cucumber Avocado Gazpacho is a refreshing and creamy chilled soup thats perfect for a light and nutritious meal. Enjoy the cool and vibrant flavors!

Garlic Roasted Broccoli

Prep Time: 10 minutes / Cook Time: 20 minutes
Yield: 4 serving

Ingredients

- 2 bunches of fresh broccoli, cut into florets
- 4 cloves garlic, minced, 2 tablespoons olive oil
- Salt and pepper to taste, 1 lemon, zested and juiced
- Grated Parmesan cheese (optional, for garnish)

Directions

1. Preheat your oven to 425°F (220°C). Line a baking sheet with parchment paper.

2. In a large bowl, toss the broccoli florets with minced garlic and olive oil until they are evenly coated.

3. Spread the broccoli in a single layer on the prepared baking sheet.

4. Season the broccoli with salt and pepper to taste.

5. Roast the broccoli in the preheated oven for about 15-20 minutes, or until it becomes tender and slightly crispy, stirring once or twice during cooking.

6. Remove the roasted broccoli from the oven and immediately drizzle with lemon juice and zest.

7. If desired, garnish with grated Parmesan cheese.

Nutritional Information
(per serving, without optional Parmesan cheese)

Calories	80	Dietary Fiber	3g
Protein	3g	Sodium	40mg
Carbohydrates	9g	Cholesterol	0mg
Total Fat	5g	Potassium	350mg
Saturated Fat	1g		

Rainbow Chard with Garlic and Pine Nuts

Prep Time: 10 minutes / Cook Time: 10 minutes
Yield: 4 serving

Ingredients

- 1 bunch rainbow chard, stems and leaves separated and chopped
- 2 tablespoons olive oil, 2 cloves garlic, minced
- 1/4 cup pine nuts, salt and pepper to taste
- Red pepper flakes (optional, for heat)
- Lemon wedges (for garnish)

Directions

1. Heat the olive oil in a large skillet over medium heat.

2. Add the minced garlic and cook for about 1 minute, or until fragrant.

3. Stir in the chopped rainbow chard stems and sauté for 2-3 minutes, or until they begin to soften.

4. Add the rainbow chard leaves to the skillet and sauté for another 2-3 minutes, or until they wilt and become tender.

5. Stir in the pine nuts and cook for an additional 2 minutes, or until they are lightly toasted.

6. Season the rainbow chard with salt, pepper, and red pepper flakes (if desired). Toss to combine.

7. Serve the Rainbow Chard with Garlic and Pine Nuts hot, garnished with lemon wedges for an extra burst of flavor.

Nutritional Information (Approximate)

Calories	110	Dietary Fiber	2g
Protein	3g	Sodium	170mg
Carbohydrates	5g	Cholesterol	0mg
Total Fat	9g	Potassium	395mg
Saturated Fat	1g		

Sautéed Spinach with Garlic and Lemon

Prep Time: 5 minutes / Cook Time: 5 minutes / Yield: 4 serving

Ingredients

- 1 pound fresh spinach leaves, washed and trimmed
- 2 cloves garlic, minced, 2 tablespoons olive oil
- Zest and juice of 1 lemon
- Salt and pepper to taste
- Red pepper flakes (optional, for heat)

Nutritional Information

Calories	700	Dietary Fiber	2g
Protein	3g	Sodium	60mg
Carbohydrates	4g	Cholesterol	0mg
Total Fat	6g	Potassium	470mg
Saturated Fat	1g		

Directions

1. In a large skillet, heat the olive oil over medium heat.

2. Add the minced garlic to the skillet and sauté for about 30 seconds, or until it becomes fragrant but not browned.

3. Add the fresh spinach leaves to the skillet. You may need to do this in batches, as spinach cooks down quickly.

4. Sauté the spinach for 2-3 minutes, tossing it gently with tongs, until it wilts and becomes tender.

5. Remove the skillet from heat and immediately drizzle with lemon juice and zest.

6. Season the Sautéed Spinach with Garlic and Lemon with salt, pepper, and red pepper flakes (if desired). Toss to combine.

7. Serve the sautéed spinach hot, as a nutritious side dish.

Spaghetti Squash with Tomato and Basil Sauce

Prep Time: 15 minutes / Cook Time: 45 minutes
Yield: 4 serving

Ingredients

- 2 medium spaghetti squash, 2 tablespoons olive oil
- 1 small onion, finely chopped
- 2 cloves garlic, minced, salt and pepper to taste
- 1 (28-ounce) can crushed tomatoes
- 1/4 cup fresh basil leaves, chopped
- Grated Parmesan cheese (optional, for garnish)

Directions

1. Preheat your oven to 375°F (190°C).

2. Carefully cut the spaghetti squash in half lengthwise. Scoop out the seeds and pulp from the center using a spoon.

3. Brush the inside of each squash half with olive oil and season with salt and pepper.

4. Place the squash halves, cut side down, on a baking sheet lined with parchment paper.

5. Roast the spaghetti squash in the preheated oven for 35-45 minutes, or until the flesh is tender and easily shreds into strands with a fork.

6. While the squash is roasting, prepare the tomato and basil sauce. In a saucepan, heat the remaining olive oil over medium heat. Add the chopped onion and sauté for 3-4 minutes, or until it becomes translucent.

7. Stir in the minced garlic and cook for an additional 30 seconds, until fragrant.

8. Add the crushed tomatoes to the saucepan and bring the mixture to a simmer. Allow it to cook for about 15 minutes, stirring occasionally.

9. Stir in the chopped fresh basil and season the sauce with salt and pepper to taste. Simmer for another 5 minutes to allow the flavors to meld.

10. Once the spaghetti squash is done roasting, use a fork to scrape the flesh into strands.

11. Serve the spaghetti squash topped with the tomato and basil sauce. If desired, garnish with grated Parmesan cheese.

Nutritional Information
(per serving, without optional Parmesan cheese)

Calories	120	Dietary Fiber	4g
Protein	2g	Sodium	340mg
Carbohydrates	19g	Cholesterol	0mg
Total Fat	5g	Potassium	500mg
Saturated Fat	1g		

This heart-healthy Spaghetti Squash with Tomato and Basil Sauce is a low-carb and satisfying alternative to traditional pasta. Enjoy the natural sweetness of the squash paired with the bright flavors of the tomato and basil sauce!

Green Bean Almondine

Prep Time: 10 minutes / Cook Time: 10 minutes
Yield: 4 serving

Ingredients

- 1 pound fresh green beans, ends trimmed
- 2 tablespoons unsalted butter
- 2 cloves garlic, minced
- 1/4 cup sliced almonds
- 1 tablespoon lemon juice
- Zest of 1 lemon, salt and pepper to taste
- Fresh parsley leaves (optional, for garnish)

Directions

1. Bring a large pot of salted water to a boil. Add the green beans and cook for 3-4 minutes, or until they are bright green and crisp-tender. Drain and immediately transfer the green beans to a bowl of ice water to stop the cooking process. Drain again and set aside.

2. In a large skillet, melt the unsalted butter over medium heat.

3. Add the minced garlic to the skillet and sauté for about 1 minute, or until it becomes fragrant.

4. Stir in the sliced almonds and cook for another 2-3 minutes, or until they are lightly toasted and the butter turns a golden brown color.

5. Add the blanched green beans to the skillet and toss to coat them in the garlic-butter mixture. Cook for an additional 2-3 minutes, or until the green beans are heated through.

6. Drizzle the green beans with lemon juice and sprinkle with lemon zest. Season with salt and pepper to taste. Toss to combine.

7. Serve the Green Bean Almondine hot, garnished with fresh parsley leaves (if desired).

Nutritional Information

Calories	120	Dietary Fiber	3g
Protein	2g	Sodium	15mg
Carbohydrates	7g	Cholesterol	15mg
Total Fat	10g	Potassium	180mg
Saturated Fat	4g		

This heart-healthy Green Bean Almondine is a classic side dish with a delightful combination of tender-crisp green beans, toasty almonds, and zesty lemon. Enjoy the vibrant flavors!

Stuffed Acorn Squash with Quinoa and Cranberries

Prep Time: 20 minutes / Cook Time: 45 minutes
Yield: 4 serving

Ingredients

- 2 acorn squash, halved and seeds removed
- 1 cup quinoa, rinsed, 2 cups vegetable broth
- 1/2 cup dried cranberries, 1/2 cup chopped pecans
- 1/2 cup chopped fresh parsley
- 2 tablespoons olive oil, 2 cloves garlic, minced
- 1 small onion, finely chopped
- 1 teaspoon ground cinnamon
- salt and pepper to taste
- Fresh sage leaves (optional, for garnish)

Directions

1. Preheat your oven to 375°F (190°C).

2. Place the acorn squash halves, cut side down, on a baking sheet. Bake in the preheated oven for 30-35 minutes, or until the squash is tender when pierced with a fork.

3. While the squash is baking, rinse the quinoa under cold water in a fine-mesh strainer.

4. In a medium saucepan, combine the rinsed quinoa and vegetable broth. Bring to a boil, then reduce the heat to low, cover, and simmer for 15 minutes, or until the quinoa is cooked and the liquid is absorbed. Remove from heat.

5. In a large skillet, heat the olive oil over medium heat. Add the finely chopped onion and sauté for about 3-4 minutes, or until it becomes translucent.

6. Stir in the minced garlic and ground cinnamon and cook for an additional 30 seconds, until fragrant.

7. Add the cooked quinoa, dried cranberries, chopped pecans, and chopped fresh parsley to the skillet. Season with salt and pepper to taste. Stir to combine and cook for 2-3 minutes to heat through.

8. Once the acorn squash halves are done baking, remove them from the oven and carefully turn them over.

9. Fill each acorn squash half with the quinoa and cranberry stuffing, pressing it down gently.

10. Return the stuffed acorn squash halves to the oven and bake for an additional 10 minutes to heat the stuffing through.

11. Serve the Stuffed Acorn Squash with Quinoa and Cranberries hot, garnished with fresh sage leaves if desired.

Nutritional Information

Calories	440	Dietary Fiber	10g
Protein	9g	Sodium	390mg
Carbohydrates	76g	Cholesterol	0mg
Total Fat	15g	Potassium	1220mg
Saturated Fat	2g		

Creamy Cauliflower and Leek Soup

Prep Time: 15 minutes / Cook Time: 25 minutes
Yield: 4 serving

Ingredients

- 1 large cauliflower head, chopped into florets
- 2 leeks, white and light green parts only, sliced
- 2 cloves garlic, minced, 1 tablespoon olive oil
- 4 cups low-sodium vegetable broth
- 1 cup unsweetened almond milk
  (or any unsweetened plant-based milk)
- Salt and pepper to taste
- Fresh chives or parsley (optional, for garnish)

Directions

1. In a large pot, heat the olive oil over medium heat.

2. Add the sliced leeks and minced garlic to the pot. Sauté for 3-4 minutes, or until the leeks become soft and fragrant.

3. Add the cauliflower florets to the pot and sauté for another 2-3 minutes, coating them in the leek and garlic mixture.

4. Pour in the low-sodium vegetable broth, ensuring that it covers the cauliflower and leeks. If necessary, add more broth or water to cover.

5. Bring the mixture to a boil, then reduce the heat to low, cover, and simmer for about 15-20 minutes, or until the cauliflower is tender when pierced with a fork.

6. Use an immersion blender or regular blender to puree the soup until smooth. If using a regular blender, be sure to allow the mixture to cool slightly before blending, and blend in batches if needed.

7. Return the pureed soup to the pot and stir in the unsweetened almond milk. Heat the soup over low heat for an additional 5 minutes, stirring occasionally.

8. Season the Creamy Cauliflower and Leek Soup with salt and pepper to taste.

9. Serve the soup hot, garnished with fresh chives or parsley if desired.

Nutritional Information

Calories	1100	Dietary Fiber	5g
Protein	4g	Sodium	270mg
Carbohydrates	18g	Cholesterol	0mg
Total Fat	3g	Potassium	710mg
Saturated Fat	0g		

This heart-healthy Creamy Cauliflower and Leek Soup is a comforting and velvety soup with a mild, nutty flavor. It's perfect for a cozy and nutritious meal. Enjoy!

chapter 11
DIABETIC MAINS

Grilled Lemon Herb Chicken Breast 88

Baked Salmon with Dill and Asparagus 88

Quinoa & Black Bean Stuffed Bell Peppers ... 89

Turkey & Vegetable Stir-Fry 89

Baked Cod with Mediterranean Salsa 90

Lentil & Vegetable Curry 90

Spinach & Feta Stuffed Chicken Breast 91

Zucchini Noodles
with Pesto & Cherry Tomatoes 91

Grilled Shrimp & Vegetable Skewers 92

Stuffed Acorn Squash
with Quinoa & Cranberries 92

Chickpea & Spinach Curry 93

Balsamic Glazed Chicken Thighs 93

Broiled Tilapia with Mango Salsa 94

Cauliflower Fried Rice with Tofu 94

Grilled Portobello Mushrooms
with Balsamic Reduction 95

Lemon Garlic Shrimp with Quinoa 95

Tofu and Vegetable Stir-Fry
with Ginger Sauce 96

Mediterranean Chickpea Salad
with Grilled Chicken 96

Baked Eggplant Parmesan 97

Spaghetti Squash with Turkey Meatballs 97

Grilled Lemon Herb Chicken Breast

Prep Time: 10 minutes / Cook Time: 15 minutes
Yield: 2 serving

Ingredients

- 2 boneless, skinless chicken breasts
- 2 tablespoons olive oil, 2 cloves garlic, minced
- Zest of 1 lemon, juice of 1 lemon
- 1 teaspoon dried oregano
- 1 teaspoon dried thyme
- Salt and pepper to taste
- Lemon slices for garnish (optional)
- Fresh herbs (e.g., parsley or basil) for garnish (optional)

Directions

1. In a small bowl, combine the olive oil, minced garlic, lemon zest, lemon juice, dried oregano, dried thyme, salt, and pepper. This will be your marinade.

2. Place the chicken breasts in a resealable plastic bag or a shallow dish. Pour the marinade over the chicken, making sure it's well coated. Seal the bag or cover the dish and refrigerate for at least 30 minutes, allowing the chicken to marinate.

3. Preheat your grill to medium-high heat. Make sure the grates are clean and lightly oiled to prevent sticking.

4. Remove the chicken from the marinade, allowing any excess to drip off. Discard the marinade.

5. Grill the chicken breasts for about 6-7 minutes per side, or until the internal temperature reaches 165°F (74°C) and the chicken is no longer pink in the center. Cooking times may vary depending on the thickness of your chicken breasts.

6. Once done, remove the chicken from the grill and let it rest for a few minutes before slicing.

7. Garnish with lemon slices and fresh herbs if desired.

Nutritional Information

Calories	250	Dietary Fiber	1g
Protein	25g	Sodium	330mg
Carbohydrates	70g	Cholesterol	70mg
Total Fat	16g	Potassium	330mg
Saturated Fat	3g		

Enjoy your heart-healthy Grilled Lemon Herb Chicken Breast! This dish is low in carbohydrates and saturated fat, making it suitable for a diabetic diet while promoting heart health.

Baked Salmon with Dill and Asparagus

Prep Time: 10 minutes / Cook Time: 15 minutes
Yield: 2 serving

Ingredients

- 2 salmon fillets (6-8 ounces each)
- 1 bunch of asparagus, trimmed
- 2 tablespoons olive oil, 2 cloves garlic, minced
- 1 tablespoon fresh dill, chopped
- 1 lemon, thinly sliced, salt and pepper to taste
- Lemon wedges and additional dill for garnish (optional)

Directions

1. Preheat your oven to 375°F (190°C).

2. Place the trimmed asparagus on a baking sheet and drizzle with 1 tablespoon of olive oil. Season with salt and pepper, and toss to coat evenly.

3. In a small bowl, mix the minced garlic and chopped dill with the remaining 1 tablespoon of olive oil.

4. Season the salmon fillets with salt and pepper. Place them skin-side down on the baking sheet with the asparagus.

5. Brush the salmon fillets with the garlic and dill oil mixture, ensuring they are evenly coated.

6. Arrange lemon slices on top of the salmon fillets for extra flavor.

7. Bake in the preheated oven for about 12-15 minutes or until the salmon flakes easily with a fork and reaches an internal temperature of 145°F (63°C).

8. Once done, remove from the oven and let it rest for a minute.

9. Garnish with lemon wedges and additional fresh dill if desired.

Nutritional Information

Calories	350	Dietary Fiber	3g
Protein	30g	Sodium	80mg
Carbohydrates	8g	Cholesterol	80mg
Total Fat	22g	Potassium	680mg
Saturated Fat	3g		

Enjoy your heart-healthy Baked Salmon with Dill and Asparagus! This dish is rich in omega-3 fatty acids from the salmon and provides a good amount of fiber and antioxidants from the asparagus. It's a delicious and nutritious choice for those with diabetes and those looking to support heart health.

Quinoa and Black Bean Stuffed Bell Peppers

Prep Time: 15 minutes / Cook Time: 30 minutes
Yield: 4 serving

Ingredients

- 4 large bell peppers, any color
- 1 cup quinoa, rinsed and drained
- 2 cups vegetable broth (low sodium)
- 1 can (15 ounces) black beans, drained and rinsed
- 1 cup corn kernels (fresh, frozen, or canned)
- 1 cup diced tomatoes (canned or fresh)
- 1 teaspoon chili powder, 1/2 teaspoon cumin
- 1/2 teaspoon paprika, salt and pepper to taste
- 1 cup shredded low-fat cheese (optional)
- Chopped fresh cilantro for garnish (optional)

Directions

1. Preheat your oven to 375°F (190°C).

2. Cut the tops off the bell peppers and remove the seeds and membranes. Set them aside.

3. In a medium-sized saucepan, combine the quinoa and vegetable broth. Bring to a boil, then reduce heat to low, cover, and simmer for about 15 minutes, or until the quinoa is cooked and the liquid is absorbed.

4. In a large bowl, combine the cooked quinoa, black beans, corn, diced tomatoes, chili powder, cumin, paprika, salt, and pepper. Mix until well combined.

5. Stuff each bell pepper with the quinoa and black bean mixture, pressing it down gently to pack the filling.

6. Place the stuffed bell peppers in a baking dish and cover with aluminum foil.

7. Bake in the preheated oven for 20-25 minutes, or until the peppers are tender.

8. If using cheese, remove the foil, sprinkle the shredded cheese on top of each stuffed pepper, and return them to the oven for an additional 5 minutes, or until the cheese is melted and bubbly.

9. Garnish with chopped cilantro if desired.

Nutritional Information (per serving without cheese)

Calories	280	Dietary Fiber	11g
Protein	10g	Sodium	290mg
Carbohydrates	54g	Cholesterol	0mg
Total Fat	3g	Potassium	710mg
Saturated Fat	0g		

Enjoy your heart-healthy Quinoa and Black Bean Stuffed Bell Peppers! This dish is packed with fiber, protein, and essential nutrients, making it an excellent choice for a diabetic and heart-healthy meal.

Turkey and Vegetable Stir-Fry

Prep Time: 15 minutes / Cook Time: 15 minutes
Yield: 4 serving

Ingredients

- 1 pound lean ground turkey
- 2 tablespoons low-sodium soy sauce
- 2 cloves garlic, minced, 1 teaspoon sesame oil
- 1 tablespoon hoisin sauce
- 1 teaspoon fresh ginger, minced
- 1 red bell pepper, thinly sliced
- 1 yellow bell pepper, thinly sliced
- 1 cup broccoli florets, 1 cup snow peas, trimmed
- 1 cup sliced carrots, 1 tablespoon cornstarch
- 2 tablespoons water, cooking spray
- Sesame seeds for garnish (optional)
- Sliced green onions for garnish (optional)

Directions

1. In a small bowl, whisk together the soy sauce, hoisin sauce, and sesame oil. Set aside.

2. In a large skillet or wok, heat a little cooking spray over medium-high heat. Add the ground turkey and cook, breaking it into crumbles, until browned and cooked through. Remove the turkey from the skillet and set it aside.

3. In the same skillet, add a bit more cooking spray if needed. Add the minced garlic and ginger and stir-fry for about 30 seconds until fragrant.

4. Add the sliced bell peppers, broccoli florets, snow peas, and carrots to the skillet. Stir-fry for about 4-5 minutes or until the vegetables are crisp-tender.

5. In a small bowl, mix the cornstarch and water until smooth to create a slurry.

6. Return the cooked turkey to the skillet with the vegetables. Pour the soy sauce mixture over everything and stir well.

7. Pour the cornstarch slurry into the skillet and continue to stir-fry for another 2-3 minutes, or until the sauce thickens and coats the turkey and vegetables.

8. Serve hot, garnished with sesame seeds and sliced green onions if desired.

Nutritional Information

Calories	280	Dietary Fiber	4g
Protein	25g	Sodium	480mg
Carbohydrates	18g	Cholesterol	60mg
Total Fat	12g	Potassium	590mg
Saturated Fat	2,5g		

Baked Cod with Mediterranean Salsa

Prep Time: 15 minutes / Cook Time: 20 minutes
Yield: 2 serving

Ingredients

For the Baked Cod:
- 2 cod fillets (6-8 ounces each)
- 1 tablespoon olive oil
- 1 teaspoon dried oregano
- 1 teaspoon dried thyme
- Salt and pepper to taste
- Lemon wedges for garnish (optional)

For the Mediterranean Salsa:
- 1 cup diced tomatoes
- 1/2 cup diced cucumber
- 1/4 cup diced red onion
- 1/4 cup chopped fresh parsley
- 2 tablespoons kalamata olives, chopped
- 1 tablespoon extra-virgin olive oil
- 1 tablespoon balsamic vinegar
- 1 clove garlic, minced, salt and pepper to taste

Directions

1. Preheat your oven to 375°F (190°C).

2. Place the cod fillets on a baking sheet lined with parchment paper or lightly greased.

3. Drizzle the cod fillets with olive oil and season them with dried oregano, dried thyme, salt, and pepper.

4. Bake the cod in the preheated oven for about 15-20 minutes, or until it flakes easily with a fork and reaches an internal temperature of 145°F (63°C).

5. While the cod is baking, prepare the Mediterranean salsa. In a bowl, combine the diced tomatoes, diced cucumber, red onion, chopped parsley, chopped kalamata olives, extra-virgin olive oil, balsamic vinegar, minced garlic, salt, and pepper. Mix well.

6. Once the cod is done, remove it from the oven and let it rest for a minute.

7. Serve the baked cod with a generous spoonful of Mediterranean salsa on top. Garnish with lemon wedges if desired.

Nutritional Information

Calories	250	Dietary Fiber	3g
Protein	30g	Sodium	350mg
Carbohydrates	10g	Cholesterol	60mg
Total Fat	10g	Potassium	630mg
Saturated Fat	1,5g		

Lentil and Vegetable Curry

Prep Time: 15 minutes / Cook Time: 30 minutes
Yield: 4 serving

Ingredients

- 1 cup dried green or brown lentils, rinsed and drained
- 2 cups vegetable broth (low sodium)
- 1 tablespoon olive oil, 2 tablespoons curry powder
- 1 onion, finely chopped, 2 cloves garlic, minced
- 1 tablespoon fresh ginger, minced
- 1 cup diced zucchini, 1 cup chopped spinach or kale
- 1 cup diced bell peppers (any color)
- 1 teaspoon ground coriander, 1 teaspoon turmeric
- 1 cup diced carrots, salt and pepper to taste
- 1 can (14 ounces) diced tomatoes (no salt added)
- Fresh cilantro for garnish (optional),
  plain yogurt for garnish (optional)

Directions

1. In a medium-sized saucepan, combine the rinsed lentils and vegetable broth. Bring to a boil, then reduce heat to low, cover, and simmer for about 15-20 minutes, or until the lentils are tender but not mushy. Drain any excess liquid.

2. While the lentils are cooking, heat olive oil in a large skillet over medium heat. Add the chopped onion and sauté for 3-4 minutes, or until it becomes translucent.

3. Add minced garlic and ginger to the skillet, and cook for another 1-2 minutes until fragrant.

4. Stir in the curry powder, ground cumin, ground coriander, and turmeric. Cook for an additional 2 minutes to toast the spices.

5. Add the diced tomatoes (with their juices) to the skillet and mix well.

6. Add the diced carrots, bell peppers, and zucchini to the skillet. Cook for 5-7 minutes, or until the vegetables start to soften.

7. Add the cooked lentils and chopped spinach or kale to the skillet. Stir to combine everything.

8. Simmer the mixture for an additional 5-7 minutes, or until the vegetables are tender and the flavors are well blended. Season with salt and pepper to taste.

9. Serve hot, garnished with fresh cilantro and a dollop of plain yogurt if desired.

Nutritional Information

Calories	280	Dietary Fiber	15g
Protein	15g	Sodium	450mg
Carbohydrates	50g	Cholesterol	0mg
Total Fat	3,5g	Potassium	800mg
Saturated Fat	0,5g		

Spinach and Feta Stuffed Chicken Breast

Prep Time: 15 minutes / Cook Time: 25 minutes
Yield: 2 serving

Ingredients

- 2 boneless, skinless chicken breasts
- 2 cups fresh spinach, chopped
- 2 cloves garlic, minced, 1/4 cup plain Greek yogurt
- 1/2 cup crumbled feta cheese
- 1/4 teaspoon dried oregano
- Salt and pepper to taste, 1 tablespoon olive oil
- Lemon wedges for garnish (optional)
- Fresh parsley for garnish (optional)

Directions

1. Preheat your oven to 375°F (190°C).

2. In a mixing bowl, combine the chopped spinach, crumbled feta cheese, minced garlic, Greek yogurt, dried oregano, salt, and pepper. Mix well to create the stuffing mixture.

3. Carefully slice a pocket into the side of each chicken breast, being careful not to cut all the way through.

4. Stuff each chicken breast with the spinach and feta mixture, dividing it evenly between the two breasts. Secure the pockets with toothpicks if needed.

5. Season the outside of the chicken breasts with a little more salt and pepper.

6. In an oven-safe skillet, heat the olive oil over medium-high heat. Once hot, add the stuffed chicken breasts to the skillet and sear for 2-3 minutes on each side until they are golden brown.

7. Transfer the skillet to the preheated oven and bake for about 18-20 minutes, or until the chicken is cooked through, and the internal temperature reaches 165°F (74°C).

8. Remove the chicken from the oven and let it rest for a few minutes.

9. Serve hot, garnished with lemon wedges and fresh parsley if desired.

Nutritional Information

Calories	330	Dietary Fiber	1g
Protein	44g	Sodium	300mg
Carbohydrates	135g	Cholesterol	470mg
Total Fat	14g	Potassium	530mg
Saturated Fat	5g		

Enjoy your heart-healthy Spinach and Feta Stuffed Chicken Breast! This dish is packed with protein and low in carbohydrates, making it suitable for those managing diabetes while providing heart-healthy ingredients like spinach and lean chicken breast.

Zucchini Noodles with Pesto and Cherry Tomatoes

Prep Time: 15 minutes / Cook Time: 5 minutes
Yield: 2 serving

Ingredients

- 4 medium-sized zucchinis, spiralized into noodles
- 1 cup cherry tomatoes, halved
- 1/4 cup fresh basil leaves, chopped
- 1/4 cup grated Parmesan cheese (optional)
- 2 tablespoons pine nuts (optional)
- Salt and pepper to taste

For the Pesto:
- 2 cups fresh basil leaves, 1/2 cup extra-virgin olive oil
- 1/4 cup grated Parmesan cheese (optional)
- 1/4 cup pine nuts, 2 cloves garlic, juice of 1 lemon
- Salt and pepper to taste

Directions

Make the Pesto:

1. In a food processor, combine the fresh basil leaves, extra-virgin olive oil, grated Parmesan cheese (if using), pine nuts, garlic cloves, lemon juice, salt, and pepper.

2. Pulse until all ingredients are well blended and the pesto reaches your desired consistency. Set aside.

Prepare the Zucchini Noodles:

3. Spiralize the zucchini into noodles using a spiralizer. If you don't have a spiralizer, you can use a vegetable peeler to create thin strips resembling noodles.

4. Heat a large skillet over medium-high heat. Add the zucchini noodles to the skillet and sauté for 2-3 minutes, just until they begin to soften.

5. Add the cherry tomato halves to the skillet and cook for an additional 2 minutes, or until the tomatoes start to blister.

6. Remove the skillet from heat and stir in the chopped basil leaves.

7. Toss the zucchini noodles and cherry tomatoes with the prepared pesto until well coated. Season with salt and pepper to taste.

8. Serve hot, garnished with grated Parmesan cheese and pine nuts if desired.

Nutritional Information
(without optional Parmesan cheese and pine nuts)

Calories	210	Dietary Fiber	4g
Protein	6g	Sodium	80mg
Carbohydrates	14g	Cholesterol	0mg
Total Fat	17g	Potassium	660mg
Saturated Fat	2,5g		

Grilled Shrimp and Vegetable Skewers

Prep Time: 20 minutes / Cook Time: 10 minutes
Yield: 4 serving

Ingredients

- 1 pound large shrimp, peeled and deveined
- 2 red bell peppers, cut into chunks
- 2 zucchinis, sliced into rounds
- 1 red onion, cut into chunks
- 1 cup cherry tomatoes, 2 tablespoons olive oil
- 2 cloves garlic, minced
- 1 tablespoon fresh lemon juice
- 1 teaspoon dried oregano, salt and pepper to taste
- Wooden skewers, soaked in water for 30 minutes
- Lemon wedges for garnish (optional)
- Fresh parsley for garnish (optional)

Directions

1. In a large bowl, combine the olive oil, minced garlic, fresh lemon juice, dried oregano, salt, and pepper. This will be your marinade.

2. Add the peeled and deveined shrimp to the marinade. Toss to coat the shrimp evenly, then cover and refrigerate for 15-20 minutes to marinate.

3. Preheat your grill to medium-high heat.

4. Thread the marinated shrimp, red bell peppers, zucchini slices, red onion chunks, and cherry tomatoes onto the soaked wooden skewers, alternating between shrimp and vegetables.

5. Place the skewers on the preheated grill and cook for about 2-3 minutes per side, or until the shrimp turn pink and opaque and the vegetables are tender and slightly charred.

6. While grilling, you can baste the skewers with any remaining marinade for extra flavor.

7. Remove the skewers from the grill and let them rest for a minute.

8. Serve hot, garnished with lemon wedges and fresh parsley if desired.

Nutritional Information

Calories	200	Dietary Fiber	2g
Protein	20g	Sodium	350mg
Carbohydrates	10g	Cholesterol	150mg
Total Fat	8g	Potassium	500mg
Saturated Fat	1g		

Enjoy your heart-healthy Grilled Shrimp and Vegetable Skewers! This dish is low in saturated fat and provides a good dose of protein and essential nutrients while being light on carbohydrates, making it a great choice for a heart-healthy and diabetes-friendly meal.

Stuffed Acorn Squash with Quinoa and Cranberries

Prep Time: 15 minutes / Cook Time: 45 minutes
Yield: 4 serving

Ingredients

- 2 acorn squash, halved and seeds removed
- 1 cup quinoa, rinsed and drained
- 2 cups vegetable broth or water
- 1/2 cup dried cranberries, salt and pepper to taste
- 1/2 cup chopped pecans or walnuts
- 1/4 cup chopped fresh parsley
- 1/4 cup chopped fresh sage leaves (or 1 tablespoon dried sage)
- 2 tablespoons olive oil, 2 cloves garlic, minced
- 1/4 cup grated Parmesan cheese (optional, for garnish)

Directions

1. Preheat your oven to 375°F (190°C).

2. Place the acorn squash halves cut-side down on a baking sheet. Roast in the preheated oven for 30-35 minutes, or until the squash is tender when pierced with a fork. Remove from the oven and set aside.

3. While the squash is roasting, combine the quinoa and vegetable broth (or water) in a medium saucepan. Bring to a boil, then reduce the heat to low, cover, and simmer for about 15-20 minutes, or until the quinoa is cooked and the liquid is absorbed. Remove from heat and fluff the quinoa with a fork.

4. In a large mixing bowl, combine the cooked quinoa, dried cranberries, chopped nuts, chopped parsley, chopped sage, olive oil, minced garlic, salt, and pepper. Mix well to combine.

5. Turn the roasted acorn squash halves over, so they are cut-side up. Stuff each half with the quinoa mixture, pressing it down gently to pack it.

6. Return the stuffed squash to the oven and bake for an additional 10-15 minutes, or until the filling is heated through and slightly crispy on top.

7. If desired, garnish with grated Parmesan cheese before serving.

Nutritional Information

Calories	450	Dietary Fiber	11g
Protein	9g	Sodium	490mg
Carbohydrates	75g	Cholesterol	0mg
Total Fat	16g	Potassium	1320mg
Saturated Fat	2g		

Chickpea and Spinach Curry

Prep Time: 10 minutes / Cook Time: 20 minutes
Yield: 2 serving

Ingredients

- 1 can (15 ounces) chickpeas, drained and rinsed
- 2 cups fresh spinach leaves, washed and chopped
- 1 onion, finely chopped, 2 cloves garlic, minced
- 1-inch piece of ginger, grated
- 1 tablespoon olive oil, 1 teaspoon ground cumin
- 1 can (14 ounces) diced tomatoes
- Salt and pepper to taste
- 1/2 teaspoon turmeric powder
- 1 teaspoon ground coriander
- 1/2 teaspoon garam masala
- 1/2 teaspoon chili powder
  (adjust to your spice preference)
- 1/2 cup low-sodium vegetable broth
- Fresh cilantro leaves for garnish
- Cooked brown rice or whole-grain naan for serving
  (optional)

Directions

1. Heat the olive oil in a large skillet over medium heat. Add the chopped onion and cook for 2-3 minutes until translucent.

2. Stir in the minced garlic and grated ginger. Cook for another 1-2 minutes until fragrant.

3. Add the ground cumin, ground coriander, turmeric powder, garam masala, and chili powder. Stir well to coat the onion mixture with the spices and cook for 1-2 minutes until the spices become aromatic.

4. Pour in the diced tomatoes (with their juice) and vegetable broth. Stir to combine and bring the mixture to a simmer.

5. Add the drained chickpeas to the skillet and let it simmer for 10-12 minutes, allowing the flavors to meld and the sauce to thicken.

6. Add the chopped spinach to the skillet and cook for an additional 2-3 minutes until the spinach wilts and becomes tender.

7. Season with salt and pepper to taste. If you prefer a spicier curry, you can add more chili powder at this stage.

8. Serve hot over cooked brown rice or with whole-grain naan, if desired. Garnish with fresh cilantro leaves.

Nutritional Information

Calories	315	Dietary Fiber	13g
Protein	11g	Sodium	680mg
Carbohydrates	52g	Cholesterol	60mg
Total Fat	7g	Potassium	645mg
Saturated Fat	1g		

Balsamic Glazed Chicken Thighs

Prep Time: 10 minutes / Cook Time: 25 minutes
Yield: 4 serving

Ingredients

- 8 bone-in, skinless chicken thighs
- 2 tablespoons honey, 1/4 cup balsamic vinegar
- 1/2 teaspoon dried rosemary
- 2 tablespoons low-sodium soy sauce
- Cooking spray
- 2 cloves garlic, minced, 1 teaspoon dried basil
- 1 teaspoon dried thyme, salt and pepper to taste
- Fresh parsley for garnish (optional)

Directions

1. Preheat your oven to 375°F (190°C).

2. In a small bowl, whisk together the balsamic vinegar, honey, low-sodium soy sauce, minced garlic, dried basil, dried thyme, dried rosemary, salt, and pepper. This will be your glaze.

3. Place the chicken thighs in a large mixing bowl and pour half of the balsamic glaze over them. Toss to coat the chicken evenly.

4. Heat an oven-safe skillet over medium-high heat. Lightly coat it with cooking spray.

5. Place the chicken thighs in the skillet, skin-side down. Sear them for about 2-3 minutes until the skin becomes golden brown.

6. Flip the chicken thighs and sear the other side for an additional 2-3 minutes.

7. Pour the remaining balsamic glaze over the chicken in the skillet.

8. Transfer the skillet to the preheated oven and bake for 18-20 minutes, or until the chicken thighs are cooked through and the internal temperature reaches 165°F (74°C).

9. While the chicken is baking, you can baste it with the glaze from the skillet a couple of times during cooking for extra flavor.

10. Once done, remove the skillet from the oven and let the chicken rest for a few minutes.

11. Serve hot, garnished with fresh parsley if desired.

Nutritional Information

Calories	310	Dietary Fiber	0.5g
Protein	30g	Sodium	330mg
Carbohydrates	10g	Cholesterol	150mg
Total Fat	15g	Potassium	350mg
Saturated Fat	4g		

Broiled Tilapia with Mango Salsa

Prep Time: 15 minutes / Cook Time: 10 minutes
Yield: 2 serving

Ingredients

- 2 tilapia fillets (about 6 ounces each)
- 1 tablespoon olive oil, 1 teaspoon paprika
- 1/2 teaspoon garlic powder
- 1/2 teaspoon onion powder
- 1/2 teaspoon dried oregano
- 1/2 teaspoon dried thyme
- Salt and black pepper to taste

For Mango Salsa:

- 1 ripe mango, diced
- 1/2 red onion, finely chopped
- 1/2 red bell pepper, diced
- 1 jalapeño pepper, seeded and minced (adjust to taste)
- Juice of 1 lime, 2 tablespoons fresh cilantro, chopped
- Salt and black pepper to taste

Directions

1. Preheat your broiler to high and position the oven rack about 6 inches from the heat source.

2. In a small bowl, combine the paprika, garlic powder, onion powder, dried oregano, dried thyme, salt, and black pepper. Brush the tilapia fillets with olive oil, then sprinkle the spice mixture evenly on both sides of the fillets.

3. Place the seasoned tilapia fillets on a broiler pan or a baking sheet lined with foil. Broil for 4-5 minutes per side, or until the fish flakes easily with a fork and is lightly browned on the outside. Be careful not to overcook.

4. While the tilapia is broiling, prepare the mango salsa. In a mixing bowl, combine the diced mango, red onion, red bell pepper, jalapeño pepper, lime juice, and cilantro. Season with salt and black pepper to taste. Mix well.

5. Once the tilapia fillets are done, remove them from the oven and serve immediately, topped with a generous portion of mango salsa.

Nutritional Information

Calories	280	Dietary Fiber	3g
Protein	29g	Sodium	110mg
Carbohydrates	23g	Cholesterol	60mg
Total Fat	9g	Potassium	590mg
Saturated Fat	1.5g		

Cauliflower Fried Rice with Tofu

Prep Time: 15 minutes / Cook Time: 15 minutes
Yield: 2 serving

Ingredients

- 1 small head of cauliflower, grated
- 8 ounces extra-firm tofu, diced
- 2 cloves garlic, minced
- 1/2 cup carrots, diced, 1/4 cup scallions, chopped
- 1/2 cup green peas, 1/2 cup red bell pepper, diced
- 2 tablespoons low-sodium soy sauce
- 1 tablespoon sesame oil, 1 tablespoon olive oil
- 1/2 teaspoon ginger, minced
- Salt and pepper to taste
- 1/2 teaspoon crushed red pepper flakes (optional)

Directions

1. Prepare the Tofu: Start by pressing the tofu to remove excess moisture. Wrap the tofu block in a clean kitchen towel and place something heavy on top (like a cast iron skillet). Let it sit for 10-15 minutes. Once pressed, dice the tofu into small cubes.

2. Prepare the Cauliflower Rice: Use a food processor or a box grater to grate the cauliflower into rice-sized pieces. Set aside.

3. Stir-Fry Tofu: Heat the olive oil in a large skillet or wok over medium-high heat. Add the diced tofu and stir-fry until it turns golden brown, about 5-7 minutes. Remove the tofu from the skillet and set it aside.

4. Sauté Vegetables: In the same skillet, add the sesame oil and minced garlic. Sauté for about 30 seconds until fragrant. Then, add the diced carrots, green peas, and red bell pepper. Cook for 3-4 minutes until the vegetables begin to soften.

5. Combine Cauliflower Rice: Add the grated cauliflower to the skillet with the sautéed vegetables. Stir-fry for another 5-7 minutes until the cauliflower rice is tender but not mushy.

6. Season the Dish: Return the cooked tofu to the skillet. Drizzle low-sodium soy sauce over the mixture and add minced ginger. Toss everything together until well combined. If you like a bit of heat, add crushed red pepper flakes. Season with salt and pepper to taste.

7. Serve: Garnish the cauliflower fried rice with chopped scallions and serve hot.

Nutritional Information

Calories	250	Dietary Fiber	6g
Protein	14g	Sodium	400mg
Carbohydrates	16g	Cholesterol	0mg
Total Fat	15g	Potassium	520mg
Saturated Fat	2g		

Grilled Portobello Mushrooms with Balsamic Reduction

Prep Time: 15 minutes / Cook Time: 15 minutes
Yield: 2 serving

Ingredients

- 4 large Portobello mushrooms
- 2 tablespoons olive oil
- 2 cloves garlic, minced
- 1/4 cup balsamic vinegar
- 1 tablespoon honey
- 1 teaspoon Dijon mustard
- Salt and pepper to taste
- Fresh parsley, for garnish

Directions

1. Preheat your grill to medium-high heat.

2. Clean the Portobello mushrooms by wiping them with a damp paper towel or gently brushing off any dirt. Remove the stems and set them aside.

3. In a small bowl, whisk together the olive oil, minced garlic, honey, Dijon mustard, salt, and pepper. This will be your marinade.

4. Brush both sides of the Portobello mushrooms with the marinade, ensuring they are well coated.

5. Place the mushrooms on the grill, gill side down. Grill for about 5-7 minutes on each side, or until they are tender and have nice grill marks.

6. While the mushrooms are grilling, prepare the balsamic reduction. In a small saucepan, combine the balsamic vinegar and the reserved mushroom stems. Bring to a simmer over medium heat and cook until it reduces by half, about 5-7 minutes. Remove and discard the mushroom stems.

7. Once the mushrooms are grilled to perfection, remove them from the grill and place them on a serving platter. Drizzle the balsamic reduction over the top.

8. Garnish with fresh parsley and serve immediately.

Nutritional Information

Calories	140	Dietary Fiber	3g
Protein	4g	Sodium	20mg
Carbohydrates	15g	Cholesterol	0mg
Total Fat	7g	Potassium	650mg
Saturated Fat	1g		

Enjoy these heart-healthy Grilled Portobello Mushrooms with Balsamic Reduction as a delicious and nutritious side dish or appetizer!

Lemon Garlic Shrimp with Quinoa

Prep Time: 15 minutes / Cook Time: 15 minutes
Yield: 2 serving

Ingredients

- 1 cup quinoa, rinsed and drained
- 1 pound large shrimp, peeled and deveined
- 2 tablespoons olive oil
- 4 cloves garlic, minced
- 1 lemon, zest and juice
- 1/2 teaspoon red pepper flakes (adjust to taste)
- Salt and pepper to taste
- Fresh parsley, chopped for garnish

Directions

1. In a medium saucepan, combine 2 cups of water and the rinsed quinoa. Bring to a boil, then reduce heat to low, cover, and simmer for about 15 minutes or until the quinoa is cooked and the water is absorbed. Remove from heat and fluff with a fork.

2. While the quinoa is cooking, heat the olive oil in a large skillet over medium-high heat. Add minced garlic and red pepper flakes. Sauté for about 1 minute or until fragrant.

3. Add the shrimp to the skillet, spreading them out evenly. Cook for 2-3 minutes on each side until they turn pink and opaque.

4. Stir in lemon zest and lemon juice, making sure to scrape up any browned bits from the bottom of the skillet. Cook for an additional 1-2 minutes.

5. Season the shrimp mixture with salt and pepper to taste.

6. Serve the lemon garlic shrimp over a bed of cooked quinoa. Garnish with freshly chopped parsley.

Nutritional Information

Calories	380	Dietary Fiber	5g
Protein	30g	Sodium	310mg
Carbohydrates	35g	Cholesterol	215mg
Total Fat	1g	Potassium	500mg
Saturated Fat	1.5g		

Enjoy your heart-healthy Lemon Garlic Shrimp with Quinoa! This dish is not only delicious but also packed with protein and fiber, making it a nutritious choice for a satisfying meal.

Tofu and Vegetable Stir-Fry with Ginger Sauce

Prep Time: 15 minutes / Cook Time: 15 minutes
Yield: 2 serving

Ingredients

- 1 block (14 oz) extra-firm tofu, cubed
- 2 cups broccoli florets, 1 red bell pepper, thinly sliced
- 1 carrot, julienned, 1 cup snap peas, trimmed
- 2 cloves garlic, minced, 1 tablespoon ginger, minced
- 2 tablespoons low-sodium soy sauce
- 1 tablespoon rice vinegar, 1 teaspoon cornstarch
- 1 tablespoon honey or maple syrup
- 2 tablespoons vegetable oil
- Sesame seeds (for garnish, optional)
- Cooked brown rice or quinoa (for serving, optional)

Directions

1. Wrap the tofu block in a clean kitchen towel or paper towel.

2. Place something heavy (like a cast-iron skillet) on top to press out excess water for 10-15 minutes. Cut the tofu into bite-sized cubes.

3. In a small bowl, whisk together soy sauce, rice vinegar, honey or maple syrup, and cornstarch until well combined. Set aside.

4. Heat 1 tablespoon of vegetable oil in a large skillet or wok over medium-high heat.

5. Add the cubed tofu and cook until all sides are golden brown, about 5-7 minutes. Remove tofu from the pan and set it aside.

6. In the same skillet, add the remaining 1 tablespoon of vegetable oil.

7. Add minced garlic and ginger, and sauté for about 30 seconds until fragrant.

8. Add broccoli, bell pepper, carrot, and snap peas. Stir-fry for 5-7 minutes until the vegetables are tender-crisp.

9. Return the cooked tofu to the skillet with the vegetables.

10. Pour the ginger sauce over the tofu and vegetables, tossing to coat evenly.

11. Cook for an additional 2-3 minutes until the sauce thickens and everything is heated through.

12. Optionally, serve the tofu and vegetable stir-fry over cooked brown rice or quinoa.

13. Garnish with sesame seeds if desired.

Nutritional Information

Calories	320	Dietary Fiber	7g
Protein	16g	Sodium	400mg
Carbohydrates	35g	Cholesterol	0mg
Total Fat	15g	Potassium	670mg
Saturated Fat	2g		

Mediterranean Chickpea Salad with Grilled Chicken

Prep Time: 20 minutes / Cook Time: 15 minutes
Yield: 4 serving

Ingredients

For the Grilled Chicken:
- 4 boneless, skinless chicken breasts, 1 lemon, juiced
- 2 tablespoons olive oil, 2 cloves garlic, minced
- 1 teaspoon dried oregano, salt and pepper to taste

For the Mediterranean Chickpea Salad:
- 2 (15-ounce) cans chickpeas, drained and rinsed
- 1 cucumber, diced, 1 cup cherry tomatoes, halved
- 1 red onion, finely chopped
- 1/2 cup Kalamata olives, pitted and sliced
- 1/2 cup crumbled feta cheese
- 1/4 cup fresh parsley, chopped
- 1/4 cup fresh mint, chopped (optional)

For the Dressing:
- 1/4 cup extra-virgin olive oil, salt and pepper to taste
- 2 tablespoons red wine vinegar, 1 clove garlic, minced
- 1 teaspoon Dijon mustard

Directions

1. In a bowl, combine the olive oil, lemon juice, minced garlic, dried oregano, salt, and pepper. This will be your chicken marinade.

2. Place the chicken breasts in a resealable plastic bag or a shallow dish. Pour the marinade over the chicken and ensure it's evenly coated. Seal the bag or cover the dish and refrigerate for at least 30 minutes to marinate.

3. Preheat your grill to medium-high heat. Remove the chicken from the marinade and grill for about 6-7 minutes per side, or until the chicken reaches an internal temperature of 165°F (74°C) and has grill marks. Remove the chicken from the grill, cover with foil, and let it rest for a few minutes before slicing.

4. In a large mixing bowl, combine the drained and rinsed chickpeas, diced cucumber, halved cherry tomatoes, finely chopped red onion, sliced Kalamata olives, crumbled feta cheese, chopped fresh parsley, and fresh mint (if using).

5. In a separate small bowl, whisk together the extra-virgin olive oil, red wine vinegar, Dijon mustard, minced garlic, salt, and pepper.

6. Drizzle the dressing over the Mediterranean chickpea salad and toss to combine.

7. Slice the grilled chicken breasts and arrange them on top of the salad.

Nutritional Information

Calories	480	Dietary Fiber	9g
Protein	35g	Sodium	750mg
Carbohydrates	32g	Cholesterol	85mg
Total Fat	24g	Potassium	820mg
Saturated Fat	6g		

Baked Eggplant Parmesan

Prep Time: 25 minutes / Cook Time: 30 minutes
Yield: 4 serving

Ingredients

- 2 large eggplants, peeled and sliced into 1/2-inch thick rounds
- 1 1/2 cups whole-wheat breadcrumbs
- 1/2 cup grated Parmesan cheese, 2 large eggs, beaten
- 1 teaspoon dried basil, 1 teaspoon dried oregano
- 1/2 teaspoon garlic powder, salt and pepper to taste
- 1 1/2 cups marinara sauce (store-bought or homemade)
- 1 1/2 cups shredded part-skim mozzarella cheese
- Fresh basil leaves for garnish (optional)

Directions

1. Preheat your oven to 375°F (190°C). Line a baking sheet with parchment paper and set aside.

2. Place the eggplant slices in a single layer on paper towels. Sprinkle them lightly with salt and let them sit for about 15 minutes. This helps remove excess moisture from the eggplant. After 15 minutes, blot the eggplant slices with paper towels to remove any remaining moisture.

3. In a shallow dish, combine the whole-wheat breadcrumbs, grated Parmesan cheese, dried basil, dried oregano, garlic powder, salt, and pepper.

4. Dip each eggplant slice into the beaten eggs, allowing any excess to drip off, and then coat it with the breadcrumb mixture. Place the breaded eggplant slices on the prepared baking sheet.

5. Bake the breaded eggplant slices in the preheated oven for about 15-20 minutes, or until they are golden brown and crisp. Remove from the oven and set aside.

6. In a baking dish, spread a thin layer of marinara sauce. Arrange half of the baked eggplant slices on top of the sauce. Top with half of the shredded mozzarella cheese. Repeat with another layer of sauce, the remaining eggplant slices, and the remaining mozzarella cheese.

7. Cover the baking dish with foil and bake for 15 minutes. Then, remove the foil and bake for an additional 15 minutes, or until the cheese is bubbly and golden.

8. Remove from the oven and let it rest for a few minutes. Garnish with fresh basil leaves if desired. Serve hot.

Nutritional Information

Calories	400	Dietary Fiber	1g
Protein	21g	Sodium	750mg
Carbohydrates	45g	Cholesterol	85mg
Total Fat	15g	Potassium	900mg
Saturated Fat	6g		

Spaghetti Squash with Turkey Meatballs

Prep Time: 20 minutes / Cook Time: 45 minutes
Yield: 4 serving

Ingredients

For the Turkey Meatballs: 1 pound lean ground turkey
- 1/4 cup chopped fresh parsley, 1 egg, cooking spray
- 1/2 cup breadcrumbs (whole wheat or gluten-free)
- 1/4 cup grated Parmesan cheese (optional)
- 1/4 cup diced onion, 2 cloves garlic, minced
- 1/2 teaspoon dried oregano

For the Spaghetti Squash:
- 2 medium-sized spaghetti squashes, 1 tablespoon olive oil

For the Tomato Sauce: 1 teaspoon dried basil
- 1 can (14 ounces) crushed tomatoes (no salt added)
- 1 teaspoon dried oregano, 1/2 teaspoon garlic powder

Salt and pepper to taste

Directions

1. In a large mixing bowl, combine the lean ground turkey, breadcrumbs, grated Parmesan cheese (if using), chopped fresh parsley, diced onion, egg, minced garlic, dried oregano, salt, and pepper.

2. Form the mixture into 1-inch meatballs, and place them on a baking sheet lined with parchment paper or lightly greased. You should have about 20 meatballs. Preheat your oven to 375°F (190°C).

3. Bake the turkey meatballs in the preheated oven for 20-25 minutes, or until they are cooked through and browned on the outside.

4. While the meatballs are baking, cut the spaghetti squashes in half lengthwise and scoop out the seeds. Brush the inside of the squash halves with olive oil and season with salt and pepper.

5. Place the squash halves cut-side down on a baking sheet lined with parchment paper or lightly greased. Bake in the same oven alongside the meatballs for about 25-30 minutes, or until the squash is tender.

6. In a saucepan, combine the crushed tomatoes, dried basil, dried oregano, garlic powder, salt, and pepper. Simmer over low heat for 10-15 minutes to heat through and allow the flavors to meld.

7. Once the spaghetti squash is done baking, use a fork to scrape the inside of each squash half, creating "spaghetti" strands.

8. Serve the spaghetti squash with turkey meatballs on top, and drizzle with the tomato sauce.

Nutritional Information
(including tomato sauce but excluding optional Parmesan cheese)

Calories	270	Dietary Fiber	7g
Protein	22g	Sodium	620mg
Carbohydrates	30g	Cholesterol	100mg
Total Fat	8g	Potassium	950mg
Saturated Fat	2g		

chapter 12
DESSERT

Dark Chocolate-Dipped
Strawberries 99

Chia Seed Pudding 99

Berry Parfait 99

Watermelon and Mint Salad 100

Mixed Berry Sorbet 100

Oatmeal Raisin Cookies 100

Greek Yogurt and Honey 101

Avocado Chocolate Mousse 101

Baked Apples with Cinnamon 101

Banana Oat Pancakes 102

Roasted Fruit Medley 102

Lemon Poppy Seed Cake 103

Pumpkin Spice Energy Bites 103

Almond and Date Bites 104

Coconut Rice Pudding 104

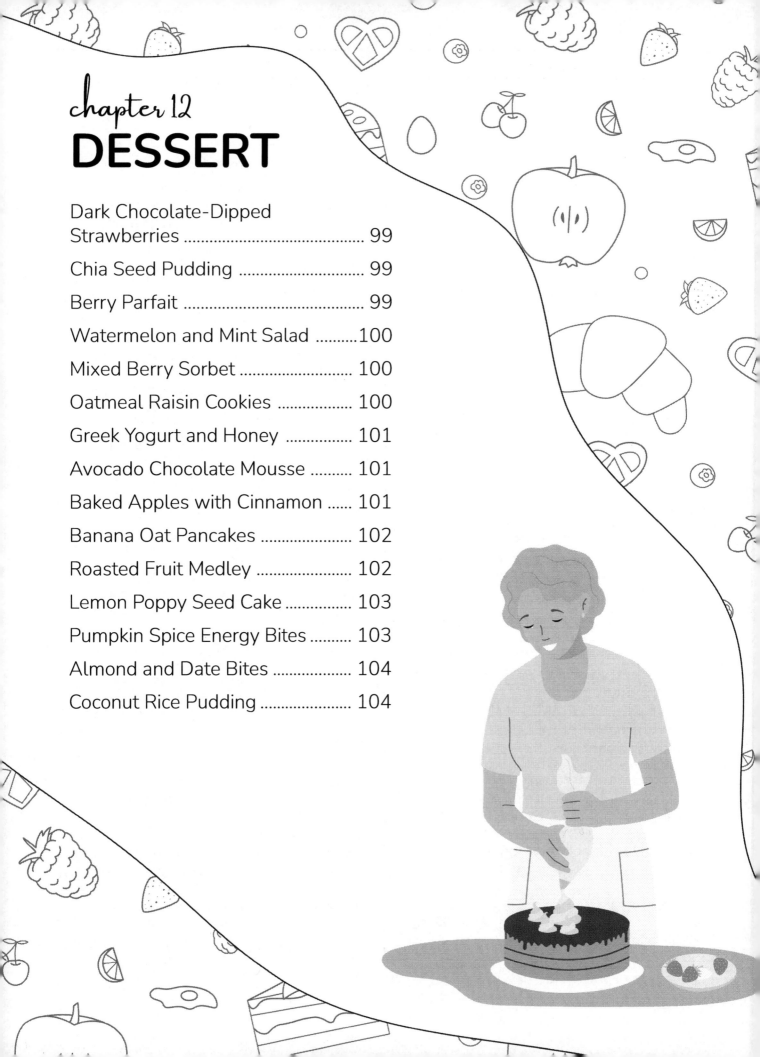

Dark Chocolate-Dipped Strawberries

Prep Time: 10 minutes / Cook Time: 5 minutes
Yield: 1 serving

Ingredients

- 5-6 fresh strawberries
- 1 ounce (about 28 grams) of dark chocolate (70% cocoa or higher)
- 1/2 teaspoon coconut oil (optional, for smoother chocolate)

Directions

1. Wash and thoroughly dry the strawberries. Make sure they are completely dry as any moisture can cause the chocolate to seize.

2. In a microwave-safe bowl or using a double boiler, melt the dark chocolate. If using a microwave, heat the chocolate in 20-second intervals, stirring in between until fully melted. If the chocolate seems too thick, you can add 1/2 teaspoon of coconut oil to achieve a smoother consistency.

3. While the chocolate is still warm, carefully dip each strawberry into the melted dark chocolate, covering about two-thirds of the strawberry.

4. Allow any excess chocolate to drip back into the bowl.

5. Place the dipped strawberries on a parchment paper-lined tray or plate.

6. Let the chocolate-coated strawberries cool and set. You can speed up the process by placing them in the refrigerator for about 15 minutes.

7. Once the chocolate is firm and the strawberries are cool, serve your heart-healthy Dark Chocolate-Dipped Strawberries as a delightful treat.

Nutritional Information

Calories	100	Dietary Fiber	3g
Protein	1g	Sodium	0mg
Carbohydrates	14g	Cholesterol	0mg
Total Fat	5g	Potassium	130mg
Saturated Fat	3g		

Chia Seed Pudding

Prep Time: 5 minutes (plus 2-3 hours for chilling)
Cook Time: 0 minutes / Yield: 1 serving

Ingredients

- 2 tablespoons chia seeds, 1/2 teaspoon pure vanilla extract
- 1/2 cup unsweetened almond milk (or any milk of your choice)
- 1 teaspoon honey or maple syrup (optional, for sweetness)
- Fresh berries or sliced fruit for topping

Directions

1. In a mixing bowl, combine the chia seeds, unsweetened almond milk, and pure vanilla extract. If you prefer your pudding to be sweet, add 1 teaspoon of honey or maple syrup at this stage.

2. Stir the mixture well to ensure the chia seeds are evenly distributed.

3. Cover the bowl and refrigerate for at least 2-3 hours, or preferably overnight. During this time, the chia seeds will absorb the liquid and form a pudding-like consistency.

4. After chilling, give the pudding a good stir to break up any clumps and achieve a smooth texture.

5. Transfer the chia seed pudding to a serving dish or a glass.

6. Top your heart-healthy Chia Seed Pudding with fresh berries or sliced fruit for added flavor and nutrition.

7. Serve chilled and enjoy!

Nutritional Information

Calories	120	Dietary Fiber	9g
Protein	4g	Sodium	80mg
Carbohydrates	14g	Cholesterol	0mg
Total Fat	6g	Potassium	130mg
Saturated Fat	0,5g		

Berry Parfait

Prep Time: 10 minutes / Cook Time: 0 minutes / Yield: 1 serving

Ingredients

- 1/2 cup low-fat Greek yogurt
- 1/2 cup mixed fresh berries (strawberries, blueberries, raspberries)
- 2 tablespoons granola (choose a low-sugar option)
- 1 teaspoon honey (optional, for drizzling)

Nutritional Information

Calories	250	Dietary Fiber	6g
Protein	12g	Sodium	70mg
Carbohydrates	45g	Cholesterol	10mg
Total Fat	4g	Potassium	300mg
Saturated Fat	0.5g		

Directions

1. In a glass or serving dish, start by adding a layer of 1/4 cup of low-fat Greek yogurt as the base.

2. Add a layer of 1/4 cup of mixed fresh berries on top of the yogurt.

3. Sprinkle 1 tablespoon of granola over the berries.

4. Repeat the layering process with the remaining yogurt, berries, and granola.

5. If desired, drizzle a teaspoon of honey over the top layer for added sweetness.

6. Serve immediately and enjoy your heart-healthy Berry Parfait!

Watermelon and Mint Salad

Prep Time: 10 minutes / Cook Time: 0 minutes
Yield: ~2 serving

Ingredients

- 2 cups cubed watermelon, 1 tablespoon lime juice
- 2 tablespoons fresh mint leaves, thinly sliced
- 1 teaspoon honey (optional, for a touch of sweetness)
- A pinch of salt, freshly ground black pepper to taste

Directions

1. Start by preparing the watermelon. Cut it into bite-sized cubes or use a melon baller for a decorative touch. Place the cubed watermelon in a mixing bowl.

2. Wash and thinly slice the fresh mint leaves. Add the sliced mint to the bowl with the watermelon.

3. In a small bowl, combine the lime juice and honey (if using). The honey is optional and can be adjusted based on your preference for sweetness.

4. Drizzle the lime juice mixture over the watermelon and mint in the bowl. Add a pinch of salt and freshly ground black pepper to taste. Be mindful not to oversalt, as the salad should be refreshing.

5. Gently toss the ingredients together to coat the watermelon and mint evenly with the lime dressing.

6. Allow the Watermelon and Mint Salad to sit for a few minutes to allow the flavors to meld together.

7. Serve your heart-healthy salad in bowls or on plates, and enjoy it as a light and refreshing appetizer or side dis

Nutritional Information

Calories	50	Dietary Fiber	1g
Protein	1g	Sodium	50mg
Carbohydrates	13g	Cholesterol	0mg
Total Fat	0g	Potassium	160mg
Saturated Fat	0g		

Mixed Berry Sorbet

Prep Time: 10 minutes / Cook Time: 0 minutes
Yield: ~2 serving

Ingredients

- cups mixed berries (such as strawberries, blueberries, and raspberries), frozen, 1 teaspoon lemon juice (freshly squeezed)
- 1/4 cup unsweetened apple juice or orange juice
- 1 tablespoon honey (optional, for added sweetness)

Directions

1. Place the frozen mixed berries, unsweetened apple juice (or orange juice), and optional honey in a blender or food processor.

2. Add the freshly squeezed lemon juice to the blender as well.

3. Blend the ingredients until the mixture is smooth and well combined. You may need to stop and scrape down the sides of the blender or processor to ensure even blending.

4. Taste the sorbet mixture and adjust sweetness if necessary by adding more honey, blending, and tasting again.

5. Once the sorbet mixture reaches your desired sweetness, transfer it to an airtight container.

6. Freeze the sorbet for about 2-3 hours, or until it firms up. You can also enjoy it immediately as a slushie-like treat.

7. Before serving, let the sorbet sit at room temperature for a few minutes to soften slightly for easier scooping.

8. Scoop the heart-healthy Mixed Berry Sorbet into bowls or glasses and serve as a refreshing and guilt-free dessert!

Nutritional Information

Calories	80	Dietary Fiber	4g
Protein	1g	Sodium	0mg
Carbohydrates	20g	Cholesterol	0mg
Total Fat	0g	Potassium	120mg
Saturated Fat	0g		

Oatmeal Raisin Cookies

Prep Time: 15 minutes / Cook Time: 10-12 minutes / Yield: ~12 cookies

Ingredients

- 1 cup old-fashioned oats
- 3/4 cup whole wheat flour
- 1/2 teaspoon baking soda
- 1/2 teaspoon ground cinnamon
- 1/4 teaspoon salt
- 1/4 cup honey or maple syrup
- 1/4 cup unsweetened applesauce
- 1/4 cup unsalted butter, softened
- 1 large egg
- 1 teaspoon vanilla extract
- 1/2 cup raisins

Nutritional Information

Calories	100	Dietary Fiber	4g
Protein	1g	Sodium	0mg
Carbohydrates	27g	Cholesterol	0mg
Total Fat	0g	Potassium	195mg
Saturated Fat	0g		

Directions

1. Preheat your oven to 350°F (175°C) and line a baking sheet with parchment paper. In a mixing bowl, combine the old-fashioned oats, whole wheat flour, baking soda, ground cinnamon, and salt. Mix them together and set aside.

2. In another bowl, beat together the unsweetened applesauce, honey (or maple syrup), softened unsalted butter, egg, and vanilla extract until well combined. Add the dry ingredients mixture to the wet ingredients and stir until a cookie dough forms. Gently fold in the raisins into the cookie dough.

3. Drop rounded tablespoons of cookie dough onto the prepared baking sheet, spacing them about 2 inches apart. Use the back of a fork to flatten each cookie slightly. Bake in the preheated oven for 10-12 minutes or until the cookies are golden brown around the edges.

4. Remove the cookies from the oven and let them cool on the baking sheet for a few minutes before transferring them to a wire rack to cool completely. Once cooled, enjoy your heart-healthy Oatmeal Raisin Cookies as a delicious treat!

Greek Yogurt and Honey

Prep Time: 5 minutes / Cook Time: 0 minutes
Yield: 1 serving

Ingredients

- 1/2 cup plain Greek yogurt (low-fat or non-fat)
- 1 tablespoon honey (adjust to taste)
- Fresh berries or sliced fruit for topping (optional)

Directions

1. Take a serving bowl or a small dish.

2. Measure out 1/2 cup of plain Greek yogurt and add it to the bowl.

3. Drizzle 1 tablespoon of honey over the Greek yogurt. Adjust the amount of honey to your desired level of sweetness.

4. If desired, top your Greek Yogurt and Honey with fresh berries or sliced fruit for added flavor and texture.

5. Give it a gentle stir to combine the honey with the yogurt.

6. Your heart-healthy Greek Yogurt and Honey is now ready to enjoy!

Nutritional Information

Calories	~150	Dietary Fiber	0g
Protein	10g	Sodium	40mg
Carbohydrates	20g	Cholesterol	10mg
Total Fat	0g	Potassium	150mg
Saturated Fat	0g		

Avocado Chocolate Mousse

Prep Time: 10 minutes / Cook Time: 0 minutes
Yield: ~2 serving

Ingredients

- 2 ripe avocados, peeled and pitted
- 1/4 cup unsweetened cocoa powder
- 1/4 cup honey or maple syrup (adjust to taste)
- 1 teaspoon pure vanilla extract, a pinch of salt
- Fresh berries or sliced fruit for topping (optional)

Directions

1. In a food processor or blender, combine the ripe avocados, unsweetened cocoa powder, honey (or maple syrup), pure vanilla extract, and a pinch of salt.

2. Blend the ingredients until the mixture becomes smooth and creamy. You may need to stop and scrape down the sides of the blender or processor to ensure even blending.

3. Taste the mousse and adjust the sweetness by adding more honey or maple syrup if desired.

4. Once the mousse reaches your desired level of sweetness, transfer it to serving dishes or glasses.

5. If desired, top your heart-healthy Avocado Chocolate Mousse with fresh berries or sliced fruit for added flavor and freshness.

6. Serve immediately or refrigerate for a short time to chill, and enjoy your delicious and nutritious dessert!

Nutritional Information (based on 2 servings)

Calories	~250	Dietary Fiber	9g
Protein	3g	Sodium	10mg
Carbohydrates	34g	Cholesterol	0mg
Total Fat	15g	Potassium	720mg
Saturated Fat	2g		

Baked Apples with Cinnamon

Prep Time: 10 minutes / Cook Time: 30 minutes / Yield: 1 serving

Ingredients

- 1 medium-sized apple
  (choose a heart-healthy variety like Granny Smith or Pink Lady)
- 1/2 teaspoon ground cinnamon
- 1 teaspoon honey (optional)
- 1 teaspoon chopped nuts (such as almonds or walnuts, optional)

Nutritional Information

Calories	100	Dietary Fiber	4g
Protein	1g	Sodium	0mg
Carbohydrates	27g	Cholesterol	0mg
Total Fat	0g	Potassium	195mg
Saturated Fat	0g		

Directions

1. Preheat your oven to 350°F (175°C).

2. Wash the apple, then core it using an apple corer or a knife, leaving the bottom intact. This will create a well in the apple.

3. Place the cored apple in a small baking dish. Sprinkle 1/2 teaspoon of ground cinnamon evenly over the apple.

4. If you prefer your baked apple to be a bit sweeter, drizzle 1 teaspoon of honey over the top.

5. Bake the apple in the preheated oven for approximately 30 minutes, or until it becomes soft and slightly golden.

6. Remove the baked apple from the oven and, if desired, sprinkle 1 teaspoon of chopped nuts over the top for added texture and heart-healthy fats.

7. Serve your heart-healthy Baked Apple with Cinnamon warm, and enjoy!

Banana Oat Pancakes

Prep Time: 10 minutes / Cook Time: 10 minutes
Yield: ~2 serving

Ingredients

- 1 ripe banana
- 1 cup rolled oats
- 1/2 cup unsweetened almond milk (or any milk of your choice)
- 1 large egg
- 1/2 teaspoon pure vanilla extract
- 1/2 teaspoon ground cinnamon
- 1/2 teaspoon baking powder
- Cooking spray or a small amount of oil for the pan
- Fresh berries or sliced fruit for topping (optional)

Directions

1. In a blender or food processor, combine the ripe banana, rolled oats, unsweetened almond milk, egg, pure vanilla extract, ground cinnamon, and baking powder. Blend until the mixture forms a smooth batter.

2. Heat a non-stick skillet or griddle over medium heat and lightly grease it with cooking spray or a small amount of oil.

3. Pour small portions (about 1/4 cup) of the pancake batter onto the heated skillet to form pancakes. You can adjust the size based on your preference.

4. Cook the pancakes for about 2-3 minutes on one side, or until you see small bubbles forming on the surface.

5. Carefully flip the pancakes with a spatula and cook for an additional 2-3 minutes on the other side until they are golden brown and cooked through.

6. Remove the pancakes from the skillet and stack them on a plate.

7. If desired, top your heart-healthy Banana Oat Pancakes with fresh berries or sliced fruit for added flavor.

8. Serve the pancakes warm, and enjoy!

Nutritional Information (based on 2 servings)

Calories	~210	Dietary Fiber	5g
Protein	8g	Sodium	120mg
Carbohydrates	35g	Cholesterol	95mg
Total Fat	5g	Potassium	300mg
Saturated Fat	1g		

Roasted Fruit Medley

Prep Time: 10 minutes / Cook Time: 20 minutes
Yield: ~2 serving

Ingredients

- 2 cups mixed fresh fruit (such as apples, pears, and grapes), washed and chopped
- 1 tablespoon honey or maple syrup
- 1/2 teaspoon ground cinnamon
- A pinch of salt
- 1/4 cup chopped nuts (such as almonds or walnuts, optional)

Directions

1. Preheat your oven to 375°F (190°C).

2. In a mixing bowl, combine the mixed fresh fruit, honey (or maple syrup), ground cinnamon, and a pinch of salt. Toss them together until the fruit is evenly coated.

3. Spread the fruit mixture in a single layer on a baking sheet lined with parchment paper.

4. Roast the fruit in the preheated oven for approximately 20 minutes, or until it becomes tender and slightly caramelized. Stir the fruit halfway through the cooking time to ensure even roasting.

5. While the fruit is roasting, you can optionally toast the chopped nuts in a dry skillet over medium heat for a few minutes until they become fragrant and lightly golden. Keep an eye on them to prevent burning.

6. Once the fruit is done roasting, remove it from the oven and transfer it to a serving dish.

7. If you toasted nuts, sprinkle them over the roasted fruit for added texture and heart-healthy fats.

8. Serve your heart-healthy Roasted Fruit Medley warm as a delightful dessert or a nutritious side dish.

Nutritional Information

Calories	~160	Dietary Fiber	5g
Protein	2g	Sodium	60mg
Carbohydrates	36g	Cholesterol	0mg
Total Fat	1g	Potassium	280mg
Saturated Fat	0g		

Lemon Poppy Seed Cake

Prep Time: 15 minutes / Cook Time: 30-35 minutes
Yield: 8 serving

Ingredients

- 1 1/2 cups whole wheat flour
- 1/2 cup almond flour, 2 tablespoons poppy seeds
- 1/2 cup granulated sugar (or a sugar substitute)
- 1 tablespoon baking powder, zest of 2 lemons
- 1/2 teaspoon baking soda
- Juice of 2 lemons, 1/4 teaspoon salt
- 1/4 cup unsweetened applesauce
- 1/4 cup plain Greek yogurt (low-fat or non-fat)
- 1/4 cup unsalted butter, melted
  (or a heart-healthy oil like canola or olive oil)
- 2 large eggs, 1 teaspoon pure vanilla extract

Directions

1. Preheat your oven to 350°F (175°C). Grease and flour a 9-inch round cake pan or line it with parchment paper for easier removal.
2. In a large mixing bowl, combine the whole wheat flour, almond flour, granulated sugar (or sugar substitute), poppy seeds, baking powder, baking soda, salt, and lemon zest. Mix them together.
3. In another mixing bowl, whisk together the lemon juice, unsweetened applesauce, plain Greek yogurt, melted unsalted butter (or heart-healthy oil), eggs, and pure vanilla extract.
4. Pour the wet ingredients mixture into the dry ingredients mixture and stir until just combined. Be careful not to overmix; a few lumps are okay.
5. Pour the cake batter into the prepared cake pan and spread it evenly.
6. Bake in the preheated oven for 30-35 minutes or until a toothpick inserted into the center comes out clean and the cake is golden brown.
7. Remove the cake from the oven and let it cool in the pan for about 10 minutes before transferring it to a wire rack to cool completely.
8. Once the Lemon Poppy Seed Cake has cooled, you can optionally dust it with powdered sugar or frost it with a heart-healthy icing.
9. Slice, serve, and enjoy your heart-healthy Lemon Poppy Seed Cake!

Nutritional Information (based on 8 servings)

Calories .... ~240	Dietary Fiber 4g
Protein 6g	Sodium 330mg
Carbohydrates 29g	Cholesterol 65mg
Total Fat 12g	Potassium 180mg
Saturated Fat 4g	

Pumpkin Spice Energy Bites

Prep Time: 15 minutes / Cook Time: 0 minutes
Yield: ~ 12 energy bites

Ingredients

- 1 cup old-fashioned oats, 1/2 cup pumpkin puree
- 1/4 cup almond butter
  (or any nut or seed butter of your choice)
- 1/4 cup ground flaxseed, 1/4 cup honey or maple syrup
- 1 teaspoon pumpkin pie spice
  (or a mix of cinnamon, nutmeg, and cloves)
- 1/2 teaspoon pure vanilla extract, a pinch of salt
- 1/4 cup chopped nuts
  (such as almonds or walnuts, optional)
- 1/4 cup dried cranberries or raisins (optional)

Directions

1. In a mixing bowl, combine the old-fashioned oats, pumpkin puree, almond butter, ground flaxseed, honey (or maple syrup), pumpkin pie spice, pure vanilla extract, and a pinch of salt.

2. Stir the ingredients together until they are well combined.

3. If desired, fold in the chopped nuts and dried cranberries or raisins for added texture and flavor.

4. Once the mixture is well mixed and forms a dough-like consistency, cover the bowl and refrigerate for about 15-20 minutes. Chilling the mixture will make it easier to handle.

5. After chilling, remove the mixture from the refrigerator and use your hands to roll it into approximately 1-inch energy bites. You can adjust the size based on your preference.

6. Place the energy bites on a plate or tray lined with parchment paper.

7. Refrigerate the energy bites for another 10-15 minutes to firm them up.

8. Once the Pumpkin Spice Energy Bites are firm, they are ready to enjoy! You can store them in an airtight container in the refrigerator for longer shelf life.

Nutritional Information (based on 12 servings)

Calories .... ~90	Dietary Fiber 2g
Protein 2g	Sodium 25mg
Carbohydrates 11g	Cholesterol 0mg
Total Fat 4g	Potassium 150mg
Saturated Fat 0,5g	

Almond and Date Bites

Prep Time: 15 minutes / Cook Time: 0 minutes
Yield: ~ 12 bites

Ingredients

- 1 cup pitted dates
- 1 cup unsalted almonds
- 2 tablespoons unsweetened cocoa powder
- 1/2 teaspoon pure vanilla extract
- A pinch of salt
- 1-2 tablespoons water (if needed)
- Unsweetened shredded coconut for rolling (optional)

Directions

1. Place the pitted dates, unsalted almonds, unsweetened cocoa powder, pure vanilla extract, and a pinch of salt in a food processor.

2. Pulse the ingredients together until they start to come together. The mixture should have a crumbly texture.

3. Check the consistency of the mixture. If it's too dry and not sticking together, add 1-2 tablespoons of water and pulse again until the mixture becomes sticky and holds together well.

4. Once the mixture is ready, use your hands to roll it into approximately 1-inch bites. You can adjust the size based on your preference.

5. If desired, roll the Almond and Date Bites in unsweetened shredded coconut for added texture and flavor.

6. Place the bites on a plate or tray lined with parchment paper.

7. Refrigerate the bites for about 15-20 minutes to firm them up.

8. Once the bites are firm, they are ready to enjoy! Store them in an airtight container in the refrigerator for longer shelf life.

Nutritional Information (based on 12 servings)

Calories	80	Dietary Fiber	2g
Protein	2g	Sodium	0mg
Carbohydrates	11g	Cholesterol	0mg
Total Fat	4g	Potassium	120mg
Saturated Fat	0g		

Coconut Rice Pudding

Prep Time: 10 minutes / Cook Time: 25 minutes
Yield: ~4 serving

Ingredients

- 1/2 cup arborio rice (short-grain rice)
- 1 can (13.5 oz) light coconut milk
- 2 cups unsweetened almond milk (or any milk of your choice)
- 1/4 cup honey or maple syrup (adjust to taste)
- 1/2 teaspoon pure vanilla extract
- 1/4 teaspoon ground cinnamon
- A pinch of salt
- Unsweetened shredded coconut and fresh berries for topping (optional)

Directions

1. In a medium saucepan, combine the arborio rice, light coconut milk, unsweetened almond milk, honey (or maple syrup), pure vanilla extract, ground cinnamon, and a pinch of salt.

2. Place the saucepan over medium heat and bring the mixture to a boil, stirring frequently to prevent sticking.

3. Once the mixture comes to a boil, reduce the heat to low and simmer for about 20-25 minutes, or until the rice is tender and the pudding has thickened. Stir occasionally to prevent sticking and ensure even cooking.

4. Taste the pudding and adjust the sweetness by adding more honey or maple syrup if desired.

5. Remove the saucepan from the heat and let the Coconut Rice Pudding cool slightly.

6. If you prefer a creamier texture, you can blend a portion of the pudding in a blender or with an immersion blender and then mix it back into the rest.

7. Serve the Coconut Rice Pudding in individual dishes, garnished with unsweetened shredded coconut and fresh berries if you like.

8. Enjoy your heart-healthy Coconut Rice Pudding warm or chilled!

Nutritional Information (based on 4 servings)

Calories	~250	Dietary Fiber	2g
Protein	3g	Sodium	120mg
Carbohydrates	45g	Cholesterol	0mg
Total Fat	6g	Potassium	200mg
Saturated Fat	4g		

Chapter 13
Measurement conversion

Volume Conversions:

1 teaspoon (tsp) = 5 milliliters (ml)
1 tablespoon (tbsp) = 15 milliliters (ml)
1 fluid ounce (fl oz) = 30 milliliters (ml)
1 cup = 240 milliliters (ml)
1 pint (pt) = 480 milliliters (ml) or 2 cups
1 quart (qt) = 960 milliliters (ml) or 4 cups
1 gallon (gal) = 3.8 liters (L) or 16 cups

Weight Conversions:

1 ounce (oz) = 28 grams (g)
1 pound (lb) = 454 grams (g)
1 kilogram (kg) = 2.2 pounds (lbs)
For smaller measurements,
use fractions or decimals of ounces
or grams (e.g., ½ oz or 15 g)

Temperature Conversions:

Fahrenheit (°F) to Celsius (°C): Subtract
32 from the Fahrenheit temperature, then
multiply by 5/9.
Celsius (°C) to Fahrenheit (°F): Multiply the
Celsius temperature by 9/5, then add 32.

Cup Equivalents for Common Ingredients:

Butter: 1 cup = 226 grams (g) or 2 sticks
Flour: 1 cup = 120 grams (g)
Sugar: 1 cup = 200 grams (g)
Brown Sugar: 1 cup = 220 grams (g)
Milk: 1 cup = 240 milliliters (ml)
Honey/Syrup: 1 cup = 340 grams (g)

Oven Temperature Equivalents:

Slow Oven: 300°F (150°C)
Moderate Oven: 350°F (180°C)
Moderate-Hot Oven: 375°F (190°C)
Hot Oven: 400°F (200°C)
Very Hot Oven: 450°F (230°C)

Chapter14: 28-Day Meal plan

Day 1:
o Breakfast: Greek yogurt parfait with mixed berries and a drizzle of honey.
o Lunch: Grilled chicken breast with quinoa and roasted vegetables.
o Snack: Carrot and celery sticks with hummus.
o Dinner: Baked salmon with lemon-dill sauce, brown rice, and steamed asparagus.

Day 2:
o Breakfast: Whole-grain oatmeal with sliced banana and chopped walnuts.
o Lunch: Lentil soup with a side of mixed greens and whole-grain bread.
o Snack: Almonds and dried apricots.
o Dinner: Grilled shrimp skewers with quinoa and grilled zucchini.

Day 3:
o Breakfast: Spinach and tomato omelet with whole-grain toast.
o Lunch: Chickpea and vegetable salad with a tahini dressing.
o Snack: Sliced cucumbers with tzatziki.
o Dinner: Baked chicken breast with brown rice and sautéed spinach.

Day 4:
o Breakfast: Whole-grain pancakes with fresh blueberries and Greek yogurt.
o Lunch: Quinoa and black bean stuffed bell peppers.
o Snack: Trail mix with nuts and dried fruit.
o Dinner: Baked cod with lemon-caper sauce, quinoa, and sautéed kale.

Day 5:
o Breakfast: Whole-grain cereal with skim milk and sliced strawberries.
o Lunch: Mixed bean and vegetable stir-fry with tofu.
o Snack: Celery sticks with almond butter.
o Dinner:Herb-Roasted Pork Tenderloin

Day 6:
o Breakfast: Whole-grain pancakes with fresh blueberries and Greek yogurt.
o Lunch: Quinoa and black bean stuffed bell peppers.
o Snack: Trail mix with nuts and dried fruit.
o Dinner: Baked cod with lemon-caper sauce, quinoa, and sautéed kale.

Day 7:
o Breakfast: Whole-grain waffles with sliced peaches and a dollop of low-fat ricotta.
o Lunch: Spinach and feta stuffed chicken breast with a side of quinoa.
o Snack: Sliced bell peppers with guacamole.
o Dinner: Chili-Lime Grilled Turkey Tenderloin with sweet potato fries and a mixed green salad.

Day 8:
o Breakfast: Muesli with Almonds and Dried Fruits
o Lunch: Quinoa and vegetable stir-fry with tofu.
o Snack: Celery sticks with peanut butter.
o Dinner:Baked Salmon with Dill Sauce with brown rice and steamed broccoli.

Day 9:
o Breakfast: Whole-grain pancakes with fresh blueberries and a dollop of Greek yogurt.
o Lunch: Spinach and mushroom stuffed chicken breast with quinoa.
o Snack: Mixed fruit salad.
o Dinner: Lentil and vegetable curry with brown rice.

Day 10:
o Breakfast: Oatmeal with berries and a sprinkle of flaxseeds.
o Lunch: Grilled chicken salad with mixed greens, tomatoes, and balsamic vinaigrette.
o Snack:Smoked Salmon and Cucumber Rolls
o Dinner: Baked salmon with steamed broccoli and quinoa.

Day 11:
o Breakfast: Greek yogurt with honey and walnuts.
o Lunch: Lentil soup with a side of mixed greens.
o Snack:Hummus and Veggie Platter
o Dinner: Grilled vegetable stir-fry with tofu and brown rice.

Day 12:
o Breakfast: Banana and Almond Butter Smoothie
o Lunch: Caprese Salad with Balsamic Glaze
o Snack: Celery Sticks with Hummus
o Dinner: Herb-Roasted Chicken with Mashed Cauliflower

Day 13:
o Breakfast: Chia Seed and Green Tea Smoothie
o Lunch: Quinoa and Roasted Vegetable Bowl
o Snack: Sliced Cucumber with Greek Yogurt Dip
o Dinner: Grilled Shrimp Skewers with Quinoa Salad

Day 14:
o Breakfast: Scrambled Eggs with Spinach and Tomatoes
o Lunch: Mixed Greens Salad with Grilled Chicken
o Snack: Berries and Cottage Cheese
o Dinner: Baked Sweet Potato with Black Beans and Salsa

Day 15:
o Breakfast: Berry and Banana Whole Wheat Muffins
o Lunch: Turkey and Avocado Wrap with a Side of Carrot Sticks
o Snack: Mixed Nuts and Dried Fruits
o Dinner: Baked Cod with Quinoa and Roasted Brussels Sprouts

Day 16:
o Breakfast:Veggie Breakfast Burrito
o Lunch: Caprese Salad with Tomato, Fresh Basil, and Reduced Balsamic Glaze
o Snack: Sliced Apples with Almond Butter
o Dinner: Herb-Roasted Chicken with Mashed Sweet Potatoes and Steamed Green Beans

Day 17:
o Breakfast: Avocado and Spinach Breakfast Wrap
o Lunch:Mediterranean Chickpea Salad
o Snack: Celery Sticks with Hummus
o Dinner: Baked Sweet Potato with Black Beans, Salsa, and Guacamole

Day 18:
o Breakfast: Banana and Almond Butter Smoothie
o Lunch: Quinoa and Roasted Vegetable Bowl with Feta Cheese
o Snack: Trail Mix with Nuts and Seeds
o Dinner:Baked Eggplant Parmesan

Day 19:
o Breakfast:Sweet Potato and Spinach Breakfast Hash
o Lunch: Mixed Greens Salad with Grilled Shrimp and Citrus Vinaigrette
o Snack: Berries and Cottage Cheese
o Dinner: Vegetable Stir-Fry with Tofu and Brown Rice

Day 20:
o Breakfast: Smoothie with spinach, banana, almond milk, and a scoop of chia seeds
o Lunch: Quinoa and black bean stuffed peppers.
o Snack:. Mixed nuts
o Dinner: Baked cod with quinoa and steamed asparagus.

Day 21:
o Breakfast: Whole-grain waffles with Greek yogurt and sliced peaches.
o Lunch: Tuna salad with mixed greens and a lemon-tahini dressing.
o Snack: Sliced cucumber with tzatziki sauce.
o Dinner: Grilled chicken breast with sweet potato and sautéed kale

Day 22:
o Breakfast: Whole-grain cereal with skim milk and sliced strawberries
o Lunch: Mixed bean soup with a side of whole-grain crackers.
o Snack:. Cottage cheese with pineapple chunks
o Dinner: Lean beef stir-fry with broccoli, bell peppers, and brown rice.

Day 23:
o Breakfast: Egg White Omelet
o Lunch: Turkey and avocado wrap with a side of mixed greens.
o Snack: Almond butter and apple slices.
o Dinner: Baked chicken breast with quinoa and sautéed spinach.

Day 24:
o Breakfast: Smoothie with kale, banana, and almond milk.
o Lunch: Moroccan Spiced Chicken with Couscous
o Snack: Mixed nuts and dried fruit.
o Dinner: Grilled shrimp skewers with quinoa and roasted asparagus

Day 25:
o Breakfast: Whole grain toast with avocado and poached eggs.
o Lunch:. Gazpacho and a mixed greens salad.
o Snack:.Sliced apple with almond butter.
o Dinner: Turkey chili with a side of brown rice

Day 26:
o Breakfast:Egg White Omelet
o Lunch:Honey Mustard Glazed Chicken Thighs
o Snack:Beet and Goat Cheese Crostini
o Dinner:Crab Stuffed Mushrooms

Day 27:
o Breakfast:Sweet Potato and Spinach Breakfast Hash
o Lunch:Spinach and strawberry salad with grilled chicken breast
o Snack:Mixed berry sorbet
o Dinner:Grilled Swordfish Steaks and Steamed asparagus with Quinoa.

Day 28:
o Breakfast:Smoothie Bowl.
o Lunch:Beef and Barley Soup
o Snack:Zucchini Chips with Garlic Parmesan
o Dinner:Baked chicken thighs with roasted sweet potatoes and asparagus.

TWO BONUSES
Here are 100 practical tips for maintaining a heart-healthy lifestyle:

Diet and Nutrition:

1. Eat a variety of colorful fruits and vegetables daily.
2. Choose whole grains over refined grains.
3. Include lean proteins like poultry, fish, and legumes in your meals.
4. Limit red meat consumption and opt for lean cuts.
5. Cook with heart-healthy oils like olive oil or canola oil.
6. Reduce your intake of saturated and trans fats.
7. Cut down on added sugars and sugary beverages.
8. Control portion sizes to avoid overeating.
9. Practice mindful eating by savoring each bite.
10. Use herbs and spices to season food instead of excess salt.
11. Eat smaller, more frequent meals to stabilize blood sugar.
12. Stay hydrated with water and herbal teas.
13. Include sources of omega-3 fatty acids like salmon and walnuts in your diet.
14. Limit processed and fast food.
15. Plan your meals and snacks in advance.
16. Enjoy dark chocolate (70% cocoa or higher) in moderation.
17. Consume high-fiber foods like oats, beans, and whole fruits.
18. Choose low-fat or non-fat dairy products.
19. Be cautious of restaurant portion sizes.
20. Try meatless meals once or twice a week.

Meal Preparation and Cooking:

21. Grill or bake instead of frying foods.
22. Steam vegetables to retain nutrients.
23. Use non-stick cookware to reduce the need for added fats.
24. Make homemade sauces and dressings to control ingredients.
25. Experiment with heart-healthy recipes.
26. Prepare extra portions for leftovers.
27. Use a food scale to measure portions accurately.
28. Keep healthy snacks readily available.
29. Batch-cook and freeze healthy meals for convenience.
30. Avoid excessive use of butter and margarine.

Shopping and Grocery Choices:

31. Create a shopping list and stick to it.
32. Shop the perimeter of the grocery store for fresh items.
33. Read food labels for sodium, sugar, and trans fats.
34. Choose low-sodium or no-salt-added canned goods.
35. Buy in-season fruits and vegetables for cost savings.
36. Purchase lean cuts of meat and poultry.
37. Opt for whole grain versions of pasta and bread.
38. Buy frozen fruits and vegetables for added convenience.
39. Avoid shopping when hungry to prevent impulse buys.
40. Check for sales and discounts on heart-healthy items.

Eating Out:

41. Research restaurant menus ahead of time.
42. Choose grilled or baked entrees instead of fried.
43. Ask for salad dressings and sauces on the side.
44. Share large restaurant portions or take leftovers home.
45. Request substitutions like a side salad instead of fries.
46. Choose water or unsweetened beverages with meals.
47. Limit alcohol consumption to moderate levels.
48. Be mindful of portion sizes at restaurants.
49. Enjoy the company and conversation, not just the food.
50. Avoid all-you-can-eat buffets.

Snacking:

51. Snack on raw vegetables with hummus.
52. Choose unsalted nuts or seeds as a snack.
53. Try air-popped popcorn instead of chips.
54. Enjoy Greek yogurt with fresh berries.
55. Keep a bowl of fruit on the counter for easy access.
56. Snack on a piece of fruit or a small handful of grapes.
57. Make your own trail mix with nuts and dried fruits.
58. Avoid sugary granola bars and opt for low-sugar options.
59. Limit high-sugar snacks like candy and cookies.
60. Hydrate with water or herbal tea between meals.

Cooking Techniques:

61. Use a slow cooker for easy, healthy meals.
62. Roast vegetables with a drizzle of olive oil and herbs.
63. Prepare stir-fries with lots of colorful vegetables.
64. Make homemade soups with low-sodium broths.
65. Try steaming seafood with lemon and herbs.
66. Grill vegetables alongside your main dish.
67. Use lean protein sources like chicken or turkey.
68. Choose whole grain or vegetable-based pasta.
69. Create colorful salads with a variety of veggies.
70. Keep sauces and gravies to a minimum.

Healthy Lifestyle Choices:

71. Engage in regular physical activity, aiming for at least 150 minutes per week.
72. Incorporate both aerobic and strength training exercises into your routine.
73. Quit smoking if you smoke.
74. Limit alcohol intake to moderate levels (if you drink).
75. Manage stress through relaxation techniques like deep breathing.
76. Get sufficient sleep (7-9 hours for most adults).
77. Stay socially connected with friends and loved ones.
78. Manage chronic conditions like high blood pressure and diabetes.
79. Know your family health history.
80. Stay up-to-date with medical check-ups and screenings.

Portion Control:

81. Use smaller plates and bowls to control portions.
82. Be mindful of serving sizes when eating out.
83. Divide restaurant meals in half before starting to eat.
84. Avoid "supersized" or "extra-large" options.
85. Serve meals on individual plates instead of family style.
86. Practice intuitive eating by listening to your body's hunger cues.

87. Limit second helpings at meals.
88. Use measuring cups and scales to gauge portions.
89. Avoid mindless snacking while watching TV.
90. Stop eating when you feel satisfied, not overly full.

Heart-Healthy Habits:

91. Monitor your blood pressure and cholesterol levels regularly.
92. Take prescribed medications as directed by your healthcare provider.
93. Reduce exposure to secondhand smoke.
94. Limit caffeine intake, especially in the afternoon and evening.
95. Incorporate stress-reduction techniques into your daily routine, such as yoga or meditation.
96. Practice good hygiene to prevent infections and illnesses.
97. Stay updated on vaccinations, including flu and pneumonia shots.
98. Manage chronic conditions like diabetes and asthma with the help of healthcare professionals.
99. Stay informed about heart-healthy nutrition guidelines.
100. Make gradual changes to your lifestyle for long-term success.

Remember, it's important to consult with a healthcare provider or registered dietitian before making significant changes to your diet or exercise routine, especially if you have underlying health conditions.

- -

Shopping list

Here's a shopping list of products and ingredients for your heart-healthy cookbook. Adjust the quantities based on the number of recipes you plan to make and your personal preferences:

Proteins:
o Skinless chicken breasts or thighs
o Lean cuts of beef or pork (e.g., sirloin, tenderloin)
o Salmon or other fatty fish (e.g., salmon, mackerel)
o Tofu or tempeh (for vegetarian options)
o Eggs

Fruits and Vegetables:
o Leafy greens (e.g., spinach, kale, romaine lettuce)
o Tomatoes
o Bell peppers
o Broccoli
o Carrots
o Onions
o Garlic
o Avocado
o Berries (e.g., strawberries, blueberries, raspberries)
o Apples
o Oranges
o Lemons
o Bananas
o Watermelon
o Fresh mint leaves

Whole Grains:
o Quinoa
o Brown rice
o Whole wheat pasta
o Oats (old-fashioned)
o Whole grain bread
o Whole grain cereal (e.g., oat bran, bran flakes)

Dairy and Dairy Alternatives:
o Low-fat or non-fat Greek yogurt
o Low-fat or non-fat milk
o Unsweetened almond milk or other plant-based milk

Nuts and Seeds:
o Almonds
o Walnuts
o Chia seeds
o Flaxseeds
o Herbs and Spices:

o Olive oil (extra virgin)
o Canola oil or other heart-healthy oils
o Ground cinnamon
o Ground nutmeg
o Basil
o Thyme
o Oregano
o Paprika
o Cumin
o Black pepper
o Salt (use sparingly)

Sweeteners:
o Honey
o Maple syrup
o Stevia (as a natural sweetener)

Pantry Staples:
o Low-sodium chicken or vegetable broth
o Low-sodium soy sauce or tamari (for reduced sodium recipes)
o Tomato paste
o Balsamic vinegar
o Dijon mustard
o Whole grain mustard
o Tomato sauce (unsalted)
o Canned beans (e.g., black beans, kidney beans)
o Low-sodium canned tomatoes

Miscellaneous:
o Baking essentials (flour, baking powder, baking soda)
o Dark chocolate (70% cocoa or higher)
o Dried fruits (e.g., raisins, apricots)
o Fresh herbs (e.g., parsley, cilantro)
o Low-sodium seasoning blends (for flavor without excess salt)
o Heart-healthy nuts and seeds (e.g., pumpkin seeds, pistachios)

Remember to check nutrition labels for sodium content and choose low-sodium or no-salt-added options whenever possible to maintain a heart-healthy diet. Adjust the list based on your dietary preferences and the specific recipes you plan to prepare from your heart-healthy cookbook

Chapter 15: Conclusion

In conclusion, a heart-healthy cookbook is not just a collection of recipes; it's a powerful tool for promoting lifelong well-being. Through the pages of this cookbook, we have explored the delicious and nutritious world of heart-healthy eating. We've learned that making thoughtful choices in the kitchen can have a profound impact on our cardiovascular health, reducing the risk of heart disease and improving overall quality of life.

Throughout this culinary journey, we've discovered that heart-healthy cooking doesn't mean sacrificing flavor or enjoyment. On the contrary, it's an invitation to embrace a diverse array of fresh ingredients, herbs, and spices that can elevate every meal to a new level of taste and satisfaction.

We've also learned that heart-healthy eating is not a one-size-fits-all approach. It can be tailored to suit individual preferences, dietary restrictions, and cultural traditions. Whether you're a seasoned home chef or a beginner in the kitchen, this cookbook has provided you with the tools and inspiration to create nourishing, flavorful, and heart-protective meals for yourself and your loved ones.

In addition to delicious recipes, we've shared valuable information about the nutritional principles that underpin heart-healthy cooking. We've emphasized the importance of whole grains, lean proteins, fresh fruits and vegetables, and healthy fats in supporting heart health. We've also highlighted the role of mindful eating and portion control in maintaining a balanced diet.

Beyond the kitchen, we've touched upon the significance of a holistic approach to heart health, which includes regular physical activity, stress management, and maintaining a healthy weight. These factors, when combined with the culinary wisdom shared in this cookbook, can contribute to a long and vibrant life.

As we close the pages of this heart-healthy cookbook, let us remember that good health is not an end but a journey. It's a journey that begins with the choices we make at the grocery store and continues with the meals we prepare and savor. It's a journey that involves nurturing our bodies and nourishing our hearts.

May this cookbook serve as a trusted companion on your path to heart health, offering you a wealth of delicious recipes and nutritional guidance to inspire a lifetime of wellness. Here's to your heart and your health, and to many more delightful meals shared with those you hold dear.

Please take a few minutes and help us improve our work. **Send us your feedback.**

bon appetit.

Made in the USA
Las Vegas, NV
05 December 2024

13465388R00061